Emissions Trading

Emissions Trading

Environmental Policy's New Approach

RICHARD F. KOSOBUD
Editor

DOUGLAS L. SCHREDER AND
HOLLY M. BIGGS
Associate Editors
University of Illinois at Chicago

John Wiley & Sons, Inc.
New York • Chichester • Weinheim • Brisbane • Singapore • Toronto

Published by John Wiley & Sons, Inc.
Published simultaneously in Canada.

Library of Congress Cataloging-in-Publication Data:

Emissions trading : environmental policy's new approach / editor, Richard F. Kosobud ; associate editors, Douglas L. Schreder and Holly M. Biggs.
    p.   cm. — (National Association of Manufacturers series)
    Includes index.
    ISBN 0-471-35504-6 (cloth : alk. paper)
    1. Emissions trading—United States.   2. Air quality management—United States.   3. Acid rain—Environmental aspects—United States. I. Kosobut, Richard F.   II. Schreder, Douglas L.   III. Biggs, Holly M.   IV. Series.
HC110.A4E475   2000
363.738'7—dc21   99-43407

Contents

v

Foreword

Air pollution is in decline. Los Angeles, long regarded as the smog capital of America, is now enjoying its cleanest air in five decades. Pittsburgh has gone from being a smokestack haven to becoming a high-tech center. And in many other major cities, people are breathing freer than in years.

The advent of such emissions control devices as catalytic converters has substantially decreased air pollution. In addition, companies have worked to reduce pollutant output, often as a matter of environmental stewardship and not simply to comply with government regulations.

The Whirlpool Corporation of Benton Harbor, Michigan, is one of the most recognizable brand names in American industry. But what's perhaps less well known is Whirlpool's extensive environmental record. The federal Environmental Protection Agency recently honored Whirlpool for the company's role in voluntarily reducing the release of 17 high-priority toxic air pollutants under its "33/50" program between 1992 and 1995.

The EPA also honored Whirlpool with its Stratospheric Ozone Protection Award for the company's voluntary development of a process for servicing its older refrigerators while avoiding ozone-depleting repair practices. And Whirlpool no longer makes refrigerators that use chlorofluorocarbons that could damage the earth's layer of ozone.

It's important to underscore that a commitment to clean air has led to the development of profitable companies whose whole focus is environmental protection. Environmental Elements Corporation (EEC) of Baltimore, Maryland, is an example of a productive enterprise solely devoted to environmental quality. The company produces electrostatic precipitators (ESPs) and other air pollution control devices for solid waste plants, paper companies, and utilities.

EEC has installed more than 1,200 ESP systems on five continents, and recently joined with the U.S. Department of Energy to cooperatively research and develop leading-edge methods of cleaning particulate matter from coal-fired power plants. In the words of EEC Chairman E.H. Verdery, "More efficient power generation will save money and, at the same time, reduce combustion pollution."

But more needs to be done. The quality of our air, while improving, is not good enough. At the same time, the threat of heavy-handed federal regulation hangs over industry like the smog-filled haze that once covered too many of our urban centers.

Much of this regulation is based on weak, if not overtly inaccurate, science and a limited grasp of the effect of federal mandates on the private sector. Recently, a federal court put a stop to the 1997 Environmental Protection Agency rules that dictated new clean air quality standards because the standards could not pass regulatory muster. The proposed global climate change treaty has met with stiff opposition in Congress because of its failure to include many of the world's most unrestricted polluting countries.

All of this is welcome news. But in too many cases, excessive regulations are stifling business. The prospect of new, more costly and more burdensome mandates threatens the business community. At the same time, air quality in many regions can, despite progress, stand improvement.

The promise of emissions trading is great. Richard Kosobud, one of America's leading experts in how business can effectively address environmental concerns, notes correctly that "emissions trading holds out the promise of overcoming the cost-ineffectiveness, inflexibilities, and confrontational aspects—manifested in the present government command-and-control efforts to reduce air pollution."

Emissions Trading: Environmental Policy's New Approach makes a compelling case for the move away from rigid mandates toward a more productive and more cost-efficient process by which air quality can be improved. As environmental regulation consumes more and more of our gross domestic product—currently, about two percent—companies are finding mandates increasingly stultifying in terms of their financial cost and subsequent toll on research, productivity, and the creation of new jobs.

That's why this book is so helpful. In its chapters, careful analysis and thoughtful proposals are put forward to demonstrate that a system of emission trading incentives can and does work in the real, competitive world of the international marketplace. American firms exist in an essentially non-inflationary environment that is unlikely to change at any time in the near future. Their capacity to profit is, therefore, contingent on higher productivity. And productivity, in turn, means technologies whose viability depends on research, development, and capital investment.

As environmental mandates drain the resources for such activities, the competitiveness of U.S. manufacturers is incrementally but steadily diminished.

The contributors to this landmark study—each of them a leader in his or her field of expertise—demonstrate that a regime of emissions trading characterized by incentives, sound science, and market-based discipline can substantially redress air pollution as an industrial and urban phenomenon.

Ultimately, this book is about the creativity and dynamism inherent in an open economy where, without undue government intervention or regulation, companies, scientists, and environmental professionals can jointly develop policies that will produce a cleaner environment, foster market competitiveness, and lead to job creation and sustained overall economic growth and productivity.

It is noteworthy that many of the advances described in this book would only have been possible under an economic system in which innovation and research are encouraged. A corollary to this observation is that innovation and research are only fostered in an environment in which both intellectual curiosity and economic risk-taking are valued. In a word, environmental success is possible because the free market system works. With appropriate incentives, science and industry can join to achieve progress in areas of mutual interest.

Regulatory demands are, at times, merited. It should be emphasized that this book does not call for an elimination of any government oversight of regulatory policy. To the contrary, Professor Kosobud and his colleagues argue that the key to emissions trading is government-business cooperation, itself premised on a recognition of common interests and common goals.

But in today's economy, regulatory demands enacted more by fiat than negotiation are significantly more likely to drag down growth and thereby hurt the ability of industry to pay for the very ends the regulations seek. This unintended consequence is as real as it is common.

Professor Kosobud is to be commended for this thorough, lucid, and cogent book, which is the most important contribution to the air pollution policy debate in recent years. It is my hope that *Emissions Trading* will achieve a wide circulation and stimulate lawmakers, business leaders and members of the environmentalist community to formulate policies that simultaneously grow the economy and clean the air.

JERRY J. JASINOWSKI

October 1999

Preface

Not many years ago a leading advocate of emissions trading, after a frustrating year or two of trying to promote this market-incentive approach, told this editor that the idea of tradable permits to pollute would become but a small footnote in the economic history of environmental regulation. The approach was too anonymous for many public interest groups suspicious of the market, too radical a change from traditional regulation for parts of the government community, too competitive for segments of the business community, and too complex for the public. Only economists seemed enthused.

This book is that footnote. It has grown considerably because something unexpected, at least to the advocate, appears to be happening. Many public interest groups are now debating this new approach and some are becoming advocates themselves, the government community is finding much to praise in this decentralized approach, the affected business community is profitably trading on green spot and futures markets, and some school children are persuading their parents to let them buy tradable rights to emit sulfur dioxide. Only economists are urging caution in applying this instrument to a lengthening list of pollutants.

There is a fascinating, unfolding story behind the new popularity of emissions trading. This book is dedicated to an objective and balanced record of this history by bringing researchers and concerned publics together, each to tell their part. A few words are in order to explain how this information was put together.

Our approach is to organize the book along the lines of the format of the Workshop on Market-Based Approaches to Environmental Policy, a research unit of the editor's university. The basic idea of the Workshop is to commission studies by experts, who follow events closely, to bring together all affected groups, supporters and critics alike, and to subject the studies of emissions trading concepts and performance to a thorough discussion and critique. Environmental regulation affects many groups and individuals; few regulatory activities touch as many lives in as many ways. The Workshop approach, by incorporating many views, provides a more complete picture—a more complete benefit-cost accounting—of the use of market tools to achieve environmental goals.

Most of the contributions were first presented at two conferences sponsored by the Workshop during the summer of 1998. Studies were commissioned by foremost researchers and market participants. Studies were subject to the critique of panelists drawn from these ranks and the ranks of concerned communities, reflecting our stated intention to present a wide range of views on these developing environmental markets. Chapters were subsequently revised in the light of these comments and in the light of editorial review. In addition, the chapter by Mary Gade and Roger Kanerva on the work of the Ozone Transport Assessment Group was specially commissioned to provide a background on the emerging discussion of nitrogen dioxide emissions trading. To convey the Workshop's approach and contribution to the exchange of views, this volume includes the revised studies and selected panel commentary.

The technical level of the discussion was also chosen to fulfill our objectives. Many of our authors have made contributions to the theory of market incentives as a means of pollution control. However, this is not a book based directly on theoretical modeling and elaboration. While the theory provides invaluable background information and points the way to sorting out the facts, the contributors have been asked to enlarge our understanding of the evolution, implementation, and practical problems of emissions trading with an emphasis on an appraisal of its performance. They have been asked to make their discussion technically sound but generally accessible.

This approach requires that contributors be aware both of the expected theoretical outcomes of emissions trading and of the slippages between these expected outcomes and the record. These slippages, or failures of the assumptions of the theory to hold in all respects, could range from significant transactions costs that inhibit trading to lack of competition in the environmental market, from imperfect information to ineffective monitoring and enforcement, and from vested interest group pressures to unexpected complications. The assignment to contributors was to clarify these matters for the well-informed and professional reader. They were to further our education concerning this new tool and its potential.

It is always a pleasure to acknowledge the support given to the Workshop in its efforts to promote the study and appraisal of incentive-based regulation. The Acid Rain Division of the U.S. Environmental Protection Agency has provided financial support for the conferences, much valuable advice, and a highly informative account of the management of the sulfur dioxide tradable allowance program. Brian J. McLean, director; Joseph Kruger, branch chief, Energy Evaluation and International Branch; and Rayenne Chen, environmental protection specialist, are to be specially thanked for help, and for their written account of administrative practices. The Federal Reserve Bank of Chicago, made available efficient settings for the conferences. Michael H. Moskow, president, and Thomas H. Klier, senior economist, gave not only support but also made written contributions to this volume. William A. Testa, senior economist and vice president, once again helped in many ways. Participants from all affected groups joined in the Workshop conferences: Their critical questioning and comments have found their way into this book in many ways to the editors and readers benefit.

My associate editors, Douglas L. Schreder and Holly M. Biggs, performed a wide variety of tasks exhibiting skill and welcome good nature. Ian A. Lange and Tara M. Raghavan acted as effective student research assistants. Professor Houston H. Stokes and Jin Man Lee were indispensable consultants helping to manage the right computer software at the right time. The experienced staff at John Wiley & Sons deserves plaudits for their skilled management of this manuscript and the logistics required. My contacts with Jeanne Glasser, business editor, and Debra Alpern, editorial program assistant, were always cooperative, productive, and enlightening.

RICHARD F. KOSOBUD

PART ONE

INCENTIVE-BASED ENVIRONMENTAL QUALITY CONTROL

1

Emissions Trading Emerges from the Shadows

Richard F. Kosobud

Under emissions trading regulation, business and government share the commanding heights of environmental policy. Each makes key decisions. The former is free to trade emission rights or to choose, and to develop, air pollution control measures with the incentive in mind of minimizing control costs. The latter reserves the right to set emission rates or aggregate levels of pollution under which tradable rights can be generated, to establish trading rules, and to monitor and enforce compliance with the incentive in mind of increasing public welfare. Public interest groups also appear on these heights by exerting their influence on trading policies and government and business decisions.

On these heights, it is clear that the regulated and regulating communities have new roles to play compared with their responsibilities under traditional regulation. Emissions trading is both a simplification of regulation in that decisions are assigned to those who can carry them out best and a complication in that new rules and procedures must be established, tested, and refined. These rules and procedures have been undergoing continuing development as existing trading pro-grams to control air pollution mature, such as those to limit sulfur dioxide (SO_2) emissions, and new implementation plans get underway, such as those to reduce the emissions of nitrogen oxides (NO_x), volatile organic compounds (VOCs), and carbon dioxide (CO_2). A first objective of this book is to bring together a group of leading researchers to present their latest and most authoritative studies on these matters for the benefit of business and government.

Emissions trading as a new environmental regulatory tool is moving out of the shadows and into the arena of public scrutiny, thus attracting attention not only from the immediately affected communities, but also from a widening circle of public officials, public interest groups, academics, and the informed public itself. It is still controversial in some quarters. Emissions trading is undergoing a rapid development process, introducing unfamiliar terms and concepts into the discussion of environmental policy. We are all in school to obtain a clearer understanding of this recent arrival on the regulatory scene. Consequently, a second objective of this book is to provide authoritative studies that are clear and readable guides to the numerous and changing definitions and concepts that have come to be embodied in this regulatory mechanism.

Not all of the ever-growing audience has greeted the new arrival with enthusiasm or approval. Doubts about the market's transparency and concerns about compliance with and enforcement of trading rules, among other problems, are raised in many quarters. A third objective is to present a wide range of views about emissions trading including the commentary of public interest groups, government administrators, and academics, with the intention of reaching readers who want more information before making up their minds about the net benefits of this policy instrument and its applicability to other pollutant problems. Our aim is to help develop a more informed appraisal and discussion of this new tool.

Emissions trading has long been studied from the theoretical point of view and advocated by mainstream economists in technical journals, read only by a relative few. Its recent implementation has generated a growing body of evidence that suggests that market incentives can work in the right circumstances and that some measure of success can be claimed in the first trials. The importance of this empirical evidence is hard to overemphasize for our purposes, as there are few deductive truths on matters of regulatory policy. Therefore, a final objective is to include qualified observers to review that evidence and to appraise that claim of success in an effort to help answer the basic question: Can this new regulatory balancing act between government and the private sectors be constructed so as to provide for the public a cleaner environment in a more cost-effective, more flexible, and less confrontational way?

Fitting Emissions Trading into the Environmental Policy Context

It is easy to lose sight of the ultimate goals of environmental policy when engaged in a discussion of the merits of regulatory reform. The question of the choice of regulatory measure typically occurs well along in the logical sequence of issues that arise in the recognition and consideration of an environmental problem. Yet, resolution of issues at earlier stages can have a bearing on regulatory decisions; for example, the determination of the negative impact of a pollutant can have a bearing on the setting of a limitation on the aggregate of tradable emission allowances allocated—the cap in a cap-and-trade market. A useful device is to envision the sequence of these issues and decisions as occurring along an environmental policy decision tree and to locate the branch where this book begins.

The First Policy Decision

The rooted trunk of the decision tree represents the recognition of an environmental problem. Has some failure of the market system or government activity or some information gap given rise to a negative externality affecting air quality that merits attention? That is, are there harms to human health, especially to people suffering from heart disease, asthma, or emphysema, damages to trees and crops, and impairment of materials caused by the emission of substances into the atmosphere whose social costs are not reflected in the accounting sheets of private transactions or in the budgets of government? If so, the prices of commodities or stated costs of government activities do not accurately measure what society must give up to have these goods and services. Society suffers both damages and an inefficient allocation of resources because there is too much of the activity or commodity that gives rise to the harmful emissions. Put another way, there are inadequately defined property rights for disposal in the atmosphere and therefore no appropriate charge is being levied.

Private or Public Resolution?

The first branching of the decision tree represents the choice of mitigating the harms either by private negotiation, government intervention, or doing nothing at all if the costs of mitigation are too high. Private negotiation between affecting and affected parties, including defensive or averting maneuvers by those who suffer, represents movement along one branch. For the problems dealt with in this volume, ranging from urban smog through acid rain to global warming, it puts too much of a strain on the imagination to conceive of a site big enough, time interval long enough, and transaction negotiations simple enough that would enable all concerned parties to get together in one forum or another to resolve the matter privately. Private defensive actions by individuals to counteract air pollution would appear to fall far short of an optimal solution.

Degree of Public Intervention

Proceeding, then, along the government intervention branch, which in effect assigns air rights to the public, brings us to the next fork where the question of the appropriate extent or efficient degree of such intervention is to be answered. In principle, a full benefit-cost analysis could be very helpful at this point in providing a means of finding where the balance of the reduction in harms and increase in control costs occur. In practice, the methodology is not yet adequate to the task for these complex air quality problems nor can the estimates currently available secure agreement among contending parties (Portney, 1995). A striking lesson is available in the legislative mandate to reduce SO_2 emissions as found in Title IV of the Clean Air Act Amendments of 1990 (CAAA).

The National Acid Precipitation Assessment Program (NAPAP) was funded in the 1980s to provide Congress with evidence on acid rain harms initially with a focus on vegetation and water quality. This information was to be used in the reconsideration of clean air legislation. The massive NAPAP research effort produced, and is still producing, much useful information. As the debate began leading to the 1990 legislation, two problems with this effort became apparent. First, an important part of the research effort was not finished in time to be of use. Second, the available findings indicated that the acid rain harms or monetized damages uncovered at that time were below what some observers expected. The benefits of reducing SO_2 emissions, a major precursor of acid rain, were thus shrouded in uncertainty. The control costs, on the other hand, were perceived to be rising, particularly those of traditional regulation that required flue gas desulfurization (scrubbers).

Congress appears to have cut the SO_2 Gordian knot in the 1990 Act by reducing historical aggregate emissions in successive stages by about one-half, and by specifying a national emissions trading mechanism that hopefully could reduce the control costs of achieving this target. One has to be politically tone-deaf to fault these judgments on the grounds that a thorough benefit-cost analysis was not on hand. Equipped as we are with hindsight, the legislative decision to set this target looks to be not only defensible but also prescient. In his study, Dallas Burtraw (Chapter 7) reports that new research on the health impacts of acid rain aerosols reveals more serious damages than previously estimated. Both Burtraw and A. Denny Ellerman (Chapter 8) provide interesting new data on the cost savings achieved by the SO_2 allowance-trading program.

The voices that once argued that the extent of the 1990 reduction of SO_2 emissions was too steep, with costs exceeding benefits, have been muted, and voices are now heard that further reductions may be desirable. Similarly, the early criticisms of the mandate to establish a SO_2 allowance cap-and-trade market, if not muted, have been sounded less frequently, re-placed by reports of market successes. Studies in this volume cast much light on the events underlying these changing views and perceptions and can contribute to our understanding of like developments that may occur in the implementation of emissions trading for other pollutants.

This is not to deny the usefulness of the benefit-cost approach in framing regulatory questions and obtaining partial answers of value in policy making. William Nordhaus in his work on global warming, summarized in Chapter 3, provides a leading example of the value of modeling benefits and costs. In the case of global warming, he finds that while some cuts in greenhouse gas emissions are justified, the extent and timing of those proposed in the Kyoto Protocol will result in marginal control costs exceeding marginal benefits, as estimated in his model.

In the case of establishing regional aggregate caps on SO_2 and NO_x emissions, precursors of urban smog in Los Angeles, James Lents (Chapter 10) reports on the political judgments made by the local authority, under permissive state legislation, that cut allowable emissions by well over half in a series of year-by-year reductions. Political establishment of reduction targets, or setting the optimum amount of pollution reduction based upon a benefit-cost analysis implies a willingness to accept a certain amount of air pollution and an abandonment of zero-air pollution or zero-risk goals. Issuance of a quantity of tradable emission allowances brings out this point dramatically in comparison with traditional regulation. The quantity of allowances issued makes it clear to all that some pollution will occur. Traditional regulations, for example, a requirement that the best available control technology be used, tend to obscure the reality that some pollution also will occur in this instance. Robert Stavins (Chapter 2) discusses the ethical basis of this difference between the two types of regulation.

Centralized versus Decentralized Control?

Assuming agreement on government intervention and on the degree of reductions of pollutant emissions or concentrations does not imply agreement about the regulatory measure best able to attain these limitations. Should it be centralized direction that specifies the exact technology for control of emission rates, or establishes performance standards for these rates that are, in fact, based on specific technologies? Or should it be decentralized incentive-based management that relies on pollutant taxes or the autonomy and anonymity of tradable emission rights? Or some combination? Here in our branching process, we have come closer to the topics of this book.

While economists and market advocates had long urged the use of decentralized incentive regulation, their advice was largely unheeded in environmental legislation prior to 1990. Centralized rate-based direction that specified devices such as sulfur scrubbers on smokestacks and catalytic converters on cars dominated the regulatory roost. The reasons for this well-known domination were many and undoubtedly complex. Much environmental legislation was passed in response to public alarm over pressing environmental problems and therefore was designed to show that the alarm was being answered with centralized control that appeared to effectively eliminate the problem once and for all. This was largely true of many features of the 1970 Clean Air Act. The regulating community could argue they needed the centralized tools to make sure the job was done—after all, weren't market failures the cause in many instances? As for the regulated community, one can be suspicious that many emitters, once regulated, discovered they could live with the details of centralized regulation because it would earn them economic rents unavailable to enterprises trying to make a start. The public interest community, in large part, appeared to harbor a distrust of impersonal market forces and a suspicion that effective monitoring and enforcement of trading rules would be difficult if not impossible to implement. Besides, zero pollution still was a goal of some segments of the green community.

There also seemed to be technical or physical reasons for preferring centralized control for some pollutants. For example, urban ozone is a local and seasonally transitory pollutant that has many sources of precursor emissions. In addition, one precursor, the hydrocarbons, contains toxic elements like benzene. Can market incentives provide protection of the public's health in these instances?

In sum, there would appear to be formidable interests in support of traditional regulation. However, the winds of change are blowing through the branches. Robert Stavins (Chapter 2) provides a perspective on the reasons for a growing interest in decentralized instruments. Perhaps foremost among them was the stubborn resistance of certain atmospheric pollutants to command-and-control measures that regulate the rate but not the volume of pollution. Added to this problem was the related increase in the (marginal) costs of further required reductions. For many of the pollutants considered in this volume, control costs vary, sometimes dramatically, among emitters. Consequently, centralized direction requiring the same measure or rule across all sources sacrifices the gains to be obtained from having those who could reduce cheaply do more of the emission reduction task.

Recently, serious efforts have been made to bring low-level ozone and its precursors under the sway of incentive-based regulation. One explanation is the accumulation of knowledge about the pollutant and the spatial transport of its precursors. Another explanation is the increase in our understanding of how emissions trading can be combined with traditional control measures. Mary Gade and Roger Kanerva (Chapter 5) bring us up to date on the advanced modeling and design progress in this area as achieved by the Ozone Transport Assessment Group.

That emissions trading can result in significant savings goes a long way in explaining the heightened interest in this incentive regulation. Both static and dynamic cost-effectiveness of control can be realized. In the former case, it can be shown by a demonstration, which is an achievement of economics (Montgomery, 1972), that allowing emitters to make current control decisions on the basis of decentralized taxes or tradable emission prices can lead to a cost-effective allocation of reductions across emitters—no other allocation can do the job more cheaply. This would not mean equal reductions, but reductions in which marginal control costs were equated to tax rates or tradable emission right prices by cost minimizing emitters, some reducing more, others reducing less. In the latter case of dynamic cost-effectiveness, meaning an efficient intertemporal allocation of control efforts, it can be shown that emitters in the decentralized case can make future decisions that lead to a least-cost time path.

These results have many and powerful implications that our contributors make use of in their discussion of trading applications. Certain conditions must prevail for these results to hold, such as competitive markets and reasonable transactions costs.

Delegating flexibility to the emitters to make relevant choices in light of their detailed knowledge of their production and control possibilities opens up another avenue for cost savings. Both tax and market incentives can lead the emitter to search for and develop control innovations that could bring down associated costs even further than those achievable by existing measures. Command-and-control regimes have been criticized because they can act to stifle this innovative incentive. Should an emitter be creative in these circumstances and thus risk having lower emission rates imposed? The hypothesis that traditional regulation and innovation do not go hand-in-hand is certainly not refuted by some of the history of SO_2 command and control from 1970 through 1990. Initially, higher smokestacks were required of coal-burning utilities; then later, costly scrubber technology was imposed. The first reduced interest in other more effective measures and succeeded mainly in spreading the precursors of acid rain over a wider region. The second slowed the introduction of low-sulfur coal.

Another telling criticism of relying solely on centralized control is that it leads to undue confrontation between regulated and regulating communities that can result in behavior on both sides that detracts from the goal of achieving a cleaner environment cost-effectively. The regulated community may well feel that it knows best the details of operations bearing on emissions and that the other side would need to duplicate the entire emitter's staff to carry out detailed supervision. The regulating community may well feel that the other side is derailing the regulatory process to avoid the detailed supervision that would appear necessary to assure compliance. If confrontation does not develop under traditional regulation, then suspicions grow among observers that something shady is going on.

These criticisms of traditional regulation are often heard and frequently appealed to in discussions of regulatory policy, but they should not be pushed too far. Some designs of trading schemes require the emitter to earn tradable credits by reducing emissions below the rate required under continuing command-and-control measures. The idea is to prevent excess local pollution. That is, we have a combination of the two regulatory measures at work in a complementary fashion. In the most comprehensive market design, the SO_2 cap-and-trade allowance market, state-by-state standards for emission rate control remain in effect as a floor to local performance. Another recent and important example is found in the new U.S. EPA rules on NO_x emission reductions. Here, emissions trading is a promising option for control of stationary sources of pollution, but traditional regulation will continue as a major tool for control of emissions from mobile and area sources (U.S. EPA, 1998).

In fact, as environmental policy has evolved in the United States, all levels of government including special districts have been active in pollution control and are unlikely to willingly abdicate their roles. The issue then emerges: Will there be conflicts between the continuing layers of command and control and the incentive-based efforts impairing the effectiveness of both, or will there be a workable combination enhancing the effectiveness of each? Will the varying levels of regulating authority be able to coordinate their efforts to manage incentive-based instruments? These issues, being far from resolved, are important topics considered in this volume. They highlight the fact that part of the business before us is the question: Can increasing the role of decentralized control mesh well with the remaining layers of traditional regulation?

What Form of Decentralized Control? *Emissions Trading versus Pollution Taxes*

There are a variety of decentralized or incentive-based measures that range from exhortation for a cleaner environment, to government purchase and thus subsidy of control equipment, to stimulation of pollution prevention agreements, and finally to emissions trading and pollution taxes. We shall concentrate on the last two measures at the next fork in the branches of our decision tree. In principle, they would appear to lead to the same effects in reducing pollution and therefore would appear to be a matter of indifference as to choice. In practice, they differ significantly.

Both emissions taxes and trading, when introduced, put a price on pollution, thus internalizing the social costs of the offending substance and altering the choices of control options at the emitter's level. If emission allowance price and tax rate are equal, having been so set by the market or by environmental policy, then cost-minimizing emitters can be expected to equate marginal control costs to that price or rate. The general observer would note, in a world of certainty and full information, that emitters were making their individual reductions in the same way under either tax or trading regulation. If a tax rate were in effect, the individual emitter's least-cost decisions would lead to a minimum of taxes paid plus control expenditures on remaining emissions. If emissions trading were in effect, the sum of the prices of marketable allowances turned over to the government to cover emissions plus remaining control expenditures would be at the same minimum.

Therefore, it doesn't really matter whether we choose tax or trading regulation, we obtain the benefits of decentralized incentive-based implementation in either case. Unfortunately, it is not that simple; there are political, economic, and even moral reasons given for preferring one regulatory instrument over the other.

The above arguments about equivalence assumed a world of perfect certainty of knowledge about the relationships between the monetary values of harms and control measures and the extent of pollution reduction. If uncertainty prevails about these relationships, the government may justifiably worry about the importance of errors in choosing one instrument or the other. Potential errors depend upon the government's knowledge of how control costs and harms vary with emissions. If uncertain costs vary little with emissions, but harms vary significantly, the choice of emissions trading will lead to less serious error. That is, issuance of a limited number of allowances provides more control over harms than does the setting of a tax rate. Emitters equating the tax rate with marginal control costs could be far off the optimum extent of reduction due to the incorrect rate set under uncertainty. Continually changing the rate to reach the correct one could be unsettling, and unpopular. In contrast, the amount of tradable allowances issued could be more closely aligned with the reduction in harms desired. Control costs were not well estimated in the case of SO_2 emissions as Burtraw and Ellerman explain in detail. In the other case, where the relationship of harms to the degree of regulation is uncertain but control costs are better known and rising sharply, the reverse situation prevails (Weitzman, 1974).

There are other departures or slippages from the ideal that could lead to problems with taxes or emissions trading. The presence of large costs in searching for and negotiating with trading partners can reduce the savings achievable under tradable property right schemes. Other slippages include the presence of monopoly power, difficulties of acquisition of market knowledge, problems of managing the portfolio of tradable allowances, and uncertainties about the bearing of other forms of regulation upon emissions trading. These potential difficulties have led some observers to recommend the use of pollution taxes (Tolley and Edwards, 1997). Pollution taxes, however, have economic problems of their own including the unfavorable impact of resetting rates when circumstances change. Choosing the tax instrument raises questions of monitoring and collection expenses. Based on experience to date, emissions trading has become the preferred alternative. It is worth noting some of the reasons for this preference.

Economic factors appear to have been less important in the final determination of which decentralized instrument to use than their relative political acceptability. The economic aspects are less visible and more difficult to document; the political aspects are sitting partridges on a leafless twig. Taxes on pollutants have not been favored, to say the least, by emitters who have argued that imposing a tax rate makes them pay twice; once for the rate on emissions and once for the control of reducing emissions. The countervailing argument is that the tax paid on emissions measures the harms imposed by the remaining emissions. The method of allocating tradable emission rights to emitters can finesse these arguments.

The attraction to emitters of emissions trading over pollution taxes is due in large part, as our contributors explain, to the free allocation of tradable credits to individual sources. This free allocation has characterized applications of all emissions trading efforts to date. If these tradable entitlements were to be auctioned off rather than freely allocated, so that emitters would have to pay for their initial allocation, the difference between the financial impact of taxes and trading would diminish, as would the political support for emissions trading. There is a social cost to this free allocation, however, because it denies revenue to the government which could be used to reduce other tax rates that distort prices and lessen welfare. This may not be too high a price to pay for a cost-effective policy instrument.

We are now ready to move along the final branch of environmental policy decisions where emissions trading regulation is to be designed and implemented. New issues and choices concerning different trading schemes require clarification, new concepts and definitions of market activities and commodities require attention, and new data and other evidence on market performance require appraisal. As our authors assume some familiarity with these subjects in order to move quickly to their tasks, it is appropriate to provide a brief guide and summary to these key ideas and terminologies in this introduction. We invite the reader desiring such background to join a growing audience and us in this educational undertaking.

THE EMISSIONS TRADING LITTLE RED SCHOOLHOUSE

In an advanced capitalistic society, designing and establishing a new environmental market would seem a routine project. There are examples of functioning markets all around and our extended experience with them would seem sufficient for us to comport ourselves as buyers or sellers as if it were now part of our genetic makeup. It is also clear what we want of green markets. We want efficient mechanisms that grind out equilibrium prices that reveal marginal control costs without bias at just the right level to equate the marginal benefits of reducing pollutant harms. Or, if not that, then we want prices that reveal marginal control costs that minimize the use of society's resources for control of pollution at the targeted level. Those outcomes imply a thick market with sufficient transactions to assure that all possible savings have been realized by emitter control decisions. A few simple rules for such markets would seem to suffice to have trading activity off and running quickly.

It is not that easy. As we mentioned, not everyone is enthused about using the market mechanism for environmental policy. Resistors have included, besides those one might expect, segments of the business community, in particular segments of the electric utility industry (Rosenberg, 1997). Old vested interests are not always easily overcome. The time required to get these markets underway, the extensive efforts needed to design market features, and the complexities of securing agreements from all affected and concerned parties suggest that something even more complex is going on. In creating new-fashioned environmental markets, every design feature is a candidate for critical examination and every batch of transactions the subject of intensive scrutiny. The public and private interests are more intertwined than in most other markets and therefore green markets are likely to be more intricate in their evolution than other types.

It is no wonder, then, that a number of different market patterns or models have emerged in the implementation stage with important variations ranging from coverage of sources to the caps in the cap-and-trade markets. Some differences reflect characteristics of the pollutant, but many others reflect contrasting views about efficient or acceptable market features. As we have said in another context, there are few deductive truths in the design and implementation of environmental markets. Our contributors clarify and appraise particular model designs based on accumulating evidence. Their studies can contribute to a better understanding of the workings of these varied regulatory tools. To the extent that the results indicate that one tool can serve our environmental ends better than others, a wider understanding and acceptance of market approaches is secured. That is one of the important assignments for our contributors.

The assignment that remains for us in this part of the introduction is to describe a simple but unifying framework within which emissions trading key terms can be defined and particular market designs compared. That is, we present the first course in the political economy of trading systems preparatory to tackling the advanced material.

At one end of the framework, or spectrum, we place the cap-based or closed-system markets and at the other end, the rate-based or open system. Several features stand out for us in making this basic distinction. The former, the most comprehensive in design, is based on the fundamental rule that the emitters are required to participate and deliver to the government a tradable credit or allowance for each unit of emission during the relevant time period. The government secures control, if all goes well, of the aggregate volume of the emissions from covered sources by determining the aggregate cap or emissions budget and by making allocations to individual sources during the relevant time period. In the latter design, the open system, emitters may elect to participate, and if they do, they may earn a tradable credit by reducing emissions below the required rate set by traditional regulation. The fundamental rule is that any emissions above the regulated rate require a tradable credit be turned over to the government, such emissions creating a demand for tradable credits. The government maintains control of the rate but not the aggregate volume of emissions because the hours of operation that the rate is in effect are not controlled. The hours of operation will depend upon firm, industry, or economywide factors.

Even without intimate knowledge of trading, the reader will sense other features that distinguish the two types. The quantities of credits traded in the open system can be uncertain and the prices hard to predict. The closed system enables the government to take a more hands-off position with respect to the quality of the tradable credit maintaining only a benign monitoring and enforcement position. The open or rate-based system raises a long series of questions about the quality of the tradable credit. Was the reduction from the legal rate generated properly? Is the reduction measurable? Can the procedure once specified be enforced? To assure the reductions do in fact clear the air, the government is drawn into a detailed hands-on involvement with the transactions. We shall see from the Belanger study that this involvement can be burdensome both to the regulated and regulating communities.

Cap-and-Trade or Closed-System Emissions Trading

The major cap-based variant in use has the government assign (or auction) dated tradable allowances to emitting sources within an aggregate limit of or cap on emissions. Emission reductions can be measured from a historical benchmark or projected future period. Sources then may control their individual emissions or emit and turn over appropriately dated allowances from their portfolio or some cost-effective combination. The portfolio of allowances can be managed by trading or by banking if permitted. A less well-known and less used variant is the cap-and-credit market that is based on a performance standard set by dividing the aggregate emissions budget or cap by total heat input or capital stock utilization; those sources with individual ratios below the overall standard get marketable credits, those above must acquire them. The interesting property of this market is that the performance standard can be reset as environmental circumstances change. This resetting aspect may be one reason this variant has not been tried often as it introduces an additional element of uncertainty into emission trading plans.

We have already suggested that cap-and-trade markets have been the most widely praised and strongly advocated incentive approach to pollution reduction. They also have been among the most intently discussed and, on occasion, hotly debated instruments to be implemented. The reader will find reasons for both views as well as an introduction to the details of their design by working through their features as depicted in Table 1.1. The table describes four of the most important current applications in effect or scheduled for implementation in the near future.

Table 1.1 provides at a glance definitions of and a guide to major market characteristics. However, the entries are very simplified and omit important details and modifications. All simplifications can be dangerous if these limitations are overlooked. The general comments that follow the table are intended to minimize the dangers by adding information to the entries of the table.

The Four Markets

Of the four markets described in Table 1.1, the SO_2 allowance plan is perhaps best known, most closely watched, and most fully in operation of all. It is the only market with a nationally

Table 1.1 Features of Cap-and-Trade Closed Systems Emissions Trading

		Four Selected Markets			
Features	Title IV CAAA '90	NO$_x$ Rule U.S. EPA (OTC)	RECLAIM SCAQMD		ERMS IEPA
1. Pollutant	SO$_2$	NO$_x$	NO$_x$	SO$_2$	VOC
2. Market coverage					
2.1 Geographical	Nation	23 states + D.C. (States to determine) OTC = 12 states + D.C.	L.A. region		Chicago region
2.2 Number and kind of covered enterprises	Phase I = 110 Phase II = All large electric utilities	Larger stationary sources in various industries	313 Larger stationary sources in various industries	65	283 Larger stationary sources in various industries
2.3 Market coverage of total emissions (%)	69	33	33	75	26
3. Who may trade?	Any registered party	States to determine (OTC: any registered party)	Any registered party		Any registered party
4. Characteristics of tradable credit					
4.1 Name and denomination	Allowance (1 ton of SO$_2$)	Allowance (1 ton of NO$_x$)	RECLAIM trading credit (lbs. NO$_x$) (lbs. SO$_2$)		Allotment trading unit (200 lbs. VOC)
4.2 When usable?	Year issued and thereafter	Year and season issued and thereafter	Year issued and next annual cycle		Year and season issued and one year thereafter
4.3 Private property?	De facto rights, subject to policy change	De facto rights, subject to policy change	De facto rights, subject to policy change		De facto rights, subject to policy change
5. Cap arithmetic					
5.1 Market start date	1995	2003 (OTC = 1998)	1994	1994	2000
5.2 Baseline date for aggregate cap	1980	2007 projection (OTC = 1990)	2003 projection		Two year average (1994–1996)
5.3 Aggregate cap reduction (%)	50 by 2007	69 Electric utilities, others 12 to 15. (OTC = 75 by 2003)	75 by 2003 (in equal annual steps)	63 by 2003	12 by 2000 (further cuts possible)

(continued)

Table 1.1   *(Continued)*

		Four Selected Markets		
Features	Title IV CAAA '90	No$_x$ Rule U.S. EPA (OTC)	RECLAIM SCAQMD	ERMS IEPA
(Pollutant)	SO$_2$	NO$_x$	NO$_x$ SO$_2$	VOC
5.4 Individual baseline allocation	Average emissions 1985–1987	To be determined by states	Highest emissions from 1989 to 1992	Average of two years 1994–1996
5.5 Allocations free or auctioned?	Free (2.8% withhheld for annual auction)	To be determined by states	Free Free	Free (1% withheld for sale)
6. Price and transactions data	Price data from brokers and public auction. EPA allowance tracking	To be determined by states. EPA allowance tracking	Price and transactions data recorded by RECLAIM	Price and transactions data recorded by Illinois EPA
7. Emissions monitoring and program enforcement	EPA emissions monitoring. Fine of $2000 per ton for overages plus make-up	EPA emissions monitoring. Penalties to be determined by states	Emissions monitoring by RECLAIM. Exceedances subtracted from next allocation	Emissions monitoring by Illinois EPA. Exceedances plus penalty subtracted from next allocation
8. Continuing issues and future choices				
8.1 The "hot spot" problem	No locational constraint	Dependent on state decisions	Trading prohibited inland to coastal zone	No locational constraint
8.2 Intersource trading? (stationary, mobil, and area)	Not applicable	Possible where feasible	Possible where feasible	Possible where feasible
8.3 Integrated assessment modeling?	SO$_2$ modeling	NO$_x$ transport modeling	Regional NO$_x$ and SO$_2$ modeling	Regional NO$_x$ and VOC modeling

Notes: Column headings: Title IV of the Clean Air Act Amendments of 1990 provides for SO$_2$ emissions trading. NO$_x$ Rule refers to the U.S. EPA NO$_x$ Final Rule of 1998 that contains provisions for an optional emissions trading plan that states can adopt for intra- and interstate use. OTC = Ozone Transport Commission. RECLAIM is the Regional Clean Air Incentive Market administered by the South Coast Air Quality Management District (SCAQMD) for the extreme nonattainment Los Angeles region. ERMS is the Emissions Reduction Market System administered by the Illinois EPA for the severe nonattainment Chicago region.

1. Pollutant: SO$_2$ = sulfur dioxide. NO$_x$ = nitrogen oxides, especially nitrogen dioxide. VOC = volatile organic compounds. Market approaches apply to anthropogenic sources primarily caused by fossil fuel combustion and use.

Table 1.1 *(Continued)*

2.1 Market coverage, geographical. Nation = Continental U.S.A. The NO_x Final Rule applies to 23 states east of the Mississippi River. OTC coverage includes the twelve northeastern states plus D.C. The L.A. region includes a coastal and inland zone between which trades can flow only from the former to the latter. The Chicago region comprises the six county area plus two townships.

2.2 Number and kind of covered or included enterprises. Enterprises are legal entities to receive and trade credit allocations. Almost all enterprises operate stationary or fixed-point emission sources with one or more emitting or generating units. In the case of Title IV, most of these are electric utilities. In the case of NO_x trading, most of these are larger boilers, turbines, and combined cycle heat-driven systems in various industries. In the case of ERMS VOC trading, emission sources range over a wider variety of industries including chemical, plating, and cleaning establishments emitting over 10 tons of VOC annually.

2.3 Percentages listed are approximate shares of total anthropogenic emissions covered by market rules.

5.2 These are baseline dates for aggregate cap determination. Title IV occurs in two phases with separate caps. Title IV and ERMS programs refer to a historical period. The NO_x Final Rule refers to a projected level of emissions that would occur without a market plan. Reductions are calculated from that level. RECLAIM estimates what reductions would be required to achieve local area attainment of NAAQS by 2003 and uses that level as a cap.

5.3 Allocations to individual enterprises under the aggregate cap are made by a complex process. In the case of Title IV, the allocation is to the electricity generating unit (boiler, turbine, or combined cycle system) of which an enterprise may own more than one. These allocations, which are a series of allowances each with its own date, were based on heat inputs in the interval 1985 to 1987 and adjusted for various reasons by Congress (to encourage scrubbers, reward past control decisions, etc.). The individual allocations under the NO_x Final Rule are to be determined by state implementation plans. The OTC percentage reductions refer to stationary sources.

The RECLAIM allocations were made by the source choosing the highest emission levels from the interval 1989 through 1992, then reduced in equal annual percentage steps to reach the 2003 attainment goal. The ERMS allocation is based on an average of the highest emissions in the years 1994 to 1996; however, in justified cases a substitution of years from 1990 to 1997 could be made. Reductions were then allocated to fit the aggregate cap. A further complication in this case is that the aggregate cap may be altered if the incoming concentrations of NO_x and VOC from other areas are changed by policies such as the NO_x Final Rule. These incoming concentrations, or boundary conditions, were found to exert a significant influence on local ozone concentrations.

7. Emissions monitoring and program enforcement: Continuous emissions electronic monitoring equipment is required of larger generating or emission units wherever possible with materials balance or input data utilized in other cases. Reliable monitoring assures the value of a tradable credit and has worked satisfactorily in the case of Title IV, as Burtraw and Ellerman explain. The RECLAIM program has required discussions between regulated

(continued)

Table 1.1   *(Continued)*

and regulating community as new monitoring equipment has been installed and put in working order, as Lents reports.

8.1   The hot spot problem arises when emissions from a source at a specific location cause more or less harms at a receptor site than emissions from other locations.

8.2   Intersource trading: An important fact of life for NO_x and VOC emissions trading is that significant emissions occur from mobile and area sources not covered in the market. This motivates attempts to devise ways to give tradable credits to stationary sources that can bring about reductions in vehicle, off-road mobile, or consumer product emissions. Few of these attempts are sufficiently well along to appraise their success. Obvious difficulties are being encountered in monitoring the extent and permanence of the reductions.

8.3   Integrated assessment modeling is discussed in the text.

legislated mandate. The U.S. EPA Final Rule for NO_x reduction issued in 1998 provides for an optional but recommended use of cap-based markets as a choice by 23 affected states. We have folded the Ozone Transport Commission (OTC) cap-and-trade market into this scheme because it is very similar in design, covers the same pollutant, affects a 13 state subset of the affected states of the Final Rule, and could be incorporated into the Final Rule program at a later date. The Final Rule has been challenged in court and its implementation remains to be determined. RECLAIM programs administered by SCAQMD of the Los Angeles region for local NO_x and SO_2 control have the distinction of being first off the mark in initiation. The ERMS program was developed by the Illinois EPA, and will be, if successful, the first cap-and-trade market to control VOC stationary source emissions.

The Pollutant

We have adopted the notational convenience of SO_2 for all the sulfur oxides, NO_x for nitrogen oxides instead of the often-used NO_2, and VOC for volatile organic compounds instead of reactive organic gases (ROG), or volatile organic materials (VOM). In this choice, the frequency of use has been put above creativity. All of these molecules play complex roles in the larger ecosystem acting in some instances as nutrients and in other cases as harmful agents. NO_x also can act as a cleansing agent for urban ozone at one concentration and a precursor at another. Nothing in school should be too easy. From emission, primarily as by-products of the combustion and use of fossil fuels, to final deposition as a harmful agent, these pollutants undergo complex physical, chemical, and meteorological processes.

Air quality models capturing some of these processes preceded initiation of each of these markets. Such modeling efforts, under continuing development, are an essential scientific background to effective control in general, and to effective market design. Market designs have also drawn on clinical and epidemiological studies of the impacts on human health as an approach to the estimation of the benefits of pollution reduction. The results of this scientific activity affect market coverage, caps, and many other features. Extensive accounts of the varying model specifications and results are available or cited elsewhere (U.S. EPA, 1998). Brief reference is made from point to point on significant aspects that bear directly on emissions trading schemes.

Market Coverage

Pollutants have no respect for political boundaries but markets do. For the Title IV market, the coverage is the continental United States, thus including some areas where SO_2 deposition is light and emissions few and excluding some areas, for example, in Canada, where deposition is more serious. The extent of reductions in emissions under the cap and the gains in efficiency through trading are thought to more than offset these spatial incongruities, as we have noted. The 23-state coverage of the EPA NO_x market was guided by information on atmospheric NO_x regional transport based on air quality models built for these purposes. VOC emissions have a more local orientation in large urban areas. Chapter 5 by Mary Gade and Roger Kanerva is informative on the results of modeling these pollutant movements. Special urban airshed models were developed to assist policy decisions about coverage in the RECLAIM and ERMS markets. In the case of RECLAIM, a spatial distinction was made between NO_x and SO_2 emissions sources located along the coast and sources inland. In view of modeling results of the prevailing winds, trading was permitted from coastal sources to inland but not the other way around.

The number and kinds of covered emission sources required to participate in a cap-and-trade market have always presented the unwary observer with seemingly different counts and definitions. Typically only larger emitters with fixed-point or stationary emitting units are included in the core coverage. Biogenic emissions can be important but are beyond the direct incentive approach, although some thought has been given to awarding credits for reductions brought about in this area. Reductions from mobile and area sources by core participants is another avenue for earning credits that has been utilized to a limited extent.

For each market, we have chosen to enter the number of enterprises or legal entities that manage portfolios as of the current date (recalling that mergers and acquisitions occur from time to time). This is typically much smaller than the number of plants and emissions generating units. For example, an investor owned utility might have more than one plant and within each plant there might be more than one electricity-generating unit (boiler or turbine). SO_2 allowances were assigned in Phase I to 263 such larger boilers and turbines. Later almost 200 additional generating units were brought voluntarily under the cap. All these units were owned by 110 separately managed utilities covered by the Phase I area (generally east of the Mississippi River). Similar distinctions are necessary for NO_x and VOC emitting source arithmetic. The entity responsible for making control, trading, and compliance decisions is the legal enterprise, and that is the number we have entered in the table.

With respect to kinds of emission generating enterprises, we distinguish between stationary, mobile, and area sources. Stationary or fixed-location sources tend to be the larger emitters per unit, fewer in total number than the other sources, and the simplest to incorporate into the market. The included stationary sources do not always emit the most significant share of the total from all sources, an area of contention as one might expect. Row 2.3 in the table gives our estimates of the covered stationary source share of total emissions. Mobile and area sources are typically very numerous and small thus posing problems for allocation of tradable credits. Extensions of the market whereby stationary sources can gain tradable credits for devising ways to reduce mobile and area emissions, for example, the cash for clunkers idea, have been proposed and are undergoing testing.

Who May Trade?

Determining who is allowed to participate in the market is not as simple a matter as it seems. In addition to covered sources that receive allocations, there has been a debate about allowing brokers, speculators, and others to join in the trading. The promotion of liquidity and an efficient market would point toward allowing everybody to participate, providing competitive rules are observed. Some regulators expressed concern about the impact of speculative activity on prices and allowance availability in thin markets. The SO_x and RECLAIM markets have been generally opened to brokers, speculators, and others, with the only requirement being that they must register. The same is true of the OTC market, and likely will be true of the NO_x Final Rule dependent upon state determinations. The ERMS market design initially restricted the qualifications of traders, setting forth detailed requirements for the designation and training of account officers acting for the affected source. These restrictions on participation have been relaxed in response to criticisms that they may make the market thin.

Characteristics of the Commodity—the Tradable Right

That the government should issue a tradable permit to pollute creates ethical questions for some, an issue that surfaces from time to time. It provokes the answer that this incentive system gives the government control over the volume of pollution, that the cap is typically a significant reduction in baseline emissions, and that the reduction is achieved at a reduced cost thus freeing society's resources for other desirable purposes. Another problem sometimes mentioned is that the enabling legislation, such as the CAAA'90, or administrative rule defines tradable credits not to be private property. The idea is to allow for government policy changes affecting the quantity, and thus the value, of tradable allowances as new knowledge of harms or costs surfaces. Thus the liability of the government for actions impairing the value of the right would be limited. Despite both these concerns, allowances or credits currently being traded by emitters, brokers, speculators, environmentalists, and school children are increasing in volume as if they were free of all sin and were in fact private property.

The bankability of the tradable right is an important matter that affects the intertemporal performance of the market. For efficient management of a portfolio of allowances, each of which can be used on or after its issuance date, the cost-minimizing emitter would aim to equate future control expenditures to expected future prices of allowances. Banking enables traders to make efficient intertemporal control decisions. When tradable credits of different first-use dates are issued, as is the case for the SO_2 and RECLAIM markets, various kinds of swaps and exchanges can also be executed to achieve this intertemporal requirement. In the case of the SO_2 market, the allowances are bankable permanently after the first-use date. The large bank of allowances being built up implies that emissions will be over the cap at a future date when the bank is drawn down. In the case of the RECLAIM markets, there is the problem of a transient, hot weather pollutant like ozone that could be aggravated by bursts or spikes of use of banked RECLAIM Trading Credits. Thus, banking per se is not allowed, but by introducing overlapping 12-month cycles and allowing the use of credits allocated in one cycle to be used in another, some intertemporal flexibility is introduced and a type of limited banking is granted. In the case of the ERMS program, where the same problem emerges, banking is permitted for one year after the first use date. The NO_x Final Rule suggests that if the bank builds beyond a certain point, then trades from the bank during the ozone season may take place only at a discount.

Cap Arithmetic

Market designers know that whatever contention has taken place over features up to this point is likely to be overshadowed by the disagreements between regulated and regulating communities that occur over the aggregate cap, and individual allocations under that cap. Since the aggregate cap is a reduction, the first sensitive point is reduction from what level or baseline? We have already discussed the issue of setting the cap so that harms are reduced to an acceptable level. However, what is acceptable to one group may not be to another. We have entered in Table 1.1 the present cap reductions as a percent from the baseline. The baseline from which the reduction is calculated raises different concerns. The baseline that has been most often chosen is some historical period on the grounds that the data are (somewhat) accurately in the record. Even if this were true, the matter of which historical period is to be chosen may be debated given business cycles in the economy and changes over time in industry and firm activity. There are winners and losers in this determination.

The NO_x Final Rule attempts an interesting variation in reducing the aggregate cap by making emission projections through the year 2007 assuming no new controls and then calculating the forward-looking cap reduction from that estimated amount. RECLAIM prepared scenarios through 2003 under which attainment of air quality standards (NAAQS) in the LA region would be achieved by tightened traditional regulation, and used that goal for the aggregate cap, which takes the place of the no longer needed, tightened traditional regulation. These forward-looking cap calculations overcome the objection that few historical periods will take all factors into account or satisfy all emitters. They are open to the limitation that unforeseen events may cause the cap to depart from welfare objectives.

Given the aggregate cap, individual source allocations can be based on various considerations. The simplest would be an auction by the government requiring emitters to purchase credits. The auction has attractive aspects in that clear price signals would be obtained and, in addition, the auction revenues could be used to reduce existing taxes that distort in unfavorable ways, like the income tax. However, the regulated community has an easily understood and strong preference for free allocation of credits and that view has held sway in all markets to date. The minor exceptions have been small set-aside percentages for sale to new enterprises, or for an annual auction in the case of the

SO_2 program. Even in the latter case, the net proceeds from the auction are returned to utilities in proportion to the set-aside allowances. Free allocation may well have been a crucial gambit to secure acceptance of a market approach.

Absent an auction, the problem is to establish a reference point for calculating the individual unit's allocation of tradable credits. The reader is invited to try his or her hand at devising an efficient and fair benchmark for this allocation. A historical period suggests itself. However, some emitters may feel they have made efforts to be clean in the past only to be punished by smaller allocations in the future. Other emitters may cite the business cycle, or unusual firm or industry or economywide conditions that necessitate special adjustments. For Phase I of the SO_2 program, the allocation equation for generating units called for multiplying an emissions rate of 2.5 pounds of SO_2 per million Btu's of heat input times the 1985–1987 average heat input. Reductions were then made from this benchmark. Considerable lobbying in congress resulted in a number of modifications of this equation (Joskow and Schmalensee, 1996).

The RECLAIM and ERMS programs have tried to ease this argument in different ways. ERMS allows enterprises to choose the average of the highest two years among the years 1994 to 1996. If justified other years between 1990 and 1997 may be substituted. RECLAIM allows enterprises the choice of the highest year in the interval 1989 to 1992. This latter policy has resulted in a substantial over-the-cap allocation of NO_x credits in the early period of the market. It is instructive to note that the plans for VOC control under a RECLAIM cap-and-trade market ran into major implementation difficulties in part because of disagreement over historical caps and individual allocations, and had to be indefinitely postponed and replaced by continuing command-and-control regulation.

Price and Transactions Data

Emissions trading makes economic sense only if marginal control costs vary among emitters. Those emitters with low costs can sell credits to those with high, both enjoying savings compared with the no-trade solution. If such costs were all the same, then a smart allocation would provide each emitter with enough credits to meet its individual reduction without trading. There is more than scattered evidence that control costs do vary in each of the markets creating the potential for substantial savings in costs from trading. For example, in the SO_2 market, high-sulfur coal scrubbers of various designs, low-sulfur coal, natural gas driven turbines, and other alternatives are available to cost-minimizing utilities. In the NO_x markets, where the pollutant is not in the fuel but arises mostly in the heat chamber, there exist opportunities to modify the temperature and thus NO_x creation, or install low NO_x burners, or introduce various catalytic reduction equipment. In the VOC market, there exist after-burner technologies, substitution among inputs, and product modification options for the consideration of cost-conscious emitters.

Whether this range of control options and technologies available to sources in each of the four markets is sufficient for achieving meaningful savings is, in our view, an empirical question. These savings are not the end of the story. Cost-saving control innovations may be stimulated by market incentives. Our contributors give us valuable insights on these significant matters and alert us to the difficult questions involved in estimating these savings.

If these markets are competitive and functioning well, the resultant prices will yield knowledge about marginal control costs, and the resultant volume of transactions will yield knowledge on the extent of savings being realized. Obtaining this knowledge, and consequently obtaining the basis for an appraisal of emissions trading, will necessitate that full and accurate data on prices and transactions become generally accessible. There are notable differences among the four markets in this regard.

As the U.S. EPA does not record price data on SO_2 allowances, the interested public must resort to the annual springtime auctions managed pro bono by the Chicago Board of Trade or to the voluntary publication of prices by private brokers. While valuable as an indicator, the once-a-year auctions do not provide enough observations for extensive statistical analysis. Burtraw and Ellerman (Chapters 7, 8) rely in large part on broker-provided price data for much of their work. Transactions information for each numbered SO_2 allowance is recorded by the U.S.

EPA Allowance Tracking System that can identify the initial allocation to a source and the final retirement by an emitting source. Intermediate transactions are not recorded. Kruger, McLean, and Chen (Chapter 6) give the reader an indispensable description of the extent and electronic processing of this information that has made accurate transactions data accessible to the public in a prompt manner.

Price and transaction data on the RECLAIM markets are available from the agency itself as it records prices when it records transactions. This information is supplemented by several brokerage houses, one of which offers an electronic bulletin board for posting bids and offers, and another publishes actual price and transactions data. The Illinois EPA plans to maintain an ownership database that will contain identification numbers for each Allotment Trading Unit and a market exchange bulletin board. What kinds of price information will become available on the NO_x markets remains to be seen when state decisions are made on the nature and extent of their participation in emissions trading.

Emissions Monitoring and Program Enforcement

Public and trader confidence in the market depends in an important way upon emissions monitoring and enforcement. The tradable credit can be degraded if monitoring is inaccurate or easy to avoid, and enforcement insufficient. The SO_2 process in these regards sets a good standard. The advanced state of continuous electronic emissions monitoring of what comes out of the smokestacks of electric utilities lends credence to the belief that the emissions record is whole and correct. Our contributors report on details of this feature that yields real-time electronic processing of consequential data at small administrative cost. The financial penalty for exceedances in this instance, $2,000 per ton, is substantially above the market prices of allowances. This deterrent together with a make-up requirement for the next period has greatly diminished concern about exceedances.

The RECLAIM program, as Lents reports, has encountered start-up problems in the installation and management of emissions recording equipment, problems that are currently being addressed through negotiations between the SCAQMD and the regulated community. The NO$_x$ Final Rule follows the SO$_2$ example in proposing monitoring and enforcement provisions. The U.S. EPA has offered to participate actively in the management of the NO$_x$ cap-and-trade markets if states choose this option. The ERMS program, after initially proposing a financial penalty, accepted the regulated community's counter proposal for a penalty "excursion compensation." For the first offense of not having sufficient tradable credits to cover emissions, the source must turn over in the next period the exceedance plus 20 percent. For the second offense, the penalty is 50 percent.

Continuing Issues and Future Choices

The four markets are efforts to control atmospheric pollution. Applications to obtain cleaner water or land have proved more difficult to develop due, in part, to the locational specificity of pollutants in these instances. Most air pollutants also have locational impacts, which means that emissions from some sources are more harmful to certain receptor areas than emissions from others. A trading scheme that took the details of location into account would require that tradable allowances have weights assigned to them depending on the emitting source and on the damage receptor. In principle this could be done; in practice this introduces much complexity and large transactions costs that could undermine the market's workability (Tietenberg, 1997). The issue becomes one of balancing the aggregate reduction in harms achieved by the cap against the fact that the remaining harms do not fall like the gentle rain evenly on all areas. Only careful quantitative studies can furnish definitive answers on the net effects, although most of the evidence to date suggests that all areas have benefited.

Congress simplified the SO$_2$ allowance market by making emissions independent of location; that is, emissions could be traded one-for-one no matter where they originated. This has been challenged, but the benefits of a more efficient market have so far outweighed the costs of ignoring the regional transport of this substance, as our contributors demonstrate. The fact that SO$_2$ emissions were to be reduced by half, and the fact that

continuance of an underlying layer of traditional regulation prohibited excess local emissions have both worked to protect
against excessive acid rain formation in specific areas.

New pollutant modeling results indicate that NO_x concentrations have a regional movement while VOC concentrations are
more local. This information is valuable for designing the geographic coverage of a cap-and-trade market. Furthermore, the
depth of reductions prescribed for NO_x, the use of seasonal discounting of trading credits, and the continuance of local restrictions, are believed to provide protection against local
adverse health impacts in a cap-and-trade system. The extremely useful simplification of one-for-one trading, independent of the location of the emission, has been generally adopted
in other applications such as the VOC market for Chicago. The
exception is the RECLAIM two-zone program, as noted. Clearly
the local adverse impact or "hot spot" problem will be one for
continuing monitoring and research.

The fact that the core sources covered by the cap-and-trade
markets emit only a varying fraction of the total is also a matter
of concern. It means that the government must rely on traditional regulation for sources not covered. Therefore, some emissions are market controlled and some controlled by traditional
regulation. Coordinating these two regulatory mechanisms to
achieve cleaner air raises challenging problems. Core sources
under the cap are typically larger enterprises with stationary
emitting units. It seems plausible that these sources could find
it cost-effective to earn credits by devising ways to reduce emissions from mobile and area sources. A number of proposals have
been made to stimulate intersource tradable credit creation although the results to date have been limited by difficulties in
making arrangements with generally small sources, and in assuring that reductions are quantifiable and permanent. The
"open market" concept, discussed in the next section, attempts
to create new avenues for tradable credit creation of this type.

Some thought has also been given to interpollutant trading,
but the details of such a program have yet to be worked out in
view of such complexities as estimating the damage trade-offs
among pollutants and hence the weights for the different tradable credits. The idea does suggest the advantages of a more
comprehensive modeling of pollutant emission, formation, and

transportation that would more fully exploit common origins and interactions. Such modeling could lay the basis for a more coordinated attack on joint control of related pollutants. In the United States, we have yet to develop an integrated assessment model or system that would provide for spatial coverage and the interrelated benefits and costs of atmospheric pollution reduction of the major substances including the pollutants already mentioned plus others like carbon monoxide, ammonia, hazardous air pollutants, and fine particulate matter. We have pieces of that integrated modeling in place. Perhaps at the present stage, given our modeling state of the art, there are advantages to this piecemeal approach; the focus is sharper and the problems of market design simpler. One can envision a future date, however, when an expanded knowledge base would enable the gains of this integrated approach to outweigh the losses of added complexity.

Rate-Based (Often Called Open-System) Emissions Trading

We return to our classification of trading systems that had at one end the cap-and-trade type market. We now turn to the other end where we place rate-based schemes in which participation is voluntary. That is, traditional control regulation without trading remains an option for the emitter. This means that business must calculate whether it is worth the costs of creating, selling or buying a tradable credit, where the costs include not only estimates of marginal control expenditures and the costs of searching for and negotiating with other traders, but also the costs of securing government verification of many details of the specific transaction. This means, for the government, verifying for each proposed emissions reduction credit (ERC) that it is permanent and not due to some transitory event, that it is genuinely surplus and not otherwise required by traditional regulation, that it is quantifiable, a matter often involving complex protocols, and that it is enforceable. The concerned public must try to estimate how much pollution has been reduced and what cost savings have been realized from use of these open-system programs. Managed as they are by the varied states, the available data is not always consistent.

Table 1.2   Features of Rate-Based or Open-System Emissions Trading

Features	Emissions Reductions Credits	Selected Programs — Discrete Emissions Reductions — Connecticut Program	Open Market Trading Rule
1. Pollutants	NO_x and VOC	NO_x and VOC	NO_x and VOC
2. Market coverage			
2.1 Geographical and other restrictions	Spatial, seasonal, and directional	Spatial, seasonal, and directional	Spatial, seasonal, and directional
2.2 Emitter participation	Voluntary	Voluntary	Voluntary
2.3 Number and kind of enterprise	All sources (stationary, mobile, and area source)	All sources	All sources
3. Who may trade?	Any registered party	Any registered party	Any registered party
4. Characteristics of tradable credit	Denominated in pounds or tons	Pounds or tons	Pounds or tons
4.1 When usable? (bankable?)	Permanent life with restrictions	Discrete amount with restrictions	Discrete amount with restrictions
4.2 Private property?	De facto rights	De facto rights	De facto rights
5. Rate (open system) arithmetic	Tradable credit earned by emissions reduction below legally allowable rate. Calculation based upon netting, offsetting, or bubbling concepts.	Credit earned by discrete reduction below allowable rate	Credit earned by discrete reduction below allowable rate
6. Price and transactions data	Not systematically collected, dependent upon state programs	Collected by state	Dependent upon state programs
7. Government regulation	Detailed verification of seller credit creation, sale, and buyer use.	Detailed verification	Verification of buyer use
7.1 Emissions monitoring and enforcement	State monitoring and enforcement	State monitoring and enforcement	State determination
8. Future issues			
8.1 Intersource trading (stationary, mobile, and area)	Possible where feasible	Possible where feasible	Possible where feasible

Notes: Column headings: Emissions Reduction Credits (ERCs) are described in the text and have a permanent life for the face value of emissions when approved by the government. Discrete Emissions Reductions (DERs) are described in the text and have a variable life dependent on state rules. They may be used only for the finite amount of emissions stated on the face of the credit. The Connecticut program is explained in the Belanger study. The Open Market Trading Rule is described by U.S. EPA in the Federal Register (1998).

Table 1.2 *(Continued)*

2.1   Both ERCs and DERs may have geographic, seasonal, and directional (generally winds from the southwest blow toward the northeast of the United States) restrictions. Note the discussion by Belanger.

2.2   All sources may participate on a voluntary basis, opening up the possibility of earning credit, when approved, by enterprises organizing reductions among mobile and area sources. To date, large enterprises with stationary emitting units have been the most active in these markets.

5.   Tradable credits must be earned by reducing emissions below legally allowable or actual rates or levels as verified by the government. Verification is typically a complex determination on which Belanger's study throws much light.

6.   Price and transaction data vary in their availability from state to state. The advantages of central reporting deserve more consideration.

8.1   In principle, states may propose intersource and interpollutant trading for U.S. EPA approval. States have yet to fulfill their potential role as experimental laboratories in this regard.

Why accept such partial trading schemes when the cap-based model yields control over aggregate pollution and enables a decentralized approach to be monitored efficiently? This is a key question that has been answered by supporters of the rate-based model in the following ways. Obtaining agreements for the design features of the cap-and-trade market, as we have pointed out, have proved time consuming and, on occasion, seemingly impossible. Why not have some cost-effective trading where possible rather than none? Rate-based efforts could be a preparatory step for later cap-based implementation. Moreover, control of urban ozone and its precursors require consideration of the locale, the seasonality of formation, and the directionality of ozone and precursor transport. Cap-based designs, it is argued, could be so complicated in these circumstances as to be not worth the cost whereas the rate-based systems enable individual transactions to be evaluated in terms of these factors. It is better to have varied trading tools in the market-incentive chest that can be adapted to different situations.

To facilitate for the reader a comparison of these approaches, we have entered in Table 1.2 selected features of both the ERC and discrete emissions reductions credits (DERs), two of the major open systems. Having described cap-based systems in detail, we can refer more briefly to the main differences. Three areas deserve close attention as we proceed. The decision to participate by emitters is voluntary and the benefits and costs of participation are likely to be complex and vary by emitter, pollutant, and state characteristics. The regulating community in turn has complex matters about air quality and rules that must be resolved, illustrated in detail by the study of the Connecticut DERs program explained in Chapter 11 by Joseph Belanger. Last, obtaining comprehensive and comparable data for evaluation purposes raises problems that have yet to be resolved.

Emission Reduction Credits (ERCs)

We shall focus on the ERC and DERs designs and experience because they have a more immediate bearing on the concerns of this volume than the trading programs introduced for the removal of leaded gasoline and chlorofluorocarbons in commercial products, both of which affected only a few large enterprises. Stavins comments on these last two programs in his work. First in time of application are the various ERC stratagems whose history can throw light on emissions trading problems and lessons learned.

In 1970, the U.S. Congress amended the Clean Air Act (CAA) to require, in Title I, that EPA issue, periodically review, and if necessary revise National Ambient Air Quality Standards (NAAQS) for six criteria air pollutants, including the three of special interest to us, SO_2, NO_x, and VOC. Criteria pollutants were those acceptable at higher concentrations than toxic pollutants. States were to be the frontline regulators and for that purpose congress required that they submit State Implementation Plans (SIPs) to attain and maintain both primary (health) and secondary standards (visibility, vegetation, and materials protection). Progress toward cleaner air proved much slower than mandated under the prescribed traditional regulation, and in 1977, among other important changes, Congress established the concept of NAAQS nonattainment areas and set stringent deadlines for regions and states to reach attainment with such dramatic, but as yet unused, penalties for the states as loss of highway funds if such were not met.

Concern about penalties together with growing concerns about the increasing marginal costs of cleaning the air, created pressures on many fronts to devise new and hopefully cheaper and quicker ways to comply with the CAA mandates. While control costs were not explicitly to be considered in devising regulation, the EPA introduced over time a series of efforts to introduce emissions trading among acceptable regulatory mechanisms. These included the policies of bubbling, netting, offsetting, and banking, linked together by the tradable ERCs. The bubble policy allowed existing sources to use ERCs to meet SIP requirements in nonattainment areas. Thus, a source within the bubble could earn an ERC by a rate reduction and use that credit elsewhere in its own system or sell to a source, also within the bubble, that could then exceed the allowable rate. In a sense, the SO_2 cap-and-trade market may be viewed as a national bubble for emissions trading.

Netting permits a source to modify or expand one unit within its facility providing the source can reduce emissions at another unit and thus earn compensating ERCs. This simplified the regulatory process. Offsetting enables new sources in a nonattainment area to purchase ERCs, and banking enables sources to store ERCs earned in the above ways for future use. In each instance, the ERC must be certified to be surplus, enforceable, permanent, and quantifiable. The regulatory agency given these assignments, even if disposed favorably toward emissions trading, would find a detailed review and prior approval of the transaction a pressing responsibility. For sources required to have an operating permit under the SIP, this meant a revision of that operating permit. Trading was limited by these regulatory measures. Many trades that did occur were internal to the large firm having more than one emitting facility or unit rather than external or interfirm.

In an effort to increase use of ERCs, the U.S. EPA codified the various rules in the 1986 Emission Trading Policy Statement (ETPS), but the high level of constraints and government supervision inherent in the ERC policies was not fundamentally changed and transaction costs have remained high. The number of trades sanctioned by official state emission trading programs have been relatively small compared with expectations (Dudek, Goffman, and Wade, 1997).

Discrete Emissions Reductions Credits (DERs)

In a clear and forceful statement, the U.S. EPA turned to a new voluntary program that attempted to simplify the ERC regulatory approach and increase emissions trading and its benefits. With its 1995 Open-Market Trading Rule for Ozone Smog Precursors, the agency recommended to the states the establishment of a process whereby sources could voluntarily create discrete emissions reductions for compliance with NO_x and VOC emissions under the 1990 legislation. As with ERCs, sources generate DERs by reducing emissions below permitted levels, but for a discrete amount of emissions and not for a nonending stream. States may decide to allow the DERs to be used at any time in the future.

Furthermore, unlike ERCs, prior approval by governmental authorities is not required to generate DERs. Sellers need not obtain a SIP revision in this case. The burden of securing government approval is shifted mainly to the buyer, a significant change from the ERC policies. Once a source generates these new credits, any person may, at any time, transfer, buy, sell, or trade them to another person in accordance with state laws. They can then be used any time after the state receives notice of their generation. At the time of use, users must retire 10 percent of all DERs dedicated to that particular use as a contribution to cleaner air. Users must provide certification of their authenticity including a statement that due diligence was made to verify that DERs were not previously used and that they were generated in accordance with regulations.

States must prescribe where the DERs can be used. For example, they can be used in the same modeling area in which they were generated or, if generated inside a specified nonattainment area, they can be used outside a nonattainment area. But, if generated outside a nonattainment area, there are restrictions on their use inside the area. Interstate trading of DERs under certain directionality requirements is also covered under the 1995 Open-Market Trading Rule.

The open-market rule was based in part on commentary and trials provided by the Northeast States for Coordinated Air Use Management (NESCAUM) and the Mid-Atlantic Regional Air Management Association (MARAMA) that brought together state and local officials, the business community, and public interest groups to work through the numerous design features. The use of market incentives to achieve environmental goals has strengthened the trend to bring together all interested groups involved in regulation for serious work on changes and reforms. This has helped reduce the confrontations that occurred in some applications of traditional regulation.

This open-market trading design for DERs appears to avoid the contentious issues of cap and allocation, but it presents another set of problems and clouds the relation between trading and aggregate pollution control. One problem that is likely to be encountered is the dependence of the quality of DERs upon the documentation that the seller can provide. Hence, DERs may sell at varying prices. The EPA suggested that intermediaries could help assure quality and ease transaction costs. After a successful trade or two, the emitter may find later regulation moves more quickly. The first indications from this new program is that there are more DERs for sale than buyers' demand, apparently a disequilibrium that price alone at this initial stage cannot solve.

In an effort to bring an early appraisal for the use of DERs to the attention of interested observers, the Workshop asked Joseph Belanger to report on the Connecticut implementation of the new policy. The program has generated a number of transactions for review, primarily for NO_x, and made available price data for analysis.

The Connecticut Department of Environmental Protection has created DERs with some characteristics that differ from those recommended in the model 1995 Rule. One of the distinctions is that an important regulatory simplification has not been utilized. Detailed state regulation continues at both the seller and buyer ends of the transaction. This, as Belanger points out, results in increased administrative burden for sources, as well as for the Department, but in turn has reduced the uncertainty and administrative burden for buyers. Another distinction is that additional usage restrictions are attached to the commodity—they are not generic once created. Each trade, like a trade of ERCs, is viewed as a SIP revision. DERs may be banked for two years only and may be used at a rate per unit time that approximates the rate during which they were created. Thus, they present another distinct trading model for consideration.

The Connecticut program began in 1995 and has generated DERs that cover approximately 6 percent of NO_x emissions from the state's stationary sources. A number of credits have been purchased from sources in New Jersey and Belanger provides interesting data on the transactions. Note that DERs created in Connecticut could not be sold to sources in New Jersey. Prices reported for DERs were in the range of $750 to $850 per ton in late 1998. An instructive note in this study is the thought given to the creation of DERs among sources not ordinarily included in green markets, that is, among mobile and area sources. To the extent this type of credit is more easily adapted to these sources, the DERs credits, or more generally, the open-market can be developed jointly with the closed-market model for stationary sources. To date, these intersource transactions have not been numerous.

Belanger notes in conclusion that consideration is being given in his state to moving from the existing DERs program to the NO_x cap-and-trade policy now being recommended to the affected states, and discussed previously in this introduction. The details brought out in Belanger's account of the program in Connecticut reveal the burden placed on government and business by rate-based regulation. Can the alternative, the cap-and-trade markets, be designed to assure air quality everywhere in the ozone case? One problem is that the precursors of low–level ozone are not uniformly mixed in the atmosphere as are (generally) sulfur dioxide and carbon dioxide. However, the advances in air quality modeling that have increased our knowledge of VOC emissions and its local transport and NO_x emissions and its regional transport have increased the confidence of many that the more comprehensive designs of cap-based markets can control these pollutants. This story is by no means over.

This brings us to the end of our little red schoolhouse. Our aim has been to prepare the way for the graduate studies of our contributors who, in presenting the best answers currently available, bring us to the frontier of emissions trading knowledge, research, and implementation. We turn in this last introductory section to a brief survey of their contributions.

Survey of Contributions

Joseph Belanger's study of the Connecticut voluntary market incentive program gives the reader an insider view of the regulatory procedures in this rate-based case to compare with those of cap-and-trade markets. While the program does not make use of the open market concept that reduces pre-trade approval requirements, it does make use of time-limited discrete emissions reductions (DERs). These differ from ERCs by allowing a finite amount of emissions rather than a never-ending stream. Belanger, as a member of a regulating agency that views market incentives with favor, describes for us the many detailed approvals and considerations that take place prior to and after each transaction to assure that emissions reductions are proper and air quality is not debased. He notes that such procedures lead to large transactions costs and has limited trades to a small percentage of total emissions. His data on specific trades reveals that a few large transactions dominate the scene to date.

Dallas Burtraw has been a close and acute observer of the SO_2 market. He was among the first to recognize that control cost savings were being realized before extensive inter-firm trading occurred as electric utilities reallocated allowances among their own boilers, and as utilities took advantage of the new flexibility afforded by decentralized regulation. His study extends this analysis to a period of increasing transactions. While additional savings are being achieved, he points out that prior events such as the availability of cheaper low-sulfur coal must be given considerable credit. His study includes new research results that reveal the increased health benefits of reducing acid rain precursors that can carry tiny particles deep into the lungs. This finding provides additional support for the legislative cuts in SO_2 emissions by half, and may point toward even deeper reductions. Another finding based on an explicit model is that the congressional mandate of free allocation of allowances to emitters has reduced the potential welfare gains of the market as the government is not able to use revenues received from an auction to reduce other taxes that distort in unfavorable ways.

A. Denny Ellerman is able to draw on the extensive empirical studies his MIT research group has made of the SO_2 cap-and-trade market in his account of the electric utility response to allowance prices. He reports that market information has enabled many utilities to correct early mistakes such as overestimating the prices of allowances and overlooking profitable trades with other emitters. Lower than expected prices for low-sulfur coal and for improved scrubbers have reduced the marginal cost of emissions reductions. Trading and price mistakes were among the reasons for over-compliance that led to an unexpected large bank of unused allowances. Utilities have shown their capacity to learn from these developments in managing their control options both currently and in the post-2000 year phase of tighter restrictions on emissions. They are trading more heavily in the market, and building portfolios of future-dated allowances for cost-effective intertemporal control. Ellerman believes market-based flexibility facilitates the correction of mistakes.

Mary Gade and **Roger Kanerva** share with us the hopes and achievements of the Ozone Transport and Assessment Group where Gade led the overall effort and Kanerva the emissions trading discussion. This remarkable degree of cooperation among the states, the U.S. EPA, the regulated community, and public interest groups left a technical database on NO_x regional transport that has extended our knowledge markedly, and a set of useful recommendations on control measures. Many of these have found their way into the new NO_x control requirements placed on the states by the U.S. EPA and into the recommended cap-and-trade market. These efforts to control regional movement of NO_x need to be followed by local steps to reduce VOC. Here again Gade and Kanerva have been among the pioneers in formulating a cap-and-trade market for limiting stationary source emissions of VOC in Northeastern Illinois. While not all efforts in OTAG were agreed to by all parties, the results achieved in this study are likely to provide lasting guides to environmental policy.

Joseph Kruger, Brian McLean, and **Rayenne Chen** bring out clearly that innovations on the commanding heights of environmental policy can take place in the decisions of the regulating community as well as in those of the regulated community. The electronic processing of allowances in the SO_2 Allowance Tracking System has not only provided assurance, to the public and the market, that the rules for trading and retiring allowances are being followed, but also has provided data to the research community for analysis (as will be seen in the Burtraw and Ellerman studies). This is, of course, only half the story. Electronic monitoring of emissions by means of continuous emissions monitoring devices provides the assurance that emissions are accounted for by allowances. Setting up these systems, managing them, and maintaining contact with the regulated community are the responsibilities of a remarkably small staff at the U.S. EPA Acid Rain Division. Our authors explain what they rightly term is an administrative revolution.

James Lents as executive director of the South Coast Air Quality Management District was at the center of the detailed, sometimes contentious discussions that gave birth to early cap-and-trade markets to achieve cleaner air in the Los Angeles region, that super bowl of smog. His study gives the reader a careful, empirical review of three years of operation of the NO_x and SO_x programs, 1994–1996, plus his analysis of the problems that remain to be resolved. The programs require deep cuts in emissions by the year 2003 but allowed over-allocation of non-bankable trading credits during the first years to ease transition to a market-based approach. Actual emissions have not increased during these early years. The intertemporal price path of tradable credits, which are issued to emitters in advance of their first-use dates, exhibit a plausible rising trajectory. Increased trading of credits also is among the indicators of markets that are beginning to function. Lents notes that problems are being encountered in setting up satisfactory electronic monitoring devices to record emissions, in the slow development of inter-emitter trading, and in the delay of actual reductions of emissions.

Michael Moskow adds a closing note to the volume by highlighting the general applicability of incentive-based regulation to other economic activities outside of environmental concerns. He provides examples in the area of financial regulation, his particular field of expertise. The cost-savings and flexibility potential of this regulatory innovation could be significant in the further development of the Midwest economy, recently the subject of a comprehensive study by the Chicago Federal Reserve Branch. Well-designed public policies, including market-based approaches to regulation, will have a role to play if advances in economic well-being in the region are to continue. The author notes that the Midwest has provided its share of leadership in designing and implementing regulatory innovations for cleaner air. Prominent examples include plans for NO_x control by emissions trading proposed by OTAG, and plans for VOC control by implementation of the Emissions Reduction Market System for the Chicago region.

William Nordhaus has been the developer of sophisticated models of environmental control that have influenced the economics profession and policy-makers alike. These models have boldly included ways of estimating the benefits and costs of alternative control strategies and thus thrown a bright and often critical light on current policy proposals. In his study, he writes for the informed but not technically trained reader, first describing the long history of the evolution of new financial commodities, and then bringing us up to date on the development of the current innovation—tradable emission credits. He finds reasons to rate the U.S. sulfur dioxide allowance program a success to date, but his analysis of the proposals to use tradable credits as a tool to limit greenhouse gas emissions, a global problem, raises important problems. Any realistic analysis of the future contribution of emissions trading to global warming control will do well to heed his cautions.

Richard Sandor is known inside and outside financial circles as a leading creator of new financial products, a skill he now brings to the generation of new environmental financial products. He and his colleague, **Michael Walsh,** have participated in the early stages of work on the sulfur dioxide market, and are now fully engaged in the early stages of the development of the carbon dioxide markets. Their chapter does hit more optimistic notes than that of Nordhaus, but the reader will find that both have a clear understanding of the opportunities and problems that lie ahead in applying market incentives to this, arguably, our most important environmental problem. The differences between their studies may be found mostly in their estimates of the political feasibility of securing agreement among the nations, or subsets of them, on an emissions quota or cap–and–trade plan that could exploit the large differences in control costs among emitters. The issues and choices are squarely met in these studies.

Robert Stavins is well qualified to explain the recent history of market-based approaches, a history that can be puzzling to the newcomer. His work has been in the forefront of our understanding of the potential of market incentives. He applies positive and normative analysis to regulatory innovations that once interested only a few academics but now have become topics of general discussion, and application. Readers will find why traditional regulation had, and still has, an appeal, and why emissions trading has secured additional and influential advocates. Readers will also find a valuable summary of the lessons to be learned from the performance of emissions trading applications to date. He presents guidelines for design features and for implementation in those circumstances where this innovation is likely to work best.

Panelists are vital contributors to the Workshop exchange of ideas, and continue that role in this volume. They provide both commentaries on the studies and original views and information on incentive-based regulation. A few examples among many will suffice in this introduction; all are worth close attention. **Vincent Albanese** shares his extensive knowledge of the various control measures that can reduce NO_x emissions. This information lends support to the idea that marginal control costs vary among emitters, and also provides an inkling of the potential innovations that may be stimulated by incentive-based regulation. **Thomas Klier** brings the tools of economic analysis to bear on the Los Angeles RECLAIM markets and finds that many enterprises are on the rapidly rising portion of the learning curve. **Kenneth Rose** from his vantage point overlooking electric utilities, and having access to comprehensive data, reports on how this twice regulated industry may not yet be taking full advantage of all the profitable trading opportunities in the sulfur dioxide allowance program. **Sarah Wade** explains how one large enterprise has introduced a carbon dioxide emissions-trading program within its own far-flung and diverse activities. It is an internal cap-and-trade type design which takes as its cap a percentage reduction from the firm's historical emissions. This reduction exceeds the average agreed to at the Kyoto conference on this topic. **Thomas Zosel** has had a long experience with all types of regulation and points out the importance of a clear delegation of responsibility between regulated and regulating communities. Mr. Zosel died shortly after completing his study which the editors publish as one of his last contributions to regulatory implementation.

REFERENCES

Dudek, Daniel J., Joseph Goffman, and Sarah M. Wade. 1997. "Emissions Trading in Nonattainment Areas: Potential, Requirements, and Existing Programs." Pp. 15–46 in *Market-Based Approaches to Environmental Policy*, edited by Richard F. Kosobud and Jennifer M. Zimmerman. New York: Van Nostrand Reinhold.

Joskow, Paul L. and Richard Schmalensee. 1996. "The Political Economy of Market-Based Environmental Policy: The U.S. Acid Rain Program." Working paper 96-003, Center for Energy and Environmental Policy Research, Massachusetts Institute of Technology, Cambridge, MA, March.

Montgomery, W. David. 1972. "Markets in Licenses and Efficient Pollution Control Programs." *Journal of Economic Theory* 5: 395–418.

Portney, Paul R. 1993. "EPA and the Evolution of Federal Regulations." Pp. 57–74 in *Economics of the Environment*, edited by Robert Dorfman and Nancy S. Dorfman. Third edition. New York: W.W. Norton Company.

Rosenberg, William G. 1997. "An Insiders View of the SO_2 Allowance Trading Legislation." Pp. 95–100 in *Market-Based Approaches to Environmental Policy*, edited by Richard F. Kosobud and Jennifer M. Zimmerman. New York: Van Nostrand Reinhold.

Tietenberg, Thomas H. 1997. *Environmental and Natural Resources Economics*. New York: HarperCollins College Publishing.

Tolley, George S. and Brian K. Edwards. 1997. "Slippage Factors in Emissions Trading." Pp. 187–197 in *Market-Based Approaches to Environmental Policy*, edited by Richard F. Kosobud and Jennifer M. Zimmerman. New York: Van Nostrand Reinhold.

U.S. Environmental Protection Agency. 1998. "Open Market Trading Rule for Ozone Smog Precursors." *Federal Register* 60 (149) (3 August): 39668–39694.

Weitzman, Martin L. 1974. "Prices and Quantities." *Review of Economic Studies* XLI: 477–491. October.

PART TWO

APPRAISING ENVIRONMENTAL POLICY'S NEW APPROACH

2

What Do We Really Know about Market-Based Approaches to Environmental Policy?

Lessons from Twenty-Five Years
of Experience

Robert N. Stavins

Μy goal is to review lessons that can be learned from three decades of experience with tradable permit systems for pollution control in the United States. I examine both positive and normative lessons: lessons about why we regulate as we do, and lessons about how we can do it better.[1]

I begin with positive lessons by noting that 30 years of political reality in the United States has diverged strikingly from economists' recommendations regarding environmental policy instrument choice. Those departures can be described in terms of three anomalies. First, economists have consistently urged the use of market-based or economic-incentive policy instruments because of the cost effectiveness potential and the dynamic incentives for technological change that can be associated with these approaches. On the other hand, the stock of environmental regulations renders the amount of pollution affected by implemented market-based instruments little more than trivial. Second, when market-based instruments have been employed, one specific form has nearly always been used in the United States: freely-distributed tradable permits, not auctioned permits, nor emission taxes. Third, in recent years, the political process has become much more receptive to using market-based instruments, despite three decades of effective resistance to these ideas.

How can we explain these three anomalies? We may start by considering the predominance of command-and-control over market-based instruments despite the apparent economic superiority of the latter. From an economic perspective, we can examine the political process through the lens of a market metaphor, treating the regulatory process as having a demand side and a supply side (Keohane, Revesz, and Stavins, 1998). Beginning with the regulatory demand side, we note that firms often prefer command-and-control to auctioned permits and taxes because, first of all, standards produce economic rents for firms. When rents (returns above normal profits) are produced for firms, those rents are eventually dissipated because other firms enter the markets, but if command-and-control standards are combined with more stringent standards for new sources, then an effective barrier to entry is created and those rents become sustainable. In fact, if we examine actual command-and-control regulations, we note that command-and-control standards are often coupled with so-called "new source performance standards," which have the perverse consequences of driving up the costs of environmental protection by retarding technological change and thereby—in some cases—reducing environmental protection. In addition, with auctioned permits and taxes, firms are paying not only abatement costs, but also taxes for residual emissions or costs of purchasing permits.

So, even though market-based instruments are cheaper than command-and-control from an economywide perspective, from the perspective of private industry, that is not necessarily the case. Those taxes, which in a social benefit-cost analysis are simply transfers from the private sector to the public sector, are very much counted by the private sector. Also, on the regulatory demand side, environmental interests groups have preferred command-and-control to market-based instruments because of philosophical, strategic, and technical objections to market-based approaches.[2]

Now, we turn to the regulatory supply side. Here, command-and-control regulations are essentially easier for legislators to supply because those legislators' training and experience, which is essentially within the law, makes them comfortable with thinking in terms of command-and-control regulations. Furthermore, standards are very effective for hiding the costs of pollution control and emphasizing the benefits (McCubbins and Sullivan, 1984). And politicians are fond of passing out benefits, but abhor the notion of passing out identifiable costs.

For example, think about Corporate Average Fuel Economy (CAFE) standards compared with gasoline taxes. We know that there are gasoline taxes of particular magnitude that would accomplish the same as existing CAFE standards, but at a lower cost, yet we continue to use CAFE standards. Ask anyone on the street how much CAFE standards cost them in terms of the price of a new car. On the other hand, try to implement a small gasoline tax that would have the same effect on fuel efficiency and note how those same consumers will respond.

Also, on the regulatory supply side, standards are much more consistent with symbolic politics (McCubbins, Noll, and Weingast, 1987). Consider the preambles to the Clean Air Act or the Clean Water Act. Can we really claim with a straight face that we will make all waters in America fishable and swimmable in the near future and that we will do it with a pollution tax or a tradable permit system? On the other hand, we can with a straight face, although it is fundamentally dishonest, talk about making all waters in America fishable and swimmable in the near future using the "best available technology" to get there.

Finally, on the regulatory supply side, command-and-control standards offer more control over the distributional effects of environmental regulation. It is not left up to the market. Regulators in the past were understandably reticent to turn any kind of environmental policy over to an economic instrument because that means leaving it to the market to allocate costs among firms and, more importantly in our representative democracy, among geographic areas (congressional districts).

Those are my attempts to explain briefly the first anomaly of predominance of command-and-control over market-based instruments, despite the overwhelming evidence of the economic superiority of market-based instruments for environmental protection.

The second anomaly is that we have used freely distributed permits exclusively, when there are a number of other market-based policy instruments that we can also use to address these issues. On the regulatory demand side, freely distributed tradable permits, like command-and-control, distribute rents to regulated firms. The property rights involved in the SO_2 tradable permit program are worth about $1 billion. This is a gift bestowed on private firms by the federal government. In addition to that, like new source performance standards, freely distributed permits give rise to entry barriers, and if there are entry barriers together with rents, those rents are sustainable, just as in the case of command-and-control. In addition, freely distributed permits offer much greater degrees of political control, compared with auctioned permits or taxes, over the distribution of costs. One of the attributes of freely distributed permits is that we can leave it up to the legislature to give them out however they wish; they can essentially bribe the constituencies. Think about the 3.5 million bonus allowances in the Clean Air Act Amendments of 1990, on top of what was a 10 million ton program for reducing SO_2 emissions. Those 3.5 million tons of bonus allowances were fundamental to creating the constituencies that were necessary to move the legislation through Congress (Joskow and Schmalensee, 1998).

The third anomaly is the relatively recent rise, despite years of resistance, in interest and activity with market-based instruments in general, and specifically, tradable permits. Why has this happened? One way to reflect on this change is to think back nearly two decades ago, when a colleague of mine, Steven Kelman, wrote a book that was rather critical of market-based instruments (Kelman, 1981). He sought to understand policy makers' perceptions of these instruments. He interviewed Democratic and Republican Congressional staff. He found that Democrats were hostile toward market-based approaches to environmental protection, but that they really did not understand them. He found that Republicans thought that market-based instruments for environmental protection were a great idea, but that they did not understand them either. My refutable hypothesis is that if we were to replicate Kelman's study today, we would find dramatic increases in support among Democrats, relatively small increases in support from Republicans, but not sufficient increases in understanding from either party to explain these dramatic changes. So what else has mattered?

First, we should acknowledge that there has been some increase in knowledge of these instruments among policy makers. Part of this is attributable to the growing number of public policy schools across the United States. In these schools, students receive a heavy dose of economics, and economics in a very political context. In addition to that, there has been the emergence and ascendancy of the law and economics movement within U.S. law schools. It is now difficult to get a law degree without exposure to an economic perspective of regulation. So there is an increased understanding of market-based approaches to environmental protection.

But there is more to it than that. The second fact that helps explain the change is that pollution control costs have been increasing. We are essentially marching up the marginal abatement cost function.[3] We addressed the lower cost problems first, for example, point sources in the case of water, as opposed to nonpoint sources. Whether it is air pollution, water pollution, or surface disposal, we naturally address the cheaper problems first. When one is addressing problems that are relatively low cost, it is not as important to focus on cost effectiveness, but as we move up the marginal abatement cost curve, cost effectiveness becomes a more important criteria for selection of policy instruments, and therefore we have given more policy attention to market-based instruments, because they can be cost-effective.

Third, environmental advocacy groups have played an exceptionally important role in this debate. In particular, the Environmental Defense Fund has been absolutely crucial in the process. They had a direct effect on legislation in the Bush administration when the Environmental Defense Fund split off from the rest of the environmental community and worked with the White House to design the SO_2 tradable permit system. Furthermore, whereas the Natural Resources Defense Council, the Sierra Club, the Audubon Society, and the Wilderness Society opposed market-based instruments 10 to 15 years ago, they have all moved to somewhere between limited acceptance and outright enthusiasm.

Fourth, there has been an unmistakable shift of the political center toward a much more favorable view of using the market to solve social problems, whether it is introducing competition to the telecommunications industry, or deregulation of railroads, trucking, or airlines.

Fifth, it is interesting to note that the major national market-based environmental instruments have addressed previously unregulated problems. Hence, there was no constituency politically for the *status quo* approach, because there was no *status quo* approach. The leaded gasoline phase-down was the first truly great success with market-based instruments. In the leaded gasoline phase-down, the lead reduction credits were used by refineries to phase out leaded gasoline and to cut lead content in the 1980s to 10 percent of previous concentrations through a tradable permit system. But, although airborne lead is a pollutant under the Clean Air Act, we were not phasing down the lead in gasoline until then. This was a new program. The chlorofluorocarbon (CFC) phase down—obviously a new program—was another success. And third, the most recent success has been the SO_2 allowance trading system under the 1990 Clean Air Act Amendments for acid rain control.

This should make us more optimistic about introducing market-based instruments for "new problems"—for example, carbon dioxide emissions and the greenhouse effect—than for regulated problems that have significant constituencies associated with the *status quo* regulatory approach, such as addressing the problem of abandoned hazardous waste sites. I conclude this part of this chapter, the positive part, with the following prediction regarding the likely future adoption of market-based instruments: global climate, yes; Superfund, no.

We now turn to the normative lessons from 25 years of experience with market-based instruments for environmental protection. I do this within three categories: lessons broadly for environmental policy; lessons for the design of tradable permit systems; and lessons for identifying new applications.

First, there are two broad lessons for environmental policy. One is that tradable permit systems work. To most economists, this may not be much of a surprise, but it is a very significant lesson. The emissions reduction credit trading program of the EPA, started in the 1970s, had great problems associated with it and this was one of the reasons why there was much skepticism about tradable permit programs in the policy community; they looked good in theory, but we had not witnessed a real success. Later, the lead reduction program failed to convince people, simply because the program lacked prominence. But the SO_2 allowance trading program received tremendous public attention, and this success has brought new credibility (Ellerman et al., 1997).

One other broad lesson is that the performance of these systems highlights the great value of regulatory flexibility. An important virtue of a tradable permit system is simply that it is not a technology standard. It is, in a sense, a form of performance standard. And that in itself—moving from a technology standard to a performance standard—is a tremendous improvement, which is why under tradable permit systems, one can have cost-effective improvements, even when there is no trading. An example of this is found in the SO_2 program (Burtraw, 1996). One of the principle reasons SO_2 controls have turned out to be so inexpensive is that railroad deregulation greatly reduced the price of low sulfur coal from the Powder River Basin. Had there been a technology standard in place, such as a scrubber requirement, such cost savings would not have been realized.

Next I consider several lessons for the design and implementation of tradable permit systems. The first is to keep it simple and keep it flexible. The temptation to address other problems by adding on complexities to tradable permit systems leads to problems. This is the history of the EPA's Emissions Trading Program for criteria air pollutants. We can think about flexibility in two ways: technologically and temporally. Technologically, for example, if we were considering a CO_2 tradable permit system, it should include not only emissions, but also sequestration, that is, land use (Stavins, 1999). On the temporal side, the evidence from the SO_2 program (Ellerman et al., 1997) and the lead trading program (Kerr and Maré, 1997) is that banking—intertemporal trading—is an exceptionally large part of the potential gains from trade. So, intertemporal flexibility is also very important.

In terms of simplicity, unique allocation formulas based on historical data are more difficult to contest or manipulate than complex formulas that address various constituencies and various concerns. Trading rules should be clearly defined up front, and there should be no requirements for government prior approval of trades.

Second, whenever possible, absolute baselines should be employed, not relative baselines. The difference is that with an absolute baseline (so-called *cap-and-trade*), sources are each allocated some number of permits (the total of which is the cap); with a relative baseline, reductions are credited from an unspecified baseline. The problem is that without a specified baseline, reductions must be credited relative to an unobservable hypothetical—what the source would have emitted in the absence of the regulation. A hybrid system—where a cap-and-trade program is combined with voluntary "opt-in provisions"—creates the possibility for *paper trades,* where a regulated source is credited for an emissions reduction (by an unregulated source) that would have taken place in any event (Montero, 1997). The result is a decrease in aggregate costs among regulated sources, but this is partly due to an unintentional increase in the total emissions cap (Atkeson, 1997). As was experienced with EPA's Emissions Trading Program, relative baselines create significant transaction costs by essentially requiring prior approval of trades as the authority investigates the claimed counterfactual from which reductions are calculated and credits generated (Nichols, Farr, and Hester, 1996).

Third, reliable monitoring and enforcement are essential. Continuous emissions monitoring pioneered by the SO_2 permit trading program and now happening in the RECLAIM program helps to build market confidence (McLean, 1995). On the other hand, such monitoring comes at a significant cost, and continuous emissions monitoring will not be worthwhile for all environmental problems. On the enforcement side, sanctions are very important; stiff penalties are required. But it is equally important not to make the penalty too stiff; the question is what is the optimal penalty. If it is too small it will not be effective. The penalty must be greater than the marginal abatement cost faced by private industry or it will have no effect. On the other hand, if the penalty is too high, it will not be credible. So, a good penalty is in the Clean Air Act of 1990, where it is set at $2000 per ton of excess SO_2 emissions, and marginal abatement costs are about $100 per ton of emissions. An example of an ineffective penalty that is set too high, is under the Clean Air Act, where the legal sanction is to withhold state highway funds. It is the *optimal* sanction that is needed, not necessarily the greatest sanction.

Fourth, I commented on the political advantages of freely distributed tradable permits in the context of positive political economy. It turns out the same political advantages, mainly that rents are conveyed to the private sector (which build a constituency for the program), can create normative efficiency concerns at the same time. In contrast to auctioned tradable permits, which can be made revenue-neutral, it is now understood that freely distributed tradable permits can exacerbate existing distortions in the economy due to interactions with existing taxes (Goulder, Parry, and Burtraw, 1997). They can, therefore, be more costly than other approaches.

Fifth, in the presence of transactions costs, the initial allocation can affect the equilibrium allocation and hence costs. Recall that one of the positive attributes of a tradable permit system is that it can, in theory, be left to the political process to determine the allocations, since according to Montgomery's seminal article (1972), the same equilibrium allocation will result from any initial distribution. Unfortunately, it turns out that in the presence of certain types of transaction costs, the post-trading allocation depends very much on the initial distribution (Stavins, 1995). So, both this transaction cost effect and the tax interaction effect mean that one perverse result of efforts to build a political constituency by allocating permits in a creative way can be to unintentionally drive up program costs.

Sixth, another lesson that has become clear from our experience with implemented systems is that private brokerage is sufficient. Government need not interfere.

Finally, I turn to four basic lessons for identifying new applications. The first is that the degree of abatement cost heterogeneity among sources is likely to be the most important factor affecting the relative performance of a tradable permit system compared with command-and-control (Newell and Stavins, 1998). If every firm has the same costs, a uniform performance standard will be cost effective. But even if all firms were the same, tradable permits are still better than a technology standard.

The second important factor in identifying new applications is the degree of pollutant mixing in the receiving airshed or watershed. That is, is the problem a uniformly mixed pollutant or does it produce so-called "hot spots"? The closer it is to being uniformly mixed, the more likely it is that a market-based instrument will be attractive. Ultimately, it is not simply an issue of whether the environmental problem under consideration is uniformly mixed or not, but whether or not the convenient fiction of it being uniformly mixed—the convenient fiction that we use in SO_2 and to some degree in RECLAIM—is worth the cost savings or not. In both of those cases, it was worth it.

Third, political feasibility considerations and experience point to the wisdom of proposing tradable permit systems for reducing emissions, not simply for reallocating them under an existing regulatory or statutory level. If one attempts to do the latter, the environmental advocacy community will perceive that it is getting nothing in the bargain and will fight the new system tooth and nail, and possibly seek to modify the program in problematic ways—such as with the infamous 20 percent rule that became part of EPA Emissions Trading Program—to make sure there are environmental gains (Hahn and Stavins, 1991). The time to introduce a market-based instrument, in my view, is when improvements are to be made in environmental quality.

Fourth and finally, there is an important caveat I wish to offer regarding new applications. The successes, whether qualified successes or otherwise, of previous tradable permit systems, such as for acid rain, leaded gasoline, and CFCs, cannot simply be extrapolated to new applications. In some cases, tradable permits will be a good instrument, in some cases not. In some cases, we should use other market-based instruments, and in some cases, we should be using conventional command-and-control instruments. In the case of market-based instruments, in particular, the magnitude and diversity of sources of carbon dioxide emissions raises significant problems even for a domestic carbon rights system to address global climate change (Stavins, 1997). And the design of a carbon trading system at the international level brings forth an entirely new set of economic problems, political problems, and institutional challenges (Schmalensee, 1996) that researchers have barely begun to consider.

REFERENCES

Atkeson, Erica. 1997. "Joint Implementation: Lessons from Title IV's Voluntary Compliance Programs." Working paper 97-003, Center for Energy and

Environmental Policy Research, Massachusetts Institute of Technology, MIT, Cambridge, MA, May.

Burtraw, Dallas. 1996. "The SO_2 Emissions Trading Program: Cost Savings Without Allowance Trades." *Contemporary Economic Policy* 14 (April): 79–94.

Ellerman, A. Denny, Richard Schmalensee, Paul L. Joskow, Juan Pablo Montero, and Elizabeth M. Bailey. 1997. "Emissions Trading Under the U.S. Acid Rain Program: Evaluation of Compliance Costs and Allowance Market Performance." Center for Energy and Environmental Policy Research, MIT. Cambridge, MA. October.

Goulder, Lawrence H., Ian W. H. Parry, and Dallas Burtraw. 1997. "Revenue-Raising vs. Other Approaches to Environmental Protection: The Critical Significance of Pre-Existing Tax Distortions." *RAND Journal of Economics* (winter).

Hahn, Robert W., and Robert N. Stavins. 1991. "Incentive-Based Environmental Regulation: A New Era From An Old Idea?" *Ecology Law Quarterly* 18:1–42.

Joskow, Paul L., and Richard Schmalensee. 1998. "The Political Economy of Market-Based Environmental Policy: The U.S. Acid Rain Program." *Journal of Law and Economics*. Forthcoming.

Kelman, Steven P. 1981. *What Price Incentives?* Boston: Auburn House.

Keohane, Nathaniel O., Richard L. Revesz, and Robert N. Stavins. 1998. "The Choice of Regulatory Instruments in Environmental Policy." *Harvard Environmental Law Review* 22 (2): 313–367.

Kerr, Suzi, and David Maré. 1997. "Efficient Regulation Through Tradeable Permit Markets: The United States Lead Phasedown." Working paper 96-06, Department of Agricultural and Resource Economics, University of Maryland, College Park, January.

McCubbins, Matthew D., Roger G. Noll, and Barry R. Weingast. 1987. "Administrative Procedures as Instruments of Political Control." *Journal of Law, Economics and Organization* 3.0: 243–277.

McCubbins, Matthew and Terry Sullivan 1984. "Constituency Influences on Legislative Policy Choice." *Quality and Quantity* 18: 299–319.

McLean, Brian J. 1995. "Lessons Learned Implementing Title IV of the Clean Air Act." Paper presented at 85th Annual Meeting of the Air & Waste Management Association, 95-A120.04, San Antonio, Texas.

Montero, Juan-Pablo. 1997. "Volunteering for Market-Based Environmental Regulation: The Substitution Provision of the SO_2 Emissions Trading Program." Working paper 97–001, Center for Energy and Environmental Policy Research, MIT, Cambridge, January.

Montgomery, W. David. 1972. "Markets in Licenses and Efficient Pollution Control Programs." *Journal of Economic Theory* 395–418.

Newell, Richard G., and Robert N. Stavins. 1998. "Abatement Cost Heterogeneity and Potential Gains from Market-Based Instruments." Working paper, John F. Kennedy School of Government, Harvard University, June.

Nichols, Albert L., John G. Farr, and Gordon Hester. 1996. "Trading and the Timing of Emissions: Evidence from the Ozone Transport Region." Draft, National Economic Research Associates, Cambridge, Massachusetts, 9 September.

Sandel, Michael J. 1997. "It's Immoral to Buy the Right to Pollute." *New York Times,* 15 December 1997, p. A29.

Schmalensee, Richard. 1996. "Greenhouse Policy Architecture and Institutions." Report 13. MIT Joint Program on the Science and Policy of Global Change. November.

Stavins, Robert N. 1995. "Transaction Costs and Tradable Permits." *Journal of Environmental Economics and Management* 995 (29): 133–148.

Stavins, Robert N. 1997. "Policy Instruments for Climate Change: How Can National Governments Address a Global Problem." *The University of Chicago Legal Forum:* 293–329.

Stavins, Robert N. 1998. "What Can We Learn from the Grand Policy Experiment? Positive and Normative Lessons from SO_2 Allowance Trading." *Journal of Economic Perspectives.* 12 (3) (Summer): 69–88.

Stavins, Robert N. 1999. "The Costs of Carbon Sequestration: A Revealed-Preference Approach." *American Economic Review* 89 (4): 994–1009.

U.S. Environmental Protection Agency. 1990. *Environmental Investments: The Cost of a Clean Environment.* Washington, DC.

NOTES

1. For a more detailed discussion, with particular emphasis on the SO_2 allowance trading program, see: Stavins, 1998.

2. For a recent explication of this perspective, see: Sandel, 1997.

3. By 1990, U.S. pollution control costs had reached $125 billion annually, nearly a tripling of real costs from 1972 levels (U.S. EPA, 1990).

3

From Porcopolis to Carbopolis

William D.
Nordhaus

The Evolution from Pork Bellies to
Emissions Trading

One of the most extraordinary economic developments of the past few decades has been the explosion of paper commodities. In this chapter, I follow this development in what I call the transformation of Porcopolis to Carbopolis— reviewing the history of derivatives, with particular emphasis on emissions trading, and looking ahead to the possible benefits and drawbacks of an international carbon emissions trading regime. Readers who are not from Chicago might be puzzled by this reference to Porcopolis. *Porcopolis* means the city of pigs, and it was Chicago's name of a century ago when commodity markets, such as those for pork, flourished in that city.

THE RISE OF DERIVATIVES

Before turning to emissions trading, it will be useful to review briefly the history of derivatives, or synthetic assets—the family of assets to which emissions trading belongs—to demonstrate that these are actually rather complex and fragile social mechanisms. In calculus, a derivative is a mathematical operation. But in economics, a derivative is an asset that derives its value from something else. The first derivative was probably money. For example, a gold certificate represents an asset called gold, and fiat money represents an asset called trust in government policy. The history of money reveals that this asset is a very complex institution. To persuade people to accept a derivative like fiat money, there must be solid institutions behind it to ensure that it has value. A cursory glance at the recent meltdown of economies from East Asia to Russia shows how easily these fragile institutions can break down.

The successes and failures of derivative assets should remind us that we need to go about the process of establishing a market for emissions trading in a sober fashion: People can and will flee from these institutions if they are not well designed and well managed. A badly designed example can set back a good idea for many years.

William Cronan, in his history of Chicago called *Nature's Metropolis,* makes two things very clear: the great complexity of setting up these commodity and derivatives markets, and the enormous, extraordinarily beneficial consequences of those institutions for our society (Cronan, 1991). The ability to set up, maintain, and manage commodity and security markets for more than a century and a half (1998 marks the 150th anniversary of the Chicago Board of Trade) is an extraordinary achievement in the history of economics. What these markets do is allow us to spread risks. Farmers today are able to survive hardships such as weather disasters, where the farmers of 150 years ago, before the era of derivative markets, were much more subject to the vagaries of the weather. Thus, the history of Porcopolis is also the history of this wonderful institution that houses derivatives. In the last quarter of a century, there has been an explosion of innovation along the lines of securitization, derivatives, and commodization. Richard Sandor writes about these in depth in his chapter. I am going to discuss a couple of these innovations and examine the rationale behind them.

Many of the financial-market institutions that grew up in the past three decades were responses to government regulations, as is the emissions-trading program itself. For example, interest-rate caps led to financial innovations and later to the securitization of the mortgage market. There are a couple of interesting new examples of securitization: The catastrophe bond is basically a way to spread risks for insurance companies. These companies, in turn, are able to spread risks because of the contingent nature of the catastrophic events. If something terrible happens, a bond kicks in. A decade ago, many people worried that global warming would lead to multiple catastrophic events and that the insurance industry might not be able to handle the scale of the change. In my opinion, the creation of catastrophe bonds has successfully addressed that concern.

The other example of new instruments is something called *personal securitization.* Unlike catastrophe bonds and emissions trading, this is still waiting for full commercial development. In this process, individuals are securitizing themselves. I'm told that the musician David Bowie is doing just that: it is possible to buy a little piece of David Bowie. My colleague Robert Shiller, who has written widely on this subject, points out that the biggest risk we face as individuals is changes in the value of our human capital—the risk that our wages will rise or fall or that we will be out of a job. It will be interesting to see whether personal securitization will someday allow us to shed our human capital risk.

Another set of interesting developments has occurred in the realm of what I call synthetic commodities. Index futures, for example, Standard and Poor (S&P) futures, are one form of this type of commodity. It is not obvious why such an index, which is, after all, a linear sum of prices of different marketed securities, is really needed. In general, you don't deliver these things, though in some cases you do. The Federal Reserve has a dollar index that may be bought and sold as well, though I suspect that not too many people know that they are buying and selling a complex geometric average.

One cautionary note: We are not batting a thousand in this league, and, contrary to what one might think or hope, all new derivatives do not succeed. In the early 1980s, a synthetic security known as an "inflation future" was created. It was marketed for a few years and then, like the dinosaurs, it died. It did not survive the low-inflation era, probably because the transaction costs were too high and the market never got developed.

Even though the inflation future died, there was an exciting innovation a year and a half ago: the Treasury Inflation Protected Securities (TIPS), or indexed bonds. So now anyone who can buy stocks with an earnings yield of about 3.8 percent can buy absolutely safe TIPS for a real yield of 3.8 percent. I do not know why people aren't flocking to buy these bonds for their pension funds.

SULFUR DERIVATIVES

The rest of this chapter focuses on environmental derivatives. I think of the birth of these derivatives as occurring during the regulatory reform movement of the 1970s. That phenomenon really started, not in Ronald Reagan's administration, and not even in Jimmy Carter's, but in Gerald Ford's administration. When I was in the Carter administration it was just picking up steam. During that period, we saw the deregulation of the airlines and the railroads and the beginning of the deregulation of oil and gas. But it was pretty rough sledding to win support for deregulation of our new approaches to the environment. I spent most of my years at the Council of Economic Advisers from 1977 to 1979 worrying about regulatory reform—and it was a nightmare.

Take, for example, the sulfur emissions program—the cap-and-trade program. It actually has three components: There is the bubble, which extends over all the plants of a given firm across the entire nation. There is the banking, which allows that bubble to cover not only the current year but the future as well. And then there is the trading, which opens the bubble to include all other firms. By 1977, we in the Council of Economic Advisers were arguing very strenuously for banking and bubbling, but we could make no headway at all. Why did these concepts of banking and bubbling fail to evolve naturally from bilateral transactions to multilateral transactions to a market? They failed to evolve because the transaction costs were too high. I think the major turning point in the past 20 years came with the conversion of some, not all, environmental groups to the view that there is a role in their efforts for market instruments. In particular, the Environmental Defense Fund has been extremely important in this movement. With the government behind the program, the market for emissions took off.

Before going on to discuss the carbon emissions program, I would like to provide a few reflections on the sulfur cap-and-trade program. First, I regard this as a really impressive new institution. Though it looks like an obvious idea now, when it was proposed it was a leap into the unknown. We had never done anything like this before. It was similar to deregulation of the airlines. People thought, are the planes going to fly? Are half the cities in the United States going to be left without airline service in or out? It's important to recognize that it was initially a very daring idea. Second, on its face, it has been extremely successful. Sulfur emissions are well below the cap. The price of allowances is well below the projections. The total cost is way below earlier estimates. On the whole, I think that the sulfur cap-and-trade program is a brilliant institution and innovation.

Having said that, I am going to follow up with some observations that are a little gloomier. While this program has been successful, it is not cold fusion—it is not the savior of all systems, and its principles cannot be applied everywhere. Markets in the real world, it must be remembered, do not behave exactly as they do in textbooks. Denny Ellerman's chapter in this volume points out this caveat nicely. There are very complex interactions between the market and institutions, people, firms, regulators, states, and tax systems. Markets are embedded in a society, a culture, and sometimes they work and sometimes they do not. It was fortunate in the case of the sulfur emissions program that institutions had been set up so that this market would work properly.

Why was this effort successful when the bilateral trading opportunities set up in the earlier 1977 amendments were not? Perhaps the feature most important to making this market viable was its use of a national bubble as opposed to state or regional bubbles. My first reaction to the national cap was that it was a terrible idea from an environmental standpoint. In terms of damages, emissions in the Four Corners region of New Mexico are just not the same as emissions at New Haven Harbor. But what was right about a national cap was that it allowed what technicians call a *thick market*—a large number of trades leading to lower transactions costs, which got the machine running.

I happened to be sitting between Richard Sandor and Vice President Gore at the White House Climate Conference in October 1997. They were both pointing to the sulfur program as an argument against the "dismal" economists who were projecting that the costs of the Kyoto Protocol would be very high.

They were asserting that once the markets for CO_2 were opened, the costs would plummet. I demurred then and I demur now. In the first place, as the chapters in this volume demonstrate, it is not clear why the initial price was so low in the case of sulfur emissions. The low price may have come about because of over-abatement in the program's early period, as Ellerman argues in his study. Did this occur because the forecast prices were too high? If so, maybe we are dealing with a cobweb here: high initial prices, overabatement; low subsequent prices, underabatement; and so on. In addition, there is a complicated interaction between Phases I and II. People are responding to a high forecast price; they are forward-looking in their decisions rather than mechanical, which can also complicate matters. And finally, there is the very important issue of the uncertainty about the security of this property right called *emissions allowances.* Everything may go smoothly as long as emissions are below the cap, but what is going to happen when they are above the cap, as they will be in the future? Will environmental groups protest that we cannot allow emissions to be above the cap? In such a scenario, it is possible that people could wind up with worthless allowances. This possibility leads me to the conclusion that we need to conduct a very careful study of this issue rather than adopting a Pollyannaish attitude toward the environmental markets.

I would like to add one more thing to the discussion of why the projections of the sulfur prices proved higher than the actual numbers. Economists and engineers usually work in teams to make these estimates. The fact is that costs are not invariably overestimated. Chlorofluorocarbons (CFCs) presented a parallel, almost identical, situation, but early estimates by academics and EPA of costs in a tradable emissions market for CFCs were pretty much on track. If anything, costs of CFC controls may have been underestimated. And we should not forget other cases where the estimated costs were so low they would have bankrupted anyone in the forecasting business—who can forget cost estimates for oil and gas synthetics in the 1970s and early 1980s, particularly for shale oil, at $3.00 a barrel. And nuclear power— I cannot tell you how much this country and others have lost because of poor forecasts of the costs of nuclear power. Forecasting is very hazardous—especially about the future!

But even with all these provisos, my primary message is that markets may not work miracles, but they do work. They will do their job, sometimes well, sometimes badly, and almost always better than command-and-control systems. Under command-and-control systems, like the sulfur program before 1990, there was a great incentive for people to drag their heels; complain; hire lobbyists; hire lawyers; wine, dine, and bribe regulators; and just not do anything. There were a thousand different excuses: I'll go bankrupt, let's talk about it some more, let's litigate. With the incentives of command-and-control it is no surprise how little emissions were reduced. Under a market approach, the incentives are reversed. People make money from abatement instead of losing it. The markets say, "Just do it."

CLIMATE CHANGE AND THE ECONOMICS OF THE KYOTO PROTOCOL

Now I want to apply these ideas to the problem of climate change. The mainstream science involved with the climate-change problem looks pretty solid—it is pretty much where it was 20 years ago. Economics, however, is a much more recent arrival to the climate-change scene. One of its early findings, though, is that there appear to be no significant impacts from climate change for market sectors in high-income countries over the next 100 years. Economists do not yet know how to estimate the impacts in nonmarket sectors, nor do we do a very good job with the estimates for low-income countries, and these results are still highly uncertain. The real impacts of climate change are likely to be long-term and potentially catastrophic events, but these are very poorly understood.

In terms of the politics of climate change, my own sense is that we are heading toward a big impasse: The developing countries are not going to play this game. China and India are delighted for the United States to reduce its emissions, but they have no intention of doing the same. The U.S. Congress recently passed the Byrd-Hagen Resolution, which says that unless the developing countries play, the United States is not going to pay. Hence the impasse.

Going back to the economics of climate change: What exactly is the economic approach to climate-change policies? Close to a decade of research has gone into developing what are called *integrated assessment models* (IAMs), which integrate the different components of climate change—greenhouse-gas (primarily CO_2) emissions, greenhouse-gas concentrations, climate change, impacts on society, and emissions-reduction policies. Two dozen IAMs currently exist. Such models allow us to examine the economic impact of programs such as those contained in the Kyoto Protocol, signed in December 1997. The protocol, for example, calls for mandatory emissions reductions of greenhouse gases, principally CO_2, in Annex I countries (OECD, or high-income economies plus economies in transition, specifically Russia, Ukraine, and East European countries). These reductions average out to about 5 percent in the year 2010 relative to 1990. The United States' reduction would be 7 percent, about a 25 percent decrease from forecast emissions—a very substantial amount. The protocol allows trading of emissions among the Annex I countries. Another part of the protocol, called the Clean Development Mechanism, allows the high-income countries to get credits for emissions reductions in developing countries, but the mechanism is vague and will probably allow little trade.

We have recently done an extensive study of the economic impact of the Kyoto Protocol using the "RICE-98" integrated assessment model developed at Yale. The first scenario is no control, which describes the current situation. The second is what we call the *optimal run,* in which costs and benefits are balanced, or net economic impacts are minimized. A third set of runs examines the impact of the Kyoto Protocol with no international trading of national emissions quotas—that is, each of the major countries or blocks (Japan, the United States, Europe, and so on) adheres to its own national emissions limits. The fourth case is that of full trading among Annex I countries. And the final one is idealistic goal of global trading—trading between all the countries of the world.

Our major conclusion is that the Kyoto Protocol will involve very high carbon taxes in the Annex I region—the numbers rising from $200 to $500 per ton of carbon except in the unrealistic global trading case. If you want to translate these numbers into coal prices, multiply by 0.7 to get the impact on the price of coal. These are very big numbers. Just to give you some idea, if you assume a carbon price of $100 per ton, which is the lower level of current estimates, we're talking about carbon revenues in the United States, if this is a tax, of about $150 billion per year. We're talking about doubling wholesale fossil fuel prices. We're talking about a program for carbon emissions with roughly *100 times* the economic impact of the sulfur program.

I might also mention some results on overall economic abatement costs. If the Kyoto Protocol is imposed with no trading, we estimate that the global costs (in terms of the discounted value of change in global consumption) to be around $2.4 trillion in current prices. With trading among Annex I countries, the costs decline to about $1.3 trillion. Global trading yields very large gains, reducing the costs by about 85 percent relative to no trading. Within the Annex I countries, the United States is the big loser, while the big winner is Russia. In the Annex I trading case, the annual transfer from the United States to Russia is around $50 billion per year.

PROBLEMS IN AN INTERNATIONAL EMISSIONS-TRADING REGIME

This discussion gives you an impression of the scope of the economic impact of the Kyoto Protocol. I would now like to touch upon a number of the administrative issues involved. Much thought has gone into designing the domestic emissions-trading programs, but many problems will arise when this kind of program is extended to an international market. An international emissions-trading program is not a straightforward extension of the domestic sulfur cap-and-trade program. There are serious technical obstacles along with the enormous economic obstacle of tremendous costs. I discuss six of these problems next.

First, what is the commodity? It must be defined before it can be traded. Is it consumption or production? Does it include the content of fuels? Is it compatible with existing international trade laws included in the World Trade Organization (WTO)? Perhaps the most important open question is the treatment of the carbon content of imports and exports.

The second problem is that of domestic implementation. Of the six, this is the only one that is technically straightforward. But the economic impact is so large that much thought must go into the design. One issue is the size of the social costs of allocating allowances. A second question is the impact on incomes, which is particularly significant when emissions rights worth between $50 and $150 billion per year are being allocated. A further but manageable issue concerns the point in the production stream where the permits are required—mine-mouth, oil well, refinery, utility, gas station, or consumption? There's a whole chain of production and distribution, and it is not obvious where the monitoring, measuring, and allocating will take place.

The remaining problems concern international issues. The third issue is that of monitoring. While there are no major technical problems involved with the monitoring of fossil fuel emissions, the protocol actually extends beyond these to other gases, the sources of which are, in principle, more worrisome. For instance, there is the somewhat amusing case of what is politely called bovine flatulence. Cows are big methane emitters, but we don't know exactly how big. Then there's the more serious problem of incentive compatibility, or the provision to nations of incentives not to lie in their reporting. When the monitoring of emissions is done by individual countries, the reliability of the scientific systems or governments of the participating countries is an important consideration. The inclusion of forests in the protocol allows for uneconomic policies to get credit for emissions reductions.

This leads to the fourth problem, which is how to treat corrupt and nondemocratic regimes. Should countries with poor scores in other areas (commercial, military, human rights, or corruption, for example) be included in an emissions-trading regime? What about countries whose governments have broken down, like Albania? Or countries whose identities are not even clear, like Bosnia? Or those suffering from serious governance problems, like Indonesia? These questions bring up the issue of conditionality. Will there be a set of conditions that countries will have to meet in order to be included? Will there be a human-rights component? This is a very slippery slope, and there is a real danger that only three countries will still be in the running at the bottom of that slope.

The fifth issue is that of "emissions bankruptcy." For example, suppose a country sells a large number of its allowances only to realize at the end of the budget period that it cannot meet its commitments. Will the purchasing country be required to make good the excessive emissions of the seller? Are countries going to be able to repudiate their CO_2 debt the way they did their dollar debts in the 1980s?

Finally, there is the major problem of setting the benchmark for emissions for future periods. The benchmark for CO_2 emissions in the Kyoto Protocol is 1990. This means that countries like Russia, which were enormously inefficient in 1990, get a big windfall, while efficient countries like Sweden or Japan are penalized. Not only is such a setup unlikely to be politically viable, it is also a poor precedent for introducing the participation of developing countries.

As we move from Porcopolis, which launched the United States into its economic ascendancy, to Sulfopolis, where we are recognizing and internalizing the domestically harmful byproducts of production, and perhaps to Carbopolis, which involves all the nations of the globe, we face a much cloudier future. Carbopolis involves extending a program that clearly works in a single country—where you have a sovereign government, a rule of law, a well-defined commodity, and a solid system of domestic implementation—to the international arena; this translation is a vastly more difficult enterprise than what we have encountered with existing financial commodities or environmental derivatives. It is extremely costly and presents severe problems of definition and implementation. Perhaps we should step back to reflect whether we might better manage international environmental issues with an alternative approach.

POSTSCRIPT

> *Editorial note:* The Workshop tradition is to engage in a frank discussion on issues and an exchange of views. We provide the author's comments on several questions raised at the Workshop conference.

In response to a question on the possibility of low-cost benefit programs like lighting retrofit acting to lower control costs, I would respond that there are probably a dozen different classes of models that deal with low-cost abatement. Some of them do include the possibility of low-cost or high-benefit programs such as lighting retrofit. Others assume a neoclassical approach where the markets have already internalized all those costs. The RICE model I discussed is a neoclassical approach, although there have been some variants where we include a cheap lunch—but not a completely free lunch.

In response to a question about how different abatement costs were estimated, I would respond that, basically, the no-trade case is just a projection of what the abatement costs would be if each of the Annex I countries adhered to their Kyoto Protocol limits, and non-Annex I countries had no emissions limits. To go to global trade would require non-Annex I countries (China, India, etc.) to cap their emissions and then allow them to trade. So it's something like Phase II of SO_2 control. Suppose the limit for China is 1 billion tons. It is now said to China, you have 1 billion tons of allowances and, subject to your accepting that, you can sell however much you don't emit. Part of the problem with global trading, even though it is economically advantageous, is that it requires setting up the equivalent of all the institutions in developing countries that you need for trading: monitoring, allocation of rights, markets for trading rights, a legal system, bankruptcy laws—it is the setting up of these necessary institutions that I see as particularly difficult.

About the possibility of enhancing carbon sinks as a control option, I would note that there are a lot of proposals being made along these lines. The one that is allowed in the Kyoto Protocol is to increase the carbon in forests. I see that provision as useful but limited due to current technology. With the amount of land that we can economically set aside for the purpose of sequestering carbon—either through increasing the standing carbon in trees or through growing and pickling the trees—the emissions reductions are likely to be small. My estimate for the United States is that, while adhering to the Kyoto ground rules, we could sequester about 50 million tons per year compared to our total emissions of around 1.5 billion tons per year.

Another interesting possibility for a renewable fuel is biomass. In Sweden, a country that is shutting down its nuclear power plants, many people think they can make up for the lost power through the use of biomass. I'm skeptical about this, at least with current technology. Perhaps, with the biotechnology revolution, we will see oil or methane trees. But these are a quantum leap from where we are in technology now.

In response to the question that some estimates of damages from global warming have been very large, I would respond that the model we use includes estimates of the damages associated with climate change. Indeed, we estimate that in the base case the present value of damages from global warming will be substantial. Our approach is to determine the path of emissions reductions that will have a payoff in terms of *reduced* climate damages sufficient to pay for the abatement costs.

Another question raised dealt with other environmental problems being reduced by limiting fossil fuel consumption. Can we include these extra benefits in the calculation? The answer is that the model deals with just a slice of our social problems, the climate part. Other environmental concerns are not included in our models. They should be analyzed separately. So to the extent that high carbon taxes reduce coal use—and we know that coal is damaging to the public health—that would be a benefit. But I prefer to keep the analysis clean and address these questions separately.

REFERENCES

Cronan, William. 1991. *Nature's Metropolis: Chicago and the Great West.* New York: W. W. Norton & Co.

4

Some Observations on the Evolution of the International Greenhouse Gas Emissions Trading Market

Richard L. Sandor
Michael J. Walsh

This chapter addresses emissions trading in a broadened context and presents our sense of the evolutionary path that the emerging international market in greenhouse gas emissions trading is likely to follow. From a generic point of view, and from the perspective of professional investors, we have found it useful to look at a dialectic for the development of a new market. To understand how markets can evolve, we posit a seven-stage process that helps describe the many forces that accrue over time and sometimes develop into more sophisticated and efficient markets. The steps can be characterized as: (1) the occurrence of a structural change that creates a demand for capital; (2) the creation of uniform standards for a commodity or security; (3) the development of a legal instrument which provides evidence of ownership; (4) the development of informal spot markets (for immediate delivery) and forward markets (nonstandardized agreements for future

The authors would like to thank Alice M. LeBlanc and Rafael L. Marques for their comments and assistance.

delivery) in commodities and securities where "receipts" of ownership are traded; (5) the emergence of securities and commodities exchanges; (6) the creation of organized futures markets (standardized contracts for future delivery on organized exchanges) and options markets (rights but not guarantees for future delivery) in commodities and securities; and (7) the proliferation of over-the-counter (OTC) markets and deconstruction of traded instruments. Within that framework, we present some historical examples of this pattern for equities, commodities and fixed-income securities, and we consider their application to environmental markets.

EXAMPLES OF THE SEVEN-STAGE PROCESS

In 1492, the discovery of America (from the European perspective) created a tremendous structural change. The Age of Discovery demanded a great amount of financial capital as business activity expanded in both the New World and between Europe and Asia. An important by-product of this era was the formation of the Dutch East India Company. This was a critical innovation in the Schumpeterian sense which led to the creation of the limited liability corporation. Prior to it, there were partnerships that raised capital, but it was the limited liability corporation and the development of transferable equity shares that provided a standard instrument and the evidence of ownership. Its use ultimately lead to trading on a number of regional exchanges in and around Amsterdam, followed in the sixteenth century by the development of futures and options trading.

In the case of agricultural commodities, the removal of restrictions on grain imports into England and the Crimean War acted as the structural change, stimulating production in the United States, which became a large exporter of agricultural goods. Growth in demand continued as the U.S. population reached 35 million by the end of the Civil War. Capital was needed to finance the storage and shipment of grain from the Midwest to the major population centers in the East Coast. At that time, there was unorganized trading in physical sacks of grain, which had to be inspected on an individual basis. The creation of the Chicago Board of Trade (CBOT) in 1848 ushered in grain standards and grading procedures, an innovation that preceded the creation of government standards by 50 years. Ultimately, a tradable legal instrument called the *warehouse receipt* emerged, which provided evidence of ownership and facilitated both capital raising and ownership transfer. The birth of futures trading in 1865 was followed by options trading, albeit at a later stage.

A more modern example of the market evolution model is the fixed income market for mortgage-backed bonds. The post-World War II economic boom in the United Stated created a great demand for housing in California, which had to be financed by institutions in the eastern part of the country. Although standardized mortgages guaranteed by the Federal Housing Authority (FHA) and the Veterans Administration (VA) assured capital flows into the sector, it was a highly inefficient market. Mortgages were sold on an individual basis or in small packages and the buyer had to have individual documentation for each loan. The "credit crunch" of 1966 and 1969 and the uncertainty surrounding the timely payment of the principal and interest during foreclosures gave rise to the formation of the Government National Mortgage Association (GNMA). This enabled the "bundling" of small loans into securities to be collateralized by the FHA/VA and backed by the U.S. government. It provided an efficient and homogeneous evidence of ownership and conveyance vehicle, which ultimately evolved into spot and forward markets, primarily among Wall Street dealers and mortgage bankers. This informal arrangement served the function of an exchange until the world's first interest rate futures contract—based on the GNMA mortgage-backed instrument—was launched at the CBOT in 1975. From that date, financial futures secured acceptance and ultimately, in the 1980s, so did collateralized mortgages.

Therefore, looking at equities, physical commodities, and fixed income instruments, and examining their development over historical periods—from the sixteenth to twentieth century—seems to indicate that they all follow the pattern of market evolution we have outlined. We are now on the verge of a whole new field of tradable products in the form of environmental derivatives.

A REVIEW OF THE U.S. SULFUR DIOXIDE EMISSIONS TRADING PROGRAM

We are currently witnessing yet another variant of the seven-stage process with the emergence of a market in SO_2 emission allowances in the United States. A latent demand for this market in abating sulfur gases resulted from a significant increase in the burning of high-sulfur coal by electric utilities in order to satisfy the demand for electricity. Increased pollution in the form of sulfuric emissions accompanied the increased output of electricity. Generated in more densely populated sections of the United States, this pollution resulted in large increases in respiratory problems for affected populations. In addition, acidification damaged rivers, streams, and forests. Latent demand became effective demand as public concern over human health and environmental problems motivated legislators to pass the Clean Air Act Amendments of 1990.

The SO_2 legislation simultaneously performed three functions: (1) it standardized an environmental commodity (a legally-authorized allowance to emit one ton of SO_2); (2) it produced the "evidence of ownership" necessary for financial instruments; and (3) it established the infrastructure to efficiently transfer title. Ultimately, an informal forward market emerged even before the Act required compliance. Options followed. Organized exchanges entered when the CBOT, on behalf of the Environmental Protection Agency (EPA), competitively won the right to conduct the annual auctions of spot and forward allowances. The market evolution pattern is very similar to the one presented in the seven-stage process.

The 1990 legislation set a national limit on SO_2 emissions that would be consistently lowered over a 20-year period. Under traditional command-and-control regulations, coal-fired utilities would have had little choice but to purchase expensive pollution-control technologies to meet the required lower emission targets. As its major innovation, the Act provided for a market-based, "cap-and-trade" system. In this way, utilities had the flexibility either to reduce emissions directly or to purchase allowances from other utilities that were beneath their targeted cap as a result of making extraordinary emission cuts. Utilities that were most efficient in reducing emissions were motivated to do so because they could profit by selling their unused spare allowances. Utilities that did not reduce their emissions bore the cost of purchasing allowances or faced stiff fines. All rules protecting local air quality remained in force.

The SO_2 allowance was a new commodity and many argued the program was doomed to failure. There were numerous problems confronting it: monitoring issues, reporting challenges, a highly regulated industry seemingly unsuited for innovative markets, and unsupportive regulations at both the state and federal levels. The United Mine Workers said the program would destroy the U.S. economy while the Sierra Club said the program would destroy the environment. Experts estimated that these emission rights would command a very high premium. Some initial estimates ran as high as $1,500 per ton. Hahn and May (1994) report several pre-1992 estimates of forecasted prices for sulfur emission allowances, ranging from $309 (Resource Data International) to $981 (United Mine Workers). (See Table 4.1.)

The real outcome is that the first published trades occurred at prices around $300 per ton. In 1998, the CBOT auctioned off a large number of allowances at an average price of $115. The market is showing that compliance costs are 20 percent of the levels

Table 4.1   Some Prominent Pre-1992 Price Forecasts for Sulfur Dioxide Emission Allowances ("Middle" Price Projections for Phase 1)

Resource Data International	$309
American Electric Power	$392
Sierra Club	$446
Electric Power Research Institute	$688
Ohio Coal Office	$785
United Mine Workers	$981

Source: Hahn and May, *The Electricity Journal,* March 1994.

of the mid-range predictions. There has been an upward trend in prices since March 1998 (Figure 4.1).

The early environmental benefits are as impressive as the program's cost-effectiveness. From 1995 through 1997, overall emissions were 30 percent below allowed levels. Recent trades occurred at less than 10 percent of the fine level on violations (which have been non-existent) and emissions are down far ahead of schedule. The cap-and-trade system is an unambiguous success. A fluid market has evolved in terms of economically significant transfers, or those between unrelated parties. The volume of such allowances transferred rose from 1.9 million in 1995 to 4.4 million in 1996 and to 7.9 million in 1997. There has also been steady growth in the inter-utility trading of allowances from 700,000 tons in 1995 to 2.8 million in 1997 (U.S. EPA 1997). The total for 1997 exceeds the total of the three previous years combined. In 1995, the costs to reduce emissions were calculated to be $726 million, according to a study by MIT researchers (Schmalensee et al., 1998). The mid-range estimate

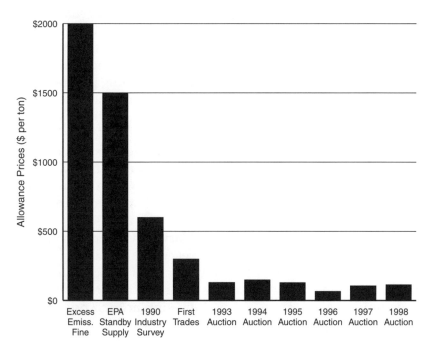

Figure 4.1   Sulfur dioxide allowance prices.

of the medical benefits of reduced SO_2 emissions—not including the benefits of improved visibility or healthier lakes, streams and forests—is \$12.5 billion per year, a very attractive return on investment ratio. Carlson et al. (1998) estimate that this innovation will save \$784 million annually beginning in the year 2000. Furthermore, they estimated the net cost of the cap-and-trade system is 43 percent of the estimated costs under a command-and-control system. The full effects of the trading are still being realized as the market continuously adjusts to this new innovation, incorporating the information contained in allowance prices.

THE INTERNATIONAL EMISSIONS TRADING MARKET FOR GREENHOUSE GASES

There is a case for extending what we have learned in the sulfur cap-and-trade program to other areas, mainly global warming. In his seminal work *Capitalism, Socialism, and Democracy* the famous economist Joseph Schumpeter described three steps in the inventive process. The first is the creation of the idea. The second is innovation, which is the commercialization of the idea. The third is the diffusion or replication and the widespread use of the idea. With the success of the sulfur trading program and other environmental markets, such as the gasoline lead phase-out and RECLAIM in Los Angeles, trading in greenhouse gases represents the replication phase.

Not surprisingly, the same kinds of predictions of economic doom trumpeted prior to launch of the SO_2 program have resurfaced when addressing global warming. As with sulfur, ominous forecasts of the cost of removing carbon dioxide from the atmosphere are now being presented. Using a top-down model, Professor Richard Cooper (1998) of Harvard University, projects the price of carbon mitigation will reach \$100 per ton. He bases his prediction on a price of \$20 for a barrel of oil, when in fact it is likely to trade below that in the future. Other academics and economic research firms are making similar high predictions while disregarding the impact of emissions trading or the role of technology in their modeling scenarios.

The industrialized world can take very meaningful steps to bring down greenhouse gas emissions at a cost that is rather small, provided we use methods that help drive down compliance costs. Consider first one measure of the magnitude of the U.S. commitment if it is to meet the targets agreed at Kyoto. The gap between emission levels under business-as-usual in year 2010 compared to the Kyoto target is roughly 600 million metric tons carbon equivalent per year. If the cost to cut carbon is US$100 per ton, the annual U.S. expenditures would total $60 billion. On the other hand, consider a US$20 per ton cost, a price in the range of many proposed offset transactions and a level which many analysts believe would generate very large emission reduction quantities. If a market system succeeds in driving the cost down to US$20 per ton, the annual U.S. cost would total US$12 billion. This total cost figure is less than 0.14 percent of current U.S. national income (1998 GDP), or 2.4 percent of the 1993 U.S. final energy bill (US$ 493 billion).

The potential for emissions trading solutions can also be extended to agriculture and forestry. In the United States, farmers can offer a highly effective system for capturing or *sequestering* carbon from the atmosphere. A major means of sequestering more carbon in cropland is through Best Management Practices (BMPs). Using the estimates of $20 to $30 per ton carbon, paying farmers to sequester 200 million tons by carbon weight per year could add $4 to $6 billion of gross income to the U.S. farm economy—and possibly up to 10 percent to overall net farm income. This figure represents one-third of the U.S. net emission reduction goal of 600 million metric tons of carbon.

According to the U.S. Census Bureau, 1992 Census of Agriculture, the United States has 590 million acres that are grassland, pasture, or rangeland. 145 million acres are forested but also serve as grazing land in the lower 48 U.S. states. In addition, there are almost 36 million acres in the U.S. Department of Agriculture Conservation Reserve Program (CRP) plan. If 50 million acres could be dedicated to reforestation and those acres could sequester 2 tons of carbon per year, 100 million tons of carbon could be captured solely through domestic reforestation. This land package could be composed from less than 10 percent of existing grassland/pasture/rangeland, or in combination with the purchase of a portion of the lands included in the CRP plan.

Full integration of agricultural mitigation activities would also generate important additional environmental benefits, such as improved water quality and animal habitat. If managed properly, participation in the international carbon market could soften farm income cycles by taking land out of crop production and putting it into conservation when relative prices favor carbon sequestration over food production. Also, leading scientists expect that climate change brought about by increased greenhouse gases may bring more extreme droughts and floods. Thus, farmers and foresters can not only sell a new "crop" in the international environmental service market, they can also help solve a problem that threatens their own livelihood.

THE MARKET IS ALREADY EMERGING

With standardization and use of existing exchanges and trading systems, a large-scale carbon emissions market including a system of quotes, hedging, and options will emerge. The market for carbon trades is already evolving. Niagara Mohawk (an electric power company in New York) and Arizona Public Service completed a swap of carbon offsets for SO_2 emission allowances in 1996. In 1998, the Japan-based Sumitomo began converting coal-fired electric power plants in Russia to natural gas to earn carbon offsets as part of the transaction. Carbon markets are being designed in the United Kingdom at the International Petroleum Exchange and in Australia at the Sydney Futures Exchange. (See Table 4.2.)

A clear example of this trend is the case of British Petroleum (BP), which is developing its own internal greenhouse gas trading process. Its first trading price was $17 per ton of CO_2, which translates into a price of $62 per ton of carbon, an initial number that includes only the internal technical options available at a dozen major production and refining facilities.[1] The program will help BP develop experience with measurement and trading issues, and will start the process of discovering its internal marginal cost of controlling emissions. This internal cost figure will be a key driver in formulating external trading strategies as a broader market emerges.

Domestically, a legislative initiative has been put forth under the auspices of Democratic and Republican Senators in advance of Senate ratification of the Kyoto Protocol.[2] The Credit for Early

Table 4.2 Examples of Recent and Pending Transactions in the Inchoate Market

1996	Niagara Mohawk and Arizona Public Service executed a swap of carbon offsets for sulfur dioxide emission allowances.
1996	A consortium involving Norwegian industry and the government of Norway purchased from the Republic of Costa Rica rainforest protection carbon offsets produced in Costa Rica's Private Forestry Project.
1997	Environmental Financial Products Limited (formerly Centre Financial Products Limited) purchased from the Republic of Costa Rica rainforest protection carbon offsets produced in Costa Rica's Private Forestry Project.
1997	Ontario Hydro agreed in principle to buy carbon offsets from Southern California Edison that resulted from efficiency improvements at various power plants.
1998	Tesco, a U.K.-based operator of retail gasoline stations, announced its intention to offset carbon emissions from selected gasoline products by carbon sequestration in a tropical forestry initiative in Uganda.
1998	Japan-based Sumitomo announced a plan to help convert numerous coal-fired electric power plants in Russia to natural gas and earn carbon offsets as part of the transaction.
1998	Canada-based Suncor Energy announced a purchase of carbon offsets from Niagara Mohawk.
1998	The government of Costa Rica is offering Certified Tradable Offsets (CTOs). These arise from carbon sequestration in a new national park. CTOs are the first monetization of environmental services produced by tropical rainforests.

Action bill would provide recognition for companies that take early action to reduce greenhouse gases emissions, allowing them to earn credit under any mechanism the government eventually establishes to limit emissions. It provides an important incentive for companies to invest in reducing their greenhouse gas emissions and will help to further stimulate trading.

The evolutionary process of market development also mirrors the history of international political cooperation. International agreements tend to grow from small beginnings—the European Coal and Steel Community has evolved to the Common Market and, now, the European Monetary Union. In the case of carbon trading, a group of countries is beginning to coalesce into what we call a *plurilateral* trading regime, involving a system of conventions and regulations evolving first among a small group of countries. Environmental markets are already occurring in this context and the Buenos Aires conference, Fourth Conference of the Parties (COP4), has given a clear action plan for advancing rules and defining standards for emissions trading and other market mechanisms by late 2000.

At the November 1998, Buenos Aires meetings, nations have also discussed in greater detail the working mechanisms of the Clean Development Mechanism (CDM), which, if properly designed, can help turn into reality the remarkable capability of tradable emission permits to deliver a "double dividend." These twin benefits would help to lower the cost to the public of addressing climate change while acting as a powerful mechanism for transferring clean energy technologies and financial resources from industrialized to developing nations.

The prospects of a market will increase this feasibility as new investments are made in the technologies and research needed to monitor and standardize carbon measurement. Active trading of carbon could prove an inexpensive insurance policy against the unknown but potentially catastrophic problems that may emerge because of the rapid increase in global carbon emissions. An effective and efficient market-based solution will become even more important if restrictions on carbon emissions are tightened.

The process of market creation starts with the private sector and the governments will follow. Because of the international requirements, we postulate an expanded 12-stage process required for the greenhouse gas market to start:

1. Clearly define the commodity;
2. Establish market oversight;
3. Define baselines;
4. Allocate permits and monitor emissions;
5. Establish uniform, nonsegmented allowances;
6. Devise an international allowance clearing house;
7. Employ existing exchanges and trading systems;

8. Develop auctions;

9. Refine trade documentation practices;

10. Foster harmonization among trade forums;

11. Prepare accounting procedures; and

12. Launch an international effort to assure that participants in emerging markets can trade as soon as possible.

CONCLUSIONS

History shows that market evolution ordinarily follows a seven-stage process that can be observed in equities, fixed income securities, physical commodities, and the SO_2 allowance trading program. The SO_2 cap-and-trade emission reduction program has been enormously successful. While most observers now say they knew the SO_2 system would be successful, there was enormous skepticism at the start, much like the skepticism now being expressed about carbon trading. The sulfur trading model can be successfully extended to carbon. Although its international dimensions add complications, we have successful environmental precedents such as the effort to slow high-level ozone depletion via the Montreal Protocol. This issue is not daunting. Transactions in carbon offsets have already occurred and trading is under way. The carbon trading history will not be unlike that of other environmental markets, where government regulation gives value to the commodity while the design and implementation are left to market forces with the governments ratifying the process.

In sum, we believe the cost of solving the global greenhouse problem will be a function of the policy choices we make. We understand those who would say that control costs of $200 billion per year will dislocate the economy, but this need not be the cost. There is growing evidence that the climate change problem is real and the benefits of reducing carbon emissions will grow larger over time. Low-cost action now is analogous to buying an insurance policy against global damages, many of which are irreversible. If designed wisely, an emissions trading program makes the insurance policy very affordable.

POSTSCRIPT

The editors continue the Workshop tradition by including selected questions and answers.

Question 1: *"How can we verify the actions needed to cut or capture
greenhouse gases?"*

It's very straightforward for sulfur, as you will learn in this
book. How does that verification occur with carbon? A good
example is the Costa Rica case. An organization called SGS
Forestry, a division of the large inspection firm Société Générale
de Surveillance, was employed to certify the carbon sequestration from tropical forests. They used satellite monitoring, field
inspection and a whole series of processes. The instruments
being sold are over-collateralized by a good margin over what
we believe to be the likely carbon sequestration rate. It took a
year to do the certification. It's very expensive and prohibitive
to use satellites alone to monitor the rainforest, so field inspection is also needed to assess reforestation growth rates, verify
avoided deforestation, and even check for landslides. You may
well ask what do landslides have to do with rainforests? It turns
out that landslides cover vegetation and as a result you have less
carbon sequestration. So we have built in a 1.7 percent risk factor for landslides. All in all, for a hundred different categories
of assessment, there's 70 percent more of safety margin. This
step is similar to that used to protect buyers of high-risk bonds.

Question 2: *Two questions. First of all, what happens to the market
in the event of forest fires and second, for how long does sequestration
continue?*

In the case of forest fires, there is a buffer reserve to account
for the risk of fires. This is one of the factors in the 70 percent
margin. If it's more than that, then the agreement with the government is to dedicate other forest lands to assure that the
promised sequestration rate is realized. The land is purchased
from the private sector and put into public parks, like Grand
Canyon National Park, in perpetuity under the program. We're
selling the carbon sequestration rights for only the first 20 years.
The parks are expected to be there in perpetuity.

Question 3: *Would you give your views on the necessity for an auction in your trade model?*

The single most important factor in markets is price transparency. People need to feel confident that there are unrigged prices. Investors and consumers make decisions based on this information. Some estimates have been made about the cost of reducing a ton of carbon emissions that seem very high to me. An auction can put such erroneous forecasts to rest. Until you get an actual exchange of money, you have little price information that is reliable; hence the strong case for an auction.

REFERENCES

Carlson, Curtis, Dallas Burtraw, Maureen Cropper, and Karen L. Palmer. 1998. "Sulfur Dioxide Controls by Electric Utilities: What are the Gains from Trade?" Resources for the Future Discussion Paper 98–44. Washington, DC July.

Cooper, Richard N. 1998. "Toward a Real Global Warming Treaty." *Foreign Affairs* 77 (March/April): 66–79.

Cushman, John H. 1999. "Industries Press Plan for Credits in Emissions Pact." *The New York Times*, 3 January, p. A1.

Hahn, Robert W. and Carol A May. 1994. "The Behavior of the Allowance Market: Theory and Evidence." *The Electricity Journal* 7 (2) (March): 28–37.

Sandor, Richard L. "The Role of the United States in International Environmental Policy." In *Preparing America's Foreign Policy for the Twenty-first Century*, ed. David L. Boren and Edward J. Perkins. Norman, Oklahoma: University of Oklahoma Press. Forthcoming.

Sandor, Richard and Jerry Skees. "Creating a Market for Carbon Emissions: Opportunities for U.S. Farmers." *Choices Magazine*. Forthcoming.

Schmalensee, Richard, Paul L. Joskow, A. Denny Ellerman, Juan Pablo Montero, and Elizabeth M. Bailey. 1998. "An Interim Evaluation of Sulfur Dioxide Emissions Trading." *Journal of Economic Perspectives* 12 (3) (summer): 53–68.

Schumpeter, Joseph A. 1942. *Capitalism, Socialism and Democracy.* New York: Harper and Brothers.

U.S. Environmental Protection Agency. 1998. *1997 Compliance Report.* Office of Air and Radiation, Acid Rain Division (6204J). Project # EPA-430-R-98–02. Washington, DC.

NOTES

1. Obtained from "Climate Change—A Role for Business," a speech by Rodney Chase, Deputy Group Chief Executive Officer and Chief Executive of BP Oil at the Royal Institute for International Affairs, Chatham House. 27 November 1998.

2. They are Senators John H. Chafee (R-R.I.), Joseph I. Lieberman (D-Conn.), and Connie Mack (R-Fla.).

PART THREE

VIEWS FROM THE MARKET DESIGNERS AND ADMINISTRATORS

5

Emissions Trading Designs in the OTAG Process

Mary A. Gade
Roger A. Kanerva

The Ozone Transport Assessment Group (OTAG) was a unique public-private collaboration between 37 state governments and the private sector to address one of the nation's most intractable environmental and public health issues—ground-level ozone—more commonly known as smog. Traditionally, the federal government has led the way on environmental policy. OTAG opened up a new path for the states to share the leading position in addressing an environmental problem of this magnitude, a problem that crosses so many state boundaries and affects so many large industrial sectors. In this account, we provide an insider's view of the work of OTAG with special emphasis on the organization of the project and on the attention given to emissions trading. We highlight both the achievements of OTAG, and the work that remains to be done.

91

OTAG Process: A New Path

The number one air pollution problem in the United States, in our view, is ground-level ozone. After 30 years of implementation of the policies of the 1970 Clean Air Act, ozone still potentially affects the health of more than one-third of all Americans, as well as damaging crops such as corn, wheat, and soybeans, and some materials. Within the OTAG region alone, states generally east of the Mississippi River, an even higher proportion of the population lives in areas still designated as nonattainment for ozone, where nonattainment is defined in terms of unhealthful concentrations of ozone. Children, the elderly, and the chronically ill are particularly at risk (OTAG, 1997a). Despite the substantial efforts by states to reduce ozone and smog-causing air emissions, these pollutants have proved stubborn and resistant to control. Only Louisiana, of the 37 states, was able to submit an ozone attainment plan to U.S. EPA by the November 1994 Clean Air Act deadline (Gade, 1997a).

One of the major reasons preventing progress was becoming more clear over time. Air monitoring data and computer modeling by Illinois and other states indicated that this problem was not a localized matter. Substantial levels of "background" ozone and its precursors were crossing state borders. An analysis by Illinois indicated that even such dramatic measures within the state as taking 2 million cars off the roads and shutting down 75 percent of industry would not produce attainment by itself. Similarly, Georgia determined that Atlanta could close all its factories and ban all cars and still not meet the standard, so affected was the local air by movement of pollutants from outside (Gade, 1997b).

When it became sufficiently clear in 1995 that most states individually could not address the regional movement of "precursor" pollutants (mainly nitrogen oxides and volatile organic compounds that potentially react with sunlight and oxygen to form ozone), the Environmental Council of the States (ECOS) proposed that OTAG be organized to search for a new approach. ECOS is an organization of state environmental commissioners and directors. The U.S. EPA pledged financial support and promised to give the states more time to further analyze and propose solutions to the ozone transport problem. ECOS saw it as a challenge and opportunity for the states to demonstrate that they could contribute to the solution of a substantial national environmental issue, while giving the private sector a greater role as well.

The OTAG process evolved into the first comprehensive multistate, multistakeholder evaluation of ozone transport. Starting as a small ad-hoc group in May 1995, OTAG grew to include active participation by nearly 1,000 representatives of industrial, scientific, and environmental groups, as well as the environmental agencies of the 37 easternmost states and the District of Columbia. Participants ranged from major utilities to automakers to the Environmental Defense Fund, representing all the affected communities. The U.S. EPA was an active advisor in the process.

OTAG provided an inclusive, open process, and as a result many of those who were initially hostile, eventually bought in and helped to achieve its success. Before the end of 1995, the Policy Group had reached consensus on the overall goal for the OTAG process. This goal was set forth in a policy paper approved on December 4, 1995 (reprinted in OTAG 1997a):

> To identify and recommend a strategy to reduce transported ozone and its precursors, which, in combination with other measures, will enable attainment and maintenance of the ozone standard in the OTAG region. A number of criteria will be used to select the strategy including, but not limited to, cost-effectiveness, feasibility, and impacts on ozone levels.

The enormous volume of work subsequently produced was not only debated within a variety of workgroups but also made available to all who were interested through the Internet. Competing regional and industrial interests threatened to derail OTAG at times. Many participants and most of the news media that covered OTAG predicted it would not be able to reach consensus on any recommendations to the U.S. EPA. Regional factions of state participants and industry groups caucused and debated, hundreds of conference calls were made outside the OTAG meetings, while the chair and other leaders used shuttle diplomacy to forge a sometimes fragile consensus and compromise among the many often competing OTAG players. From our perspective, it took a blend of political finesse and good humor, coupled with technical understanding and strong-willed determination, to keep OTAG together, and working.

The hard work paid off. This extraordinary mix of public-private expertise eventually produced the most comprehensive scientific and technical database ever compiled on what causes smog in the eastern United States. At the final OTAG meeting in Washington, DC, in June 1997, 31 of the 37 OTAG states formally voted to support 12 significant recommendations on strategies to address the smog problem, recommendations that we shall summarize after discussing the important features of the process that led to OTAG achievements.

SETTING THE STAGE FOR POLICY DEVELOPMENT

Numerous technical and policy barriers and conflicts had to be addressed during the more than two-year OTAG odyssey. Before OTAG, many of the states and private stakeholders had been wary of each other and shared little information on ground-level ozone. As chair of the Policy Group, one of the authors (Gade) sought to facilitate networking and consensus, and despite her own state's significant stake in the OTAG outcome, followed a policy of neutrality. This position avoided unproductive and potentially fatal protracted debates with some interest groups, such as the coal industry, that initially were hostile to the OTAG effort in principle. The challenge was to keep the group focused on the overall goal when disagreements over computer models, number and types of modeling runs, the specific historical ozone episodes to use for the analysis, the pollution source inventory, and other difficult technical issues threatened to derail OTAG (Gade, 1997b).

The emphasis from the beginning was to rely on sound science as a basis for future policy decisions and for resultant strategies to reduce ground-level ozone. The four major subgroups established enabled participants to become engaged in areas of special interest to them (see Figure 5.1). Workgroups were formed within each subgroup in order to hone in on

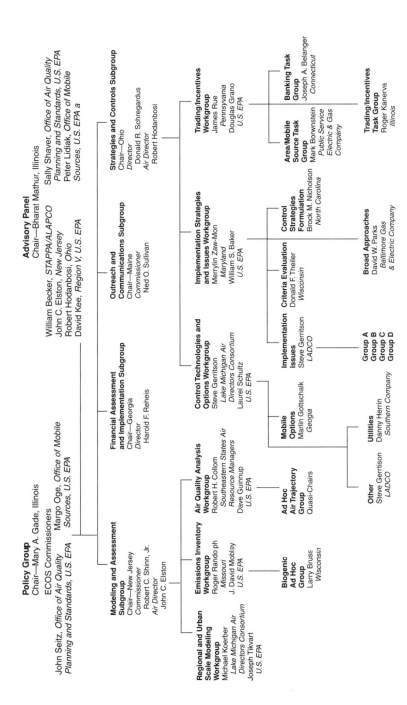

Figure 5.1 OTAG organization chart.

95

well-defined tasks. These included regional and urban scale modeling, emissions inventory, air quality analysis, control technologies and options, and trading/incentives. We shall, in a later section, go into more detail on the efforts of the last mentioned workgroup. Further subdivision of the work to task groups enabled OTAG to obtain more information on particular issues that could help minimize conflict. The subdivision of OTAG's work served as one means to attract some of the best talent in the field, from both the public and private sector, to address these specific issues and to share data and expertise. Much of this information was made available over the Internet through U.S. EPA's Technology Transfer Network.

The level of participation seemed to increase with each OTAG meeting, not only in numbers but also in the presentations and discussion. Many mentioned to us that they were astonished at the openness of the process. Anyone with an interest or stake in ground-level ozone was free to join a workgroup on an ad hoc basis and contribute and join in the debate. As noted in OTAG's final executive report: "The nature of the work and interaction of participants in the workgroups was the heart of OTAG. It was here that stakeholders were able to use their technical expertise in a development process rather than in the responsive process they normally experience when dealing with environmental agencies. The tangible and intangible contributions of all workgroup participants formed the flavor and dynamism that radiated through the subgroups to the Policy Group." If someone had a problem, we put him or her to work.

In many cases, the task groups created within workgroups were chaired by nongovernment stakeholders. When the issues were resolved, these task groups were dissolved. Recommendations were channeled up through workgroups to the subgroups, which included both government and private sector participants who had not been part of a particular workgroup. The subgroups became a forum for further debate and refinement on what the scientific research was showing and how to interpret it for policy considerations.

The final step in the process involved the Policy Group (composed of the state commissioners and U.S. EPA representatives) reviewing the reports from the subgroups and reaching, via discussion, final conclusions and recommendations. The Policy Group initially proceeded on a consensus basis. However, in the final three meetings, each state's environmental commissioner or designee was allowed to cast a vote on emerging policy recommendations as well as on the final major scientific conclusions to be forwarded to U.S. EPA. The Policy Group also invited any stakeholder to submit written comments within 10 days that were included in the package of recommendations forwarded to U.S. EPA.

The Policy Group had to make several key decisions during the two-year OTAG process, including those relating to the emissions inventory, the computer model, and determination of the runs, as well as possible control measures grouped into "control packets" for the modeling (OTAG, 1997a). One of the early key decisions was an agreement on a single uniform state-of-the-art modeling system, the Urban Airshed Model Five (UAM-V). Previously, different states and regions had used various models, making it difficult to share comparative data in a meaningful manner.

Agreement was also reached on the use of data provided by states, OTAG member organizations, and the U.S. EPA on four high ozone episodes in July of 1988, 1991, 1993, and 1995. The model was then used to simulate actual high ozone episodes with different levels of emissions. Modeling activity proceeded in three rounds. The first round allowed OTAG to set parameters for modeling; the second allowed OTAG to understand the impact of different emissions controls on different emissions sources; and the last round helped OTAG understand the regional aspects of controlling various emissions sources. Another major achievement was the first compilation of a "national" inventory of emissions sources for all ozone precursors. These inventories may be adjusted by users at a later date for future growth and controls. A final recommendation on a trading program framework provided strong support for emissions trading but recognized that several different market designs were currently in favor. The Policy Group also heard and evaluated presentations from dozens of stakeholders on a variety of issues as well. OTAG became, in effect, a marketplace for the display and testing of ideas on regional ozone policy and its implementation.

It was important to bring this marketplace of ideas and the resultant discussion to the attention of the broader public. As chair of the Policy Group, Mary Gade's role in this phase included giving progress-report speeches to major industrial sectors that had a stake in the outcome, such as the World Fuels Conference and the Edison Electric Institute. She also gave numerous interviews to the press, including many major newspapers, ABC News, and National Public Radio, as well as the avidly interested trade publications, which even included a new *Inside OTAG* newsletter. The chair also frequently had to use her contacts with U.S. EPA to make sure needed work was funded on time to meet deadlines. She also challenged individual companies, environmental groups, and industry associations to step up to the technical challenges and provide their experts. When expertise was needed on clean-burning fuels, Amoco came forward, for example. As a result of leveraging this volunteer talent, OTAG produced an astonishing volume of cutting-edge technical work that eventually filled 36 file drawers. A foundation was being laid for policy guidance, for further development and refinement, and for future research.

MAJOR CONCLUSIONS, RECOMMENDATIONS, AND LESSONS LEARNED

We believe that the OTAG process was a significant departure from previous efforts undertaken by the federal government and the states to assess and solve air pollution problems. Traditionally, the U.S. EPA has formulated regulations and standards for meeting broad congressional mandates under the Clean Air Act, and then accepted state and private input before making final decisions. OTAG turned that process on its head. With state environmental commissioners taking the policy initiating and recommending role, they were able to secure open and active participation by nongovernmental stakeholders, including industrial sectors such as utilities, automakers, petroleum refiners, and others.

We perceived that the participants came to feel that they were in the process at the very start, when all positions had a chance for full consideration. Remarkably, while also vigorously advancing their own positions, this diverse variety of interests also ended up working together to overcome initial mistrust, share information, and work productively on solutions to the smog problem. At one point, conflicting regional concerns by some state environmental commissioners, in many cases influenced by major home state industrial interests, threatened to jeopardize consensus on policy recommendations from OTAG. The chair convened regional caucuses and pushed them to clarify their positions, eventually resulting in the remarkable show of support for the final report in June 1997. Those recommendations range from some tough new standards for utility and large industrial boiler emissions of nitrogen oxides to innovative expansion of emission trading programs that could provide cost-effective alternatives while still improving air quality. The U.S. EPA is using them as one of the cornerstones of further steps to reduce the smog problem, such as in the 1998 NO_x Final Rule release and NO_x SIP call (U.S. EPA, 1998). Where consensus could not be achieved, there was agreement to pose the issue as requiring further work and discussion. OTAG's contribution in these instances, which included low emission vehicle standards and the sulfur content in gasoline, was to help clarify the differences of views in preparation for subsequent research and discussion.

Among the major conclusions reached by OTAG by consensus were (OTAG, 1997a):

- Regional NO_x reductions are effective in producing ozone benefits; the more NO_x reduced, the greater the benefit;
- Ozone benefits are greatest in the subregions where emissions reductions are made; the benefits decrease with distance;
- Both elevated (from tall stacks) and low-level NO_x reductions are effective;
- VOC controls are effective in reducing ozone locally and are most advantageous to urban nonattainment areas;
- Air quality data indicate that ozone is pervasive, that ozone is transported, and that ozone aloft is carried over and transported from one day to the next;
- The range of transport is generally longer in the North than in the South, and the range of transport is less than previously believed.

The ultimate charge to OTAG was to make recommendations. A total package of these was prepared for consideration. Stakeholder comments were welcome and a voting procedure was established for the state environmental commissioners. Thirty-one states voted for the final package, five opposed, and Nebraska was not present. Among the recommendations made on the basis of this voting procedure, in summarized form, were that (OTAG, 1997a):

- The stringency of controls for large non-utility point sources should be established in a manner equitable with utility controls, and that control targets for them should be set as recommended;
- The U.S. EPA develop, adopt, and implement national control measures on a list of mobile and area sources of VOC and NO_x;
- OTAG supports and encourages a voluntary National Low-Emission Vehicle Program;
- OTAG recommends the continued use of reformulated gasoline and an appropriate sulfur standard to further reduce emissions;
- OTAG recommends new diesel fuel standards if found beneficial and cost-effective;
- OTAG recommends effective vehicle emissions inspection and maintenance program, and recommends that states consider the adoption of enhanced inspection and maintenance programs;
- OTAG states endorse and encourage the development and implementation of ozone action days.
- OTAG recognizes the benefits of market-based approaches to control, and further recognizes that states may choose one of the two following basic tracks to NO_x emissions trading:

  Track one: States that elect emissions caps should be part of a common, interstate emissions market. A central authority such as the U.S. EPA could administer the interstate NO_x market system.

  Track two: States that elect trading without caps would be part of an alternative system starting with intrastate trading but leading possibly to multistate trading.

> OTAG recommends that a joint state/EPA workgroup be formed to address the implementation of the two tracks building on the design features developed by the Trading/Incentives Workgroup (TIW).

This last recommendation—that states may choose between two different emissions-trading markets—was the end product of a long discussion, and debate, in the TIW. This extensive exchange among all concerned parties, while clarifying some views on the features of the appropriate market design, revealed differences in views that prevented consensus on one best design. For readers interested in the design of market-based approaches and in the critical features which engender debate, we present a more detailed account of the deliberations of the TIW.

EMISSIONS TRADING DESIGNS FOR THE OTAG REGION

The TIW was established to provide information and recommendations to the Policy Group on market-based approaches that could help achieve reductions in ozone precursors, especially NO_x emissions, in a more cost-effective manner. To guide its efforts, the TIW initially agreed on the following general mission statement (OTAG, 1997b):

> This workgroup is to design market-based approaches to reduce ozone precursor emissions across the eastern half of the United States consistent with OTAG objectives. The focus of the group's efforts should be to reduce background concentrations of ozone by reducing precursors transported across and between states. It is not the intention of the group to re-examine individual SIPs, but rather to develop an interstate market-based framework. As individual states develop their own market-based strategies, the focus will be to provide mechanisms to effect trades between states. NO_x emissions have been initially chosen because of the ambient impact demonstrated by regional ozone modeling, the number of sources impacted, and the relative ease of emission estimation procedures. A NO_x

trading program will establish principles that can be extended to VOC emissions in a second phase effort.

Agreeing to this preliminary statement were workgroup members that included state officials and representatives from all parts of the OTAG domain. To facilitate the dialogue process, three task groups were formed to address subjects that posed distinct problems for emissions trading of ozone precursors: one task force was to deal with emissions from large stationary NO_x sources, another with emissions from area and mobile sources, and a third with the question of emissions banking. The chronology of the TIW and its task group efforts provides not only a convenient framework for our presentation, but also tracks the evolution of the debate about the preferred market design.

Key Policy Papers

The TIW prepared key policy papers in 1996 that set the stage for the more detailed design discussion. Three papers were consensus products and were submitted to the Policy Group where they were approved. Several papers did not achieve consensus and revealed a division among participants on several features of emissions trading.

The first consensus policy paper, entitled "Emissions Market Approaches Suitable for Accomplishing OTAG Policy Goals," described a three-step process for the workgroup to accomplish its mission. Step one was to develop basic or general principles applicable to any market-based framework, step two was to develop a market-based framework appropriate for large stationary sources of NO_x, and step three was to develop a market-based framework generally applicable to stationary, mobile, and area sources of NO_x, and eventually VOC.

Flowing from this paper were three recommendations to the Policy Group for development of NO_x and VOC market systems. The first recommendation outlined specific or guiding principles for the market system development. These guiding principles indicate the TIW's concerns about the details of an effective emissions-trading program:

- The focus should be on actual NO_x and VOC emissions during the applicable control period.
- Emissions-trading programs should be compatible among geographic areas that are suitable for common markets.
- Participation should be encouraged by sufficient NO_x and VOC sources to promote a robust market and to achieve the emissions reductions necessary for addressing background ozone air quality goals.
- Market areas should be delineated that give participating sources the widest range of compliance options consistent with air quality boundary determinations.
- Emissions currency should be designed that is fungible across the region and, with appropriate qualifications, intertemporal in nature.
- Trading rules should be designed that give sources who participate in the market maximum certainty of rules and minimum regulatory intervention.
- Enforcement and monitoring procedures should be established to yield performance assurance that will maintain the integrity of the emissions reduction objectives and the market system, and provide equitable treatment for participating sources.

The second recommendation was that the initial market design incorporating these principles should address large stationary NO_x sources. The third recommended that additional design components should address other stationary NO_x sources and mobile and area sources consistent within a multisector approach. That is, provisions should be made for appropriate integration of multiple components into a total functional market system.

The second consensus policy paper dealt with "Interstate Budget/Trading Framework for Large Stationary NO_x Sources (Utility and Industrial Boilers)." The paper described a framework or design for a "cap" type of program for total seasonal NO_x emissions from utility and industrial boilers in the OTAG region within which sources would receive "NO_x emissions allotments" (OTAG, 1997b). The paper also described generally other major features for a NO_x emissions market system, including interstate compatibility, qualification of emissions that could be traded, quantification of emissions, registry and clearinghouse arrangements, enforcement, and audit of environmental and economic impact.

The third consensus policy paper continued with the development of a budget-trading framework for large stationary NO_x sources and was entitled "Design Features Relating to Interstate Budget/Trading Framework." Consensus was reached on general matters such as a recommendation that tradable emissions rights (allotments) be bankable. It was further recommended that no restrictions should be placed on the ability to put and retain allotments in a bank but that responsible use of banked allotments is necessary to ensure that air quality is not adversely affected during major ozone periods. Two different viewpoints emerged on this major issue as follows:

1. No initial program design or initial use restrictions should be imposed, but results should be closely tracked and adjustments made if any problems develop. A flow control mechanism that would limit emissions trading during critical (high ozone) periods should be considered as a contingency measure.

2. Initial program design should include a provision to control excessive allotment withdrawals in an ozone season.

The paper also recommended that performance accountability be addressed for the whole system and for each participating source.

Several other draft policy papers were also developed dealing with allocation of NO_x emissions to individual emitters, and area and mobile source emissions trading. The allocation of tradable emission rights to sources under a cap-based design includes issues such as establishing the appropriate benchmark time period for allocation and allowing for the source's normal activity level. Area and mobile source emissions trading includes issues such as the large number of small sources and the reliability and permanence of reductions. Consensus among the TIW participants was achieved on some but not all aspects of these matters and the Policy Group did not approve these draft papers, and set the issues aside for later work.

Market System Workshops

A series of workshops were then designed to further inform members of the Policy Group about the major issues and choices flowing from the general policy papers, and to promote dialogue among all interested parties about possible detailed policy statements, and possible resolution of different viewpoints on the appropriate market design.

The first one-day workshop was held on January 23, 1997, and was planned to foster a dialogue between the TIW and the Policy Group on the following subjects (OTAG, 1997b):

- The features of specific market system designs such as the cap- and rate-based types;
- The policy issues relevant to large stationary NO_x sources compared with issues relevant to area and mobile emissions sources;
- The consideration of inter-sector trading; and
- The supporting analysis and information that would be required to appraise these policy options.

During this workshop, presentations were made by the Environmental Defense Fund, the Utility Air Regulatory Group, and the Electric Power Supply Association. It was becoming clear that there were significant differences in opinion on the merits of alternative emissions-trading programs.

As a result of these diverging views, the Policy Group requested that the TIW prepare a special paper that presented the pros and cons of market designs system types with and without emissions caps for participating sources. Addressing this request became a daunting challenge for the TIW and after a good deal of work a consensus work product, titled "Comparison of Market System Types," was presented to the Policy Group on March 14, 1997 (OTAG, 1997b).

However, a consensus was not achieved on the preferred market type. This lack of agreement was to carry through the work of the TIW, including the final recommendations. It became clear that some parties were giving a different meaning to the "consensus" reached on the second policy paper that specified a framework or design for a cap-and-trade (budget-type) market. A minority of state participants held strong views in favor of a rate-based in contrast with the majority who favored a cap-based market. Concern about accommodating growth, source expansion, and new sources, was the main reason for this minority view. The minority position was that they had only agreed in the prior policy statement to a design framework and not to a commitment to one design. This turn of events was viewed by some as a significant setback for the TIW's policy development efforts. The TIW turned its attention to developing guidelines for a regulatory system to ascertain whether such guidelines could lead to agreement on an emissions-trading model.

The second TIW workshop was held on May 29, 1997, jointly with the Policy Group with an agenda that began with a discussion of the basics of any NO_x regulatory system, centralized or decentralized. The workshop developed three desired results or performance criteria that any regulatory system design relating to NO_x emissions should achieve or meet (OTAG, 1997b):

1. The regulatory system should achieve and maintain the applicable aggregate or state wide emissions budget (where the budget means the reduced permissible amount of emissions for the state).

2. The regulatory system should maximize certainty of control and the opportunities for cost savings for participants.

3. The regulatory system should be feasible in implementation and operate efficiently.

Four question areas were put to participants to determine more precisely what system could be relied on to achieve the desired results.

1. What regulatory system do you prefer for each sector budget (stationary, mobile, or area in nature) in order to deliver the desired results?

Would market systems for appropriate sources be feasible?

Would traditional command-and-control systems be preferable?

2. What specific market system do you prefer to ensure the delivery of desired results?

A system with emissions caps [cap-and-allocation (trade) or cap-and-credit]?

A system without emissions caps (traditional rate-based or rate-tonnage)?

3. What interstate system or program do you prefer for the operation of a multistate market system?

One program for the entire area?

Regional programs for multiple control areas?

State-specific programs?

4. Should a joint Environmental Council of the States (ECOS) and EPA workgroup be chartered to undertake an appropriate market system?

Question 2 raised a central issue on the choice of two contending market systems. The TIW presented to the Policy Group an analysis comparing the pros and cons of the two major types and of two variants of each. These choices are (1) a market systems without emissions caps, specifically a rate-based system, and a rate-tonnage system; and (2) a market systems with emissions caps, specifically a cap-and-credit system, and a cap-and-allocation system.

A digression to explain briefly these different market systems or designs is in order. The rate-based and the cap-and-trade systems are most frequently proposed, but differ markedly in many respects. In the rate-based design, the fundamental rule is that the source must meet prescribed sector emission rates by controls or by tradable emission credits. Trades when they occur are voluntary and often of a bilateral character with buyer and seller requiring government approval at both ends of the transaction. In the cap-and-trade design, an aggregate sector emissions limitation is prescribed within which individual sources are required to participate and are allocated tradable allowances. The fundamental rule in this case is that a tradable allowance must be turned over to the government for each unit of emission. Trades when they occur are often of a multilateral character as the government does not require approval of each transaction.

There are less known and less used variants of these designs. In the rate-tonnage type, the prescribed emissions rate is multiplied by the source's actual activity level to determine the sources tradable allowance allocation for the period. In the cap-and-credit type, a performance standard is set by dividing the sector's emission budget by total utilization to obtain an emissions standard rate. Sources with rates below the standard earn credits, sources with rates above must buy credits. The standard may be periodically reset as activity levels change.

There are other important differences, but for many purposes the essential distinction is that the establishment of a cap gives the government authority control of the aggregate volume of emissions but not directly the rates. On the other hand, the establishment of a rate gives the government authority control of that rate but not the aggregate volume of emissions, as rates may extend over varying lengths of time. For the emitter, an important difference is that the cap-and-trade market requires participation in the allocation and monitoring process whereas participation in the rate-based market is voluntary. These two were the leading contenders for participant choice.

Not able to reach consensus on these choices, the TIW then proceeded to survey the membership to find out how the four designs would rate in terms of three criteria. First, could the design with a high degree of certainty achieve a presumed emissions budget? Second, could the design achieve cost savings, and third, could the design be feasibly implemented and efficiently operated? The following straw rating or ordered ranking for each criterion was offered for consideration:

1. Cap-and-allocation; (most certain).
2. Cap-and-credit.
3. Rate-tonnage.
4. Rate-based (least certain).

Most state participants who expressed a view sensed, in general, that the straw ranking was appropriate for the first criterion, achieving the budget, but agreement could not be reached on the cost savings and efficiency criteria. The TIW was unable to recommend a particular trading design based on these rankings.

There was more agreement on the matter of seven more general design features or proposals that were applicable to all four-market types. The TIW proposed these to be applied to large stationary sources of NO_x emissions. These proposals, or background papers, represented agreed-upon final work products. No serious concerns were raised that would justify reconsideration of this set of recommendations (OTAG, 1997a); the recommendations were:

1. The first general design proposal for stationary sources lists several issues relevant to identifying appropriate sources for inclusion in a trading program for large stationary NO_x sources. Participation should be defined on an emissions unit basis (size).

2. The second design proposal presents methodologies for determining emissions assignments (allocations to sources) in each of the four market system types and describes various policy concerns that program designers may want to consider when determining these important emissions assignments.

3. The third design proposal discusses the value of emissions banking in achieving cost effective control decisions over time and shows how the impact of potential emissions fluctuations during critical ozone periods due to the use of banked credits or allowances can be reduced.

4. The fourth design proposal describes the characteristics of a currency that is truly common among the states and facilitates a liquid, well functioning market. The problems associated with having different currencies trading at different rates are presented.

5. The fifth design proposal describes the specific data elements and procedures required to monitor and enforce compliance, and the consequences for noncompliance.

6. The sixth design proposal addresses whether a market-based system should allow inter-sector transactions (e.g., to include tradable credits for reducing vehicle emissions), and suggests possible methods for implementing these transactions.

7. The seventh design proposal for market system performance review addresses various features (price trends, quantities of transactions, degree of competition, etc.) of the market that should be assessed periodically and the types of evaluation practices that might be used.

The second workshop ended with the crafting of a final policy recommendation that could be acted on by the Policy Group. At this point, it was clear that OTAG could recommend design guidelines, but could not recommend a preferred market design for NO_x emissions control.

Final Recommendation for Trading Program Framework

A special meeting of the TIW was called for June 12, 1997, with an open invitation to the Policy Group in order to recap the important viewpoints on policy perspectives and on market design features that had surfaced. U.S. EPA also presented its views regarding the requirements of a multistate NO_x emissions market system. An initial proposed policy recommendation was distributed to the participants for discussion built around a 2-track, compromise approach (OTAG, 1997a). The first track was designed for those states that preferred to implement a cap-and-trade market and wanted to be part of a common interstate emissions market. In support of this first track, the U.S. EPA stated it would be willing to serve as the central administrator of this multistate NO_x market system. The second track was designed for those states that preferred to implement a rate-based market. In contrast to track one, however, these states would be part of "an alternative emissions market" that could take several forms from intrastate trading to possible multistate trading arrangements. For this track, U.S. EPA was not willing to be the central administrator.

Numerous useful suggestions were made, many contacts were initiated, and quite a few drafts of recommendations were written in the following days prior to the final meeting on June 19, 1997. The final product was characterized as "something we could all live with" (Kanerva, 1997). To get this support, it was necessary to sort out numerous differences. For example, it was important to note the reduced certainty of obtaining specific emission reductions associated with track two or the rate-based market. Another concern was the possible difficulties of cross-track trading. Once again, a compromise was fashioned that recognized this as a future possibility but only if further development work was done to ensure a credible system. The last major component of the recommendation dealt with the seven design proposals that the TIW had worked so hard to develop. The solution that proved acceptable to everyone was to reference these products as a sound basis for future deliberations by a joint ECOS—U.S. EPA workgroup. To round out this suggestion, an initial agenda was proposed for this future joint workgroup including the design proposals. It was felt to be a significant accomplishment to finally craft a recommendation that could be adopted by the Policy Group that provided firm guidelines for emissions trading, if not a specific market design. The actual text of the final recommendation is provided in Appendix A.

CONCLUSION

The OTAG process is a new approach to regional and national problem solving, and not limited to environmental issues. It is already being considered by western states as a model for addressing environmental concerns impacting the Grand Canyon and for other regional air quality problems. The techniques used in the OTAG process to foster an open and inclusive process that invites the private sector and public interest groups to participate as true partners with government could be used to achieve consensus on a variety of important public policy issues. OTAG also demonstrated that not all solutions have to come from Washington; that states and the private sectors can reach dynamic solutions to difficult problems. U.S. EPA Administrator Carol Browner called OTAG the ultimate "multi, multi, multistakeholder" process. Not the least significant of OTAG's achievements is that it met its specific goals, and then went out of existence. This is a refreshing contrast to many government task forces or working groups that have become so bogged down in technical issues they lose sight of their ultimate goals and deadlines. We as participants charged with our respective chair positions feel a sense of accomplishment in reviewing this work.

OTAG's work on emissions trading has been reflected in U.S. EPA's subsequent rule makings for reducing regional transport of ozone. On September 24, 1998, the U.S. EPA issued a final rule that provided for a NO_x Budget Trading Program, among other control measures that may be chosen (EPA Final Rule, 1998). This rule provides for a model cap-and-trade program for certain large stationary sources as the recommended means for states to comply with the current NO_x SIP (State Implementation Plan) call on these sources. As was the case with OTAG's work, U.S. EPA does, however, recognize that states may pursue other types of trading programs in their SIPs, provided they meet the specified SIP approval criteria. As an incentive for states to adopt the model program, U.S. EPA offers a streamlined approval process. That the model program makes numerous references to OTAG's activity not only provides us with a feeling of work well done, but also augurs well for the many decisions on emissions trading that the affected states will be making in the next several years. The chances for more healthful air obtained in a cost-effective manner seem to us to have been improved.

APPENDIX A: FINAL RECOMMENDATION: TRADING PROGRAM FRAMEWORK

Market-based approaches are generally recognized as having the following benefits in relation to traditional command-and-control regulations: They serve to (1) reduce the cost of compliance; (2) create incentives for early reduction; (3) create incentives for emissions reductions beyond those required by regulations; (4) promote innovation; and (5) increase flexibility without resorting to waivers, exemptions and other forms of administrative relief.

OTAG recognizes that states have the option to select market systems that are best suited to their policy purposes and air quality planning and program needs. In anticipation of the state-specific decisions, OTAG recognizes that states may choose one of two basic approaches to implement NO_x emissions market system:

1. *Track One:*—States that elect to implement equivalent NO$_x$ market systems with emissions caps could be part of a common, interstate emissions market. Designated sources would be authorized to participate in emissions trading. Other stationary sources could opt-in to the market under specific conditions. A central regulatory authority, such as EPA, could administer this multistate NO$_x$ market system.

2. *Track Two:*—States that elect to implement NO$_x$ market systems without emissions caps would be part of an alternative emissions market. These alternative markets could have several different forms starting with intrastate emissions trading which could possibly lead to multistate trading arrangements. Participating sources in each state would be authorized to conduct emissions trading consistent with the scope of the alternative market system. If multiple, equivalent NO$_x$ market systems are generated by states, then some central entity, in consultation with EPA, could administer the multistate NO$_x$ market system.

While OTAG recognized that the procedures for a cap-and-trade program are known and implementable, OTAG encourages the joint state/U.S. EPA workgroup(s) described herein to bring similar certainty to no-cap but SIP approved trading programs. At some point, states may be interested in cross-track trading. Further development work and more time is necessary to determine whether and how this could be credibly done. Implementation of either track should not be delayed while an approach for cross-track trading is developed. Intersector trading might be provided for as well.

EPA review and approval of specific state SIP revisions would be necessary for NO$_x$ market systems from either track that are developed in response to EPA's SIP call. States would be responsible for meeting applicable federal requirements and ensuring that the integrity of the state's emissions budget was maintained, as well as other desirable results from adoption of suitable market systems. EPA is responsible for approving state programs that meet the applicable federal requirements.

OTAG also recommends that a joint state/EPA workgroup be formed to address, with appropriate stakeholder involvement, the following tasks:

1. Appropriate provisions for implementing Tracks One and Two as described.

2. Key design features for NO$_x$ emissions market systems that could be selected by affected states.

A series of seven design proposal papers have been developed by the Trading/Incentives Workgroup and are incorporated in the OTAG final report. These papers serve as a sound basis for carrying out the work of this joint workgroup.

The following specific features should also be addressed by the joint workgroup:

- Subregional modeling and air quality analysis should be carefully evaluated to determine whether geographical constraints should be placed on emissions trading. Appropriate mechanisms, such as trading ratios or weights, could be developed if significant effects are expected.
- Market systems should be operated and evaluated, and adjustments made as needed to reflect experience gained with trading dynamics and any attendant air quality impacts. Local control requirements necessary for attainment may still be utilized for specific sources.

—Approved by the Policy Group on June 19, 1997)

References

Gade, Mary. 1997a. Speech given at World Fuels Conference, March, San Antonio, TX.

Gade, Mary. 1997b. Presentation at John F. Kennedy School of Government, Harvard University, March.

Gade, Mary. 997c. Speech given at National Conference on Environmental Strategies in a Restructured Electric Industry, April, Houston, TX.

Kanerva, Roger. 1997. Personal notes taken during Trading Incentives Workshop, 19 June.

OTAG. 1997b. Technical Support Document. Available at the web address cited.

Ozone Transport Assessment Group (OTAG). 1997a. Executive Report. Available at http://www.epa.gov/ttn/otag.

U.S. EPA. 1998. Final Rule: "Finding of Significant Contribution and Rulemaking for Certain States in the Ozone Transport Assessment Group Region for Purposes of Reducing Regional Transport of Ozone." 63 Fed. Reg. 57355. 27 October.

6

Joseph A. Kruger
Brian J. McLean
Rayenne Chen

A Tale of Two Revolutions

Administration of the SO$_2$
Trading Program

$\mathbf{M}$uch has been written about the early successes of the SO$_2$ trading program under Title IV of the Clean Air Act Amendments of 1990. There have been early emission reductions spurred by the banking provision, a sharp drop in acid deposition throughout the eastern United States, and lower than expected costs. In addition, after a slow start, emissions trading has increased steadily as Phase II of the program approaches.[1]

Less attention has been devoted to the "nuts and bolts" of administering the SO$_2$ trading program and to the valuable administrative lessons that have been learned during the program's first few years. In particular, there has been a convergence of two powerful forces that have shaped the way the program is implemented. First, there has been what one observer has called a "revolutionary" redefinition of the role of the environmental regulator (Ellerman, 1998). Under this revolutionary approach, EPA tracks environmental performance by requiring stringent monitoring and reporting of emissions. There are no compliance technology mandates, no detailed facility specific permits, and no need to negotiate over exemptions or waivers of compliance requirements. Compliance is as simple as holding enough allowances to match a facility's annual emissions. EPA maintains accountability by focusing the majority of its activities on the accurate tracking of emissions and allowances.

This first revolution has created a conceptual framework for an efficient trading program. However, the actual operation of the program has been helped immeasurably by a second revolution: the revolution in the use of computers and information technologies. In its role as the emissions and allowance "accountant," EPA must handle vast amounts of information. In addition to processing information for compliance purposes, EPA must make emissions and allowances information accessible to facilitate an efficient allowance market and to build public credibility in the emissions trading approach. Without recent advances in information technologies, these activities would be considerably more difficult if not impossible.

This chapter will explore how these two "revolutions" have shaped the implementation of the SO_2 trading program. We will conclude with a discussion of how these forces could have several important implications for future emissions trading programs.

A DIFFERENT ROLE FOR REGULATORS

The difference between the SO_2 allowance program and previous air pollution control efforts begins with how the goals and source obligations are stated. To achieve the emission reduction goal for utilities of 8.5 million tons below their 1980 level of 17.5 million tons, the program objective was established as a maximum annual emissions level (or permanent "cap") of 8.95 million tons. To constrain emissions to 8.95 million tons, only 8.95 million allowances would be issued each year, and a source would have to hold an allowance (the legal authorization to emit a ton of SO_2) for each ton it emitted. This is the first air program to limit total emissions. This "cap" on emissions not only ensures the environmental integrity of the program, it also encourages the lowest possible emissions and highest possible efficiency from facilities.

Sources in the program are required to hold allowances in amounts at least equal to the total emissions of SO_2 during each year. The program relies on a common measurement metric through rigorous continuous emissions monitoring systems (CEMS), with quarterly reporting of hourly emissions to EPA. If annual SO_2 emissions exceed the number of allowances held at the end of the year, statutory penalties of $2000 per ton exceeded (indexed to inflation) and an offset of one allowance per excess ton is assessed automatically.

The SO_2 trading program is the first air program to rely exclusively on emissions (output) for determining compliance as opposed to relying on traditional command-and-control approaches, which require a specific technology, emissions rates (mass per unit of heat input), concentrations, or percent reduction, all of which do not limit total emissions. This made the government's goal and the industry's goal the same: to limit emissions. It also allowed plants to get full credit for emissions reduced through improved efficiency or lower utilization.

Because all emissions are measured and no detailed compliance schedules are needed, permit applications are greatly streamlined compared to traditional operating permits. For the allowance program, the applicant must simply provide the name of the plant, commit to measure emissions, and commit to hold sufficient allowances to cover annual emissions. These changes dramatically reduce the cost of permitting for both the source and the government and increase the likelihood of sources seeing the allowances as a full compliance alternative.

Differences with Past Trading Programs

Unlike previous emissions trading programs, which simply added flexibility to the underlying command-and-control infrastructure, the concept with Title IV was to build an entirely new program—one that would be completely separate from other requirements. While health-based standards for sources would remain in place, they would not affect the goals of the new program or control any of the aspects of the emissions trading. In other words, the allowance program would be built on the experience of previous command-and-control programs and emissions trading programs, but not on their infrastructure.

Most existing air pollution regulations in the United States require the installation of specific control technology or specify a performance standard in terms of emission rates, for example, pounds of pollutant per million Btu of heat input (lb/mmBtu); or pollutant concentrations, such as parts per million (ppm); or pollutant removal efficiencies. In some cases, requirements are stated in terms of allowable emissions per time period, such as pounds per hour.

In most past trading programs, therefore, emissions trading required the conversion of these requirements into a tradable commodity, such as tons of a pollutant emitted. This required all parties (emissions credit generator, consumer, and governmental authority) to agree on the present (baseline) and future utilization rates for generating and consuming sources, to agree on the time over which the trade would be valid, often to agree that the reductions for which credit was being given would not have happened but for this trade, and to agree on how emissions at both sources would be quantified. It was also often necessary to ascertain that the air quality would not be worsened by the transaction.

This process could be resource intensive and time consuming with changes to the agreement often requiring renegotiation. The resources required and the uncertainty of the process created significant transaction costs and limited the number of trades (and later the creation of emission reduction credits) to those circumstances where there were clear and substantial economic benefits. Despite the considerable efforts to ensure that transactions would not worsen the environment, most air regulators and environmentalists remained suspicious of emissions trading.

Using Information Technology

The new regulatory role discussed earlier would be impossible without the extensive use of information technologies. Running a cap-and-trade program consists largely of two major activities: processing huge amounts of information and disseminating huge amounts of information. Thus, the implementation backbone of the Acid Rain Program is the data systems that track emissions and allowances and help process these two sources of data to ensure compliance. For dissemination of emissions and allowance information, the Internet has become critical over the past several years. Following is a discussion of how these information technologies are used in implementing the program.

Processing Information

EPA's goal has been to allow program participants to submit information to these databases and receive feedback more directly and quickly. For example, most utilities now submit their emissions data directly to EPA's computers via modem. Within minutes, these electronic filers receive an automated feedback report on the emissions data files they have just submitted. Work has also begun to enable utilities and others to submit allowance transfers to EPA electronically, rather than depending on paper forms and overnight mail. In addition, EPA has updated its own interfaces with its data systems, which enables EPA staff to enter and access data more efficiently. More efficient data management will ultimately speed the end-of-year reconciliation process.

Emissions data

Highly accurate emissions data is one of the pillars of the Acid Rain Program's operations. After the end of every calendar quarter, the Division receives over 1,700 reports containing the hourly emissions of SO_2, NO_x, and CO_2 and heat input data from each affected unit. By implementing advances in computer technology and information management, the Acid Rain Program has improved the speed and ease of the data reporting process, both for regulated emissions sources and EPA.

A major improvement in the data reporting process occurred when the Acid Rain Division developed, and then enhanced, ETS-PC, a software program that facilitates data submissions by modem. Previously, facilities submitted their quarterly reports to EPA on diskette, a tedious process for both parties. Over the past several years most companies have switched to using ETS-PC to electronically transmit their reports directly to EPA's mainframe ETS database. Now, over 90 percent of data submittals are by modem, allowing much more rapid data processing (see Figure 6.1). By the year 2000, we expect all quarterly reports will be submitted in this manner.

ETS-PC provides those submitting data with an important benefit: rapid feedback on their data. After each report is submitted to the EPA mainframe, it is immediately analyzed by ETS and the results are transmitted back to the user. This automated process enables sources to identify and correct errors in their submissions more quickly, and helps EPA verify receipt of all quarterly reports. If necessary, reports can be quickly resubmitted to resolve problems. EPA recently implemented a wider range of error checks to make the feedback more comprehensive. These automated improvements give companies the chance to check for, and resolve, errors in their data and enable EPA to process data more quickly, thus streamlining this integral aspect of the Acid Rain Program.

Allowance data
EPA strives to record efficiently transfers reported to the Allowance Tracking System (ATS), the Agency's accounting

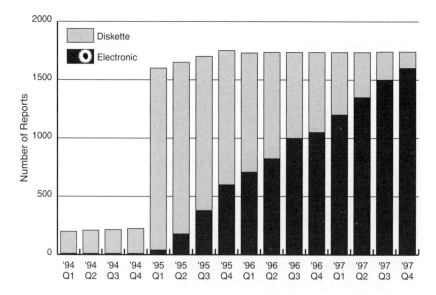

Figure 6.1 Sources are increasingly submitting emissions data by modem.

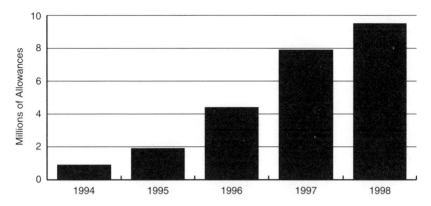

Figure 6.2　Number of private allowances transferred between economically distinct parties.

system that tracks allowance holdings. EPA processes about 90 percent of allowance transactions within 24 hours of receipt, using just two Acid Rain staff. Streamlining this process is important for minimizing transaction costs to parties trading allowances and for facilitating the trading market. Recent improvements to ATS are intended to allow EPA to maintain this quick turnaround as the program expands in 2000 and trading volumes for SO_2 allowances continue to rise.

Figures 6.2 and 6.3 illustrate the rising activity in allowance trading, in terms of both the number of private transfers and the

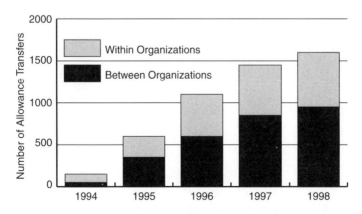

Figure 6.3　Allowance transfers have been increasing.

number of allowances transferred. Private transfers are those occurring between non-EPA parties. Not all private transfers recorded within the ATS are economically significant allowance trades. For example, in some cases, allowances may be moved back and forth between a company's different allowance accounts for accounting purposes rather than for compliance.[2] One kind of private transfer involves "economically distinct," or unrelated, companies. This category of trade has been rising, indicating market growth. EPA transfers involve transactions such as EPA deducting allowances for compliance or distributing allowances purchased at the annual auction.

To handle this growing number of transactions, the Acid Rain Program upgraded its user interface to facilitate data entry into ATS. A Windows-based program has replaced the mainframe interface, providing EPA staff with a more agile, user-friendly system (Figure 6.4). For example, users can now keep several windows open simultaneously, allowing access to other ATS data without closing out the current screen. Another feature is

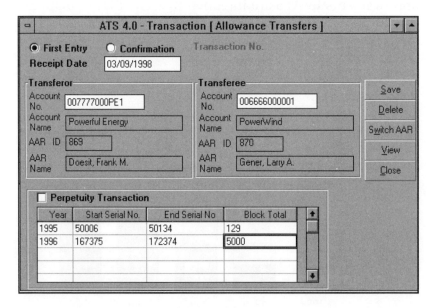

Figure 6.4   The new ATS is geared for faster data entry, enabling the operator to access more data through the same screen.

drop-down menus in entry fields, which cut down on time spent typing out plant and representative names or account numbers. While the public won't ever see the new look for ATS, the Windows-based version will allow EPA to process greater numbers of transfers with about the same amount of resources.

EPA is also making ATS more convenient for traders by developing a system to allow parties to submit allowance transfers electronically. Currently, trading parties fill out a paper form and mail it to EPA. In 1998, we introduced web-based public access to view allowance accounts, transactions, and allowance holdings. In 1999, the Acid Rain Program developed Internet-based allowance transfer capability. Functioning much like an on-line banking service, this system enables allowance holders to transfer allowances to other parties electronically from their own computer. Users log into the EPA allowance database to access their accounts, identify the account where allowances are to be transferred, and record the allowance transfer, saving both users and EPA time and resources in recording and tracking allowance transactions.

Disseminating Information

Emissions data

EPA puts the emissions data collected on its web site in several different formats. As Figure 6.5 shows, EPA publishes summary reports on the web that include SO_2, NO_x, CO_2, and other information. In the past, the quarterly data posted has been raw emissions information that has not been quality assured. Emissions data has been finalized annually and published in an Emissions Scorecard that can be downloaded from the web site. However, by the end of 1999, EPA instituted a new policy whereby quality assured quarterly data will be posted on the Acid Rain Program web site. EPA will continue to publish the annual Emissions Scorecard as well.

Emissions data has provided important information to the allowance market.[3] Quarterly emissions information has helped allowance market participants gauge potential supply and demand for allowances. For example, market observers have noted that analysis of emissions data in late 1995 led to a

State	Plant	ORISPL	Stack/Unit ID	Phase	Status	Primary Fuel	SO2 Controls	NOx Controls	SO2 (tons)	NOx Rate (lb/mmBtu)	NOx (tons)	CO2 (tons)	HEAT (mmBtu)
ALABAMA	BARRY	3 4	P2		Coal	U	U	18,182	0.62	8,676	2,871,523	27,986,995
ALABAMA	BARRY	3 5	P2		Coal	U	U	34,697	0.73	19,864	5,584,279	54,421,080
ALABAMA	BARRY	3 CS0AAN(1,2,3)	P2		Coal	U	U	22,435	0.50	8,026	3,294,332	32,105,472
ALABAMA	CHARLES R LOWMAN	56 1	P2		Coal	U	U	6,598	0.65	1,361	426,373	4,187,363
ALABAMA	CHARLES R LOWMAN	56 2	P2		Coal	DL	LNB	8,480	0.60	4,988	1,700,974	16,626,189
ALABAMA	CHARLES R LOWMAN	56 3	P2		Coal	DL	LNB	8,028	0.59	4,751	1,645,148	16,104,424
ALABAMA	CHICKASAW	5 110	P2		Gas	U	U	0	0.17	29	20,615	346,000
ALABAMA	COLBERT	47 5	P1		Coal	U	U	58,218	0.44	7,493	3,494,425	34,058,704
ALABAMA	COLBERT	47 CSCO14(1,2,3,4)	P1		Coal	U	U,LNB(3)	31,939	0.43	10,651	5,082,626	49,539,852
ALABAMA	E C GASTON	26 5	P1		Coal	U	LNB	33,819	0.43	10,339	4,935,627	48,089,378

Figure 6.5   EPA publishes summary reports that include SO_2, NO_x, and CO_2 data for every source.

sharp decline in allowance prices as analysts detected a trend for greater than expected emissions reductions for that year.

Allowance data

All allowance transfers are posted on the web site as well. Users can query the ATS database for transactions during a specified period or by allowance account, power plant, or state. This information is updated at the end of each business day with that day's transactions. As Figure 6.6 shows, the database provides information on the type of transfer (e.g., private transfer, auction), buyer name and account information, seller name and account information, confirmation data, serial numbers for the allowances traded, and the total number of allowances traded.

The allowance trading information reported to the ATS is important to many different players. Some researchers, for example, seek this information to aid in their evaluation of the performance of Title IV or to gain insights that might be used in the development of new emissions trading programs. Others are interested in this data to help determine whether there are barriers to cost effective-trading, such as state Public Utility Commission cost recovery or accounting policies. Utilities and brokers are also interested in the data, both to assess overall market activity and to determine those transactions that can be classified as economically significant. Finally, environmental groups and others have expressed interest in ATS data for purposes of analyzing the emissions implications of trades.

IMPLICATIONS FOR FUTURE PROGRAMS

Increased Administrative Efficiency

One important design issue associated with emissions trading programs is the tradeoff between the size of the universe of sources and the administrative feasibility of operating a trading system. In particular, analysts have noted that monitoring and verification of emissions data could be overwhelming to program administrators with too many sources in a system (Smith et al., 1992). To the extent that the electronic reporting, verification, and

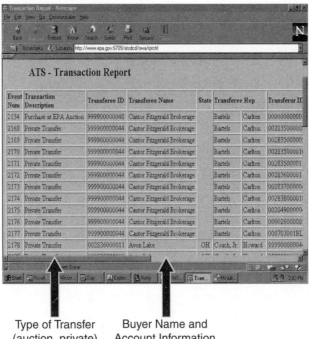

Type of Transfer
(auction, private)

Buyer Name and
Account Information

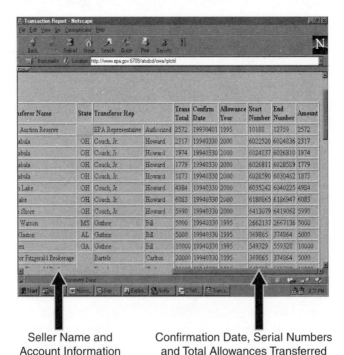

Seller Name and
Account Information

Confirmation Date, Serial Numbers
and Total Allowances Transferred

Figure 6.6 Sample results from an ATS query on the Acid Rain Program web site.

processing of emissions data becomes more prevalent, a larger universe of sources can be included in a program for a given amount of administrative resources.

The efficiency of using information technologies in an emissions trading system is illustrated by EPA's new role in administering the Ozone Transport Region's NO_x trading system. Starting in 1998, EPA has used a modified version of its existing data system infrastructure to support the 12 northeastern states in the Ozone Transport Region as they strive to meet a NO_x emissions budget through a new NO_x trading program. Through the efficiency of improved information management, EPA will be able to add more than 500 additional combustion sources to our emission tracking system and operate a new NO_x Allowance Tracking System (NATS)—with just a small net increase in staff.

It is also important to note that some programs may require substantially less data per source. For example, for CO_2, if daily data, instead of hourly data were collected, then 24 times as many sources could be handled with the same human and information technology resources.

Lower Transaction Costs

Transaction costs are a critical factor in whether an emissions trading market will operate efficiently.[4] The information revolution could have several important impacts on transactions costs in emissions trading markets. First, as larger emissions trading markets become administratively feasible, transactions costs would be expected to fall. The ability to include a larger number of sources in a system could potentially lower transactions costs because a larger universe of potential trading partners could make it easier to identify beneficial trades (Noll, 1982).

Second, the combination of the cap-and-trade model and improved information technology can reduce administrative delays associated with case-by-case review of credit-based emissions trades built on command-and-control regulations. These delays and the resultant uncertainty have contributed significantly to higher transactions costs in past emissions trading programs.[5] In contrast, several recent articles have noted the low transaction costs of the SO$_2$ allowance market.[6] Although there are a number of components to transaction costs for emissions trading, high transaction costs from long administrative reviews have not materialized under the SO$_2$ program. According to an analysis of log-in dates in the Allowance Tracking System, 98 percent of 1997 allowance transactions were processed within 5 days; 89 percent were processed within 24 hours.

Finally, although this chapter has focused on the link between program administration and information technology, the impacts of these technologies on private sector efforts to reduce compliance and transaction costs could be even more important. For example, several software programs have been developed that allow companies to better manage their emissions and allowances (U.S. EPA, 1996). In addition, brokers and traders have used the Internet, broadcast faxes, and other techniques to disseminate price information and to help match buyers with sellers.

Greater Environmental Accountability

Dissemination of emissions data is important for building public confidence in the credibility of emissions trading programs. The high-quality emissions data provided by continuous emissions monitors and its rapid dissemination lets the public know exactly what is being emitted on a unit by unit basis. This makes the "emissions" part of emissions trading transparent and has helped to dispel at least some of the traditional skepticism about the environmental benefits of trading among environmental groups.[7]

The ability to disseminate emissions information quickly could be especially important in any future international greenhouse gas program. Many observers have noted the difficulties inherent in assuring compliance in any international agreement to limit greenhouse gases (Schmalensee, 1996). International environmental compliance regimes (and international agreements in general) pose special challenges because of sovereignty issues and the lack of a strong international enforcement authority.

On the other hand, scholars of international agreements have argued that these agreements can be strengthened by requiring governments to make their performance accountable and transparent through reporting requirements (Chayes and Chayes, 1991). Thus, broad public access to emissions and trading data through the Internet could be critical to an effective greenhouse gas protocol. Scrutiny of this data by nongovernmental organizations and others could be an important force for encouraging environmental accountability. As Tietenberg has noted, adverse publicity could be one of the most important sanctions available for an international greenhouse gas agreement.[8]

No one should underestimate the challenges of implementing an international emissions trading system (or any other international effort to curb greenhouse gas emissions for that matter). However, applying the experience of the "Two Revolutions" to the design of an international trading system offers the best chance for an effective effort to control greenhouse gases. The combination of flexible compliance with strict accountability and stringent tracking of emissions can promote better environmental results as it lowers cost. Moreover, although implementing an international greenhouse gas trading program is probably an order of magnitude more difficult than implementing the U.S. SO_2 trading program, the ability to use information technologies to solve difficult problems is also considerably greater than it was a decade ago. A trading system that is built to take advantage of these technologies will have the greatest chance of success.

REFERENCES

Chayes, A. and A.H. Chayes. 1991. *Adjustment and Compliance Processes in International Leadership.* New York: W.W. Norton, 112–153. Cited in Thomas Tietenberg, "Implementation Issues: A General Survey," in *Combating Global Warming,* (New York: United Nations, 1992).

Ellerman, Denny. 1998. "Experimenting With Freer Markets." Paper presented at 21st Conference of the International Association for Energy Economics, 16 May, Quebec City, Canada.

Noll, R.G. 1982. "Implementing Marketable Emissions Permits." *American Economic Review* 72. Cited in Robert Stavins, "Transactions Costs and Tradeable Permits," *Journal of Environmental Economics and Management* 29 (1995): 133–148.

Schmalensee, Richard. 1996. "Greenhouse Policy Architectures and Institutions." MIT Joint Program on the Science and Policy of Global Change Report 13. November.

Smith, A.E., A.R. Gjerde, L.I. DeLain, and R.R. Zhang. 1992. "CO_2 Trading Issues, Vol. 2: Choosing the Market Level for Trading." Report to the Environmental Protection Agency, Decision Focus Inc. Washington, DC.

U.S. EPA. 1996. "Acid Rain Program Update No. 3." EPA-430-R-96-004. May.

U.S. EPA. 1998. "1997 Compliance Report: Acid Rain Program." EPA-430-R-98-012. August.

NOTES

1. For a summary of the early results of the Acid Rain Program see National Acid Precipitation Assessment Program, "NAPAP Biennial Report to Congress: An Integrated Assessment," (Silver Spring, Maryland, May 1998).

2. For a description of a methodology to classify allowances transactions see Joseph Kruger and Melanie Dean, "Looking Back on SO_2 Trading: What's Good for the Environment Is Good for the Market." *Public Utilities Fortnightly* 135 (15) (August 1997): 30–37.

3. See, for example, Carlton Bartels, "Recent Trends in SO_2 Allowance Marketplace," Proceedings of Acid Rain & Electric Utilities II, Air and Waste Management Association, (Scottsdale, AZ, 21–22 January 1997).

4. For a discussion of transaction costs in emissions trading programs, see Robert Stavins, "Transactions Costs and Tradeable Permits," *Journal of Environmental Economics and Management* 29 (1995): 133–148.

5. See for example Robert H. Hahn and Gordon L. Hester, "Marketable Permits: Lessons for Theory and Practice," *Ecology Law Quarterly* (16) (2) (1989).

6. See for example A. Denny Ellerman, Richard L. Schmalensee, Paul Joskow, Juan Pablo Montero, and Elizabeth Bailey, *SO_2 Emissions Trading under Title IV of the 1990 Clean Air Act Amendments: Evaluation of Compliance Costs and Allowance Market Performance*, (Center for Energy and Environmental Policy Research, Massachusetts Institute of Technology, October 1997), Bartels op. cit., and Klaus Conrad and Robert E. Kohn, "The U.S. Market for SO_2 Permits," *Energy Policy* (24) (12) (1996): 1051–1059.

7. For a discussion of the importance of monitoring in emissions trading programs see Daniel A. Seligman, "Air Pollution Emissions Trading: Opportunity or Scam?, A Guide for Activists," (The Sierra Club Center for Environmental Innovation, September 1994).

8. Tietenberg, op. cit. Note that the U.S. has advocated other important compliance provisions in international climate negotiations including the loss of the right to trade emissions and the forfeit of a portion of a party's future emissions budget if that party exceeds its target.

PART FOUR

AN APPLICATION AT CENTER STAGE

THE PIONEERING NATIONAL CAP-AND-TRADE MARKET TO REDUCE ACID RAIN

7

Appraisal of the SO₂ Cap-and-Trade Market

Dallas Burtraw

$Appraisal\ of\ the$
$SO_2\ Cap\text{-}and\text{-}Trade$
$Market$

Title IV of the 1990 U.S. Clean Air Act Amendments (CAAA) regulates emissions of sulfur dioxide (SO_2) from electric generating facilities. The widely acknowledged innovation of Title IV is the SO_2 emission trading program that is designed to encourage the electricity industry to minimize the cost of reducing emissions. The industry is allocated a fixed number of total allowances and firms are required to hold one allowance for each ton of sulfur dioxide they emit.[1] Firms are allowed to transfer allowances among facilities or to other firms, or to bank them for use in future years.

A less widely acknowledged innovation of Title IV is the annual cap on average aggregate emissions by electric generators, set at about one-half of the amount emitted in 1980. The cap

The author is grateful for the assistance of Matt Cannon, Curtis Carlson, Martin Heintzelman, Ron Lile, Erin Mansur, James McVeigh, and Terrell Stoessell, as well as the contibutions of numerous coauthors on the research that is reviewed in this paper. Financial support for this research was received from the U.S. Environmental Protection Agency.

133

accommodates an allowance bank, so that in any one year aggregate industry emissions must be equal to or less than the number of allowances allocated for the year plus the surplus that has accrued from previous years.

For years economists have urged that policy makers use market-based approaches to control pollution (taxes or tradable permits). Rather than forcing firms to emit SO_2 at a uniform rate or to install specific control technology, this approach enables firms operating at high marginal pollution abatement costs to purchase SO_2 emission allowances from firms operating at lower marginal abatement costs. The motive is that trading, by equalizing marginal abatement costs among generating units, should limit SO_2 emissions at a lower cost than traditional command-and-control approaches.

The SO_2 allowance market presents the first real test of the wisdom of economists' advice, and therefore merits careful evaluation. Has the allowance market significantly lowered the costs of abating SO_2, as economists claimed it would? How has trading affected the balance and distribution of benefits and costs in the program? How have specific features of the program and of the electricity industry affected the performance of the program and its adaptability as a model for addressing other pollution problems (e.g., control of NO_x or CO_2 emissions)?

This chapter addresses these issues through a review of several recent and some ongoing research projects. First, we report on an assessment of benefits and costs of the program, and then explore the effect of trading and banking along spatial (geographic) and temporal dimensions. Second, we discuss estimates of the cost reductions from formal trading within the emission market, and the relevance of the trading institution to cost reductions obtained outside the market. Finally, we compare the measure of compliance cost to the measure of economic cost.

The conclusion offered, in brief, is that the SO_2 program has been a remarkable success from the standpoint of comparing benefits and costs. The trading program has, on net, contributed to this success, but it is not the primary reason for this success. As a formal institution, emission allowance trading promises to deliver only a portion of the compliance cost savings originally envisioned by its proponents and, in the first years of the program, it has had difficulty achieving even this level of success. However, the flexible approach embodied in the trading program has allowed firms to capture significant cost reductions outside of the formal allowance market, which has dramatically reduced costs.

Finally, an examination of the distinction between compliance costs and economic costs suggests there is significant room for improvement in designing a market-based program that can be adapted to other pollutants. To achieve their potential, market-based instruments may need to raise revenue that can be used to reduce other taxes. Otherwise, there may be significant hidden social costs that erode or even reverse the cost savings from trading.

COMPARING BENEFITS AND COSTS

The primary measure of success of the SO_2 program, from the perspective of economics, should be the comparison of benefits and costs. A recent study (Burtraw, Krupneck, Mansur, Austin, and Farrell, 1998) reported the results of an integrated assessment of the benefits and costs through the year 2030, with benefits quantified for health, visibility, and lake recreation.[2] The cost and benefits estimates are not additive because they do not describe consistent geographic areas. Costs and health benefits are calculated for the entire nation. Visibility benefits are calculated at selected cities or states. Lake recreation benefits are calculated for the Adirondacks only. Hence, the values are expressed *per affected capita* to illustrate the potential relative magnitude of these benefits. Midpoint estimates of the benefits and costs per affected capita for the year 2010 are summarized in Table 7.1.

The study found that benefits of the SO_2 program are an order of magnitude greater than costs, a result that contrasts sharply with estimates in 1990 that pegged benefits about equal to costs (Portney, 1990).

What explains the difference between the earlier and recent estimates? On the cost side, compliance has and will cost in the future one-half or less of what was anticipated in 1990, a point we subsequently consider in detail.

Table 7.1   Benefits and Costs of SO$_2$ Emission Reductions

Effect	Benefits and Costs per Affected Capita of Expected Emission Reductions in 2010 (1995 dollars)
Benefits	
Morbidity	4
Mortality	69
Lake recreation	1
Recreational visibility	4
Residential visibility	7
Costs	6

Note: Benefits are not additive because affected populations differ. However, morbidity and mortality benefits, and costs, are calculated for the entire nation.
Source: Burtraw et al., 1998.

Meanwhile, the lion's share of benefits resulted from reduced risk of premature mortality, especially through reduced exposure to sulfates. These expected benefits measured ten times the expected costs of the program. Significant benefits are also estimated for improvements in health morbidity, recreational visibility, and residential visibility, each of which are approximately equal to costs. These areas, namely human health and visibility, were not the focus of acid rain research in the 1980s, and new information suggests these benefits are greater than were previously anticipated.

In contrast, benefit areas that were the focus of attention in the 1980s including effects to soils, forests, and aquatic systems still have not been modeled comprehensively, but evidence suggests benefits in these areas are likely to be relatively small.[3] It is surprising to many that relatively low benefits are estimated to result in the the recent study from improvements in lake recreation, or are expected to result from effects of acid rain reduction on forests and agriculture. One reason is that willingness to pay for environmental improvement depends on the availability of substitute assets. Economists would not expect changes in quality at one site to elicit large benefits if there are many sites available for comparable recreational opportunities. In contrast, individuals do not have the same kind of substitution possibilities with respect to health and visibility, which may help explain their relatively large benefit estimates. Furthermore, the low benefit estimates stem from an assessment of *use* values, or *commodity* values in the case of agriculture. Environmental changes may also yield *nonuse* values, but estimates for nonuse values are not yet available. The evidence, based on a small number of relatively narrow studies, suggests these values may be significant.

There are huge uncertainties, especially on the benefits side of the ledger, especially in valuation of mortality. Recent economic critiques have argued that the use of the value of a statistical life as the basis for valuing health risks from air pollution, instead of a more appropriate measure of quality-adjusted life years lost, could grossly overestimate mortality benefits. In addition, economists have questioned the appropriateness of using labor studies of prime-age men to value changes in life expectancy that occur among an older population (Johannesson and Johansson, 1997). On the other hand, because environmental exposures are involuntary while labor market risks are assumed to be voluntary in nature, the labor market studies may underestimate willingness to pay to avoid environmental exposures. Burtraw et al. (1998) used Monte Carlo analysis and a parametric one-sided sensitivity analysis to investigate some of these sources of uncertainties. Their analysis finds that there is no year in which health benefits alone at the 5 percent confidence interval are less than the levelized expected costs. As noted, significant benefits are also estimated for improvements in health morbidity, recreational visibility, and residential visibility, each of which measures approximately equal to costs. Despite tremendous uncertainties about benefits and costs, the main conclusion that benefits soundly outweigh costs appears to be robust.

The Effects of Banking

The banking provision of the program is expected to result in an accumulated surplus of allowances of nearly 12 million tons by the year 2000, when Phase II of the program begins. Beginning in 2000, allowance allocations to Phase I facilities will decrease and additional facilities will be covered by the program, and it is expected that the allowance bank will be diminished over a period of several years.

The opportunity to bank allowances is expected to play a significant role in reducing compliance cost because it affords firms the flexibility to plan their investment activities. However, it has an ambiguous effect on benefits. To build up a bank, firms are expected to take advantage of relatively low-cost compliance options in the early years of the program resulting in lower emissions than would occur were they not able to bank allowances. This leads to greater environmental benefits in the early years. However, after 2000 when the bank is drawn down, emissions are expected to be greater than would occur absent the opportunity to bank and hence environmental benefits are expected to be less.

The evaluation of the environmental consequences of banking is potentially complicated, depending on whether there are threshold effects in environmental or public health response and the level of effects, if any. The dominant view in health epidemiology regarding exposure to particulates is that the concentration-response function is linear over the range in which changes will occur. Hence, at least with respect to public health, there is a trading off of exposure and response in the later years for less exposure and response in the near term. From an economic perspective, benefits achieved sooner are viewed as superior to benefits achieved later due to discounting, so this would seem an unambiguously beneficial aspect of the program. The issue is complicated further, however, by population growth that implies that greater numbers of people will be potentially exposed in the future due to the banking provision.

To explore this issue, we exercised the benefit-cost model (Burtraw et al., 1998) to compare two scenarios. One is largely a default or Baseline scenario intended to represent compliance with Title IV as it is taking shape with banking permitted, with the exception that 3.5 million bonus allowances that subsidized scrubbing in Phase I under the program are omitted. The reason for the omission is that, absent the opportunity to bank, these allowances are relatively useless. To include them would unfairly bias the comparison away from banking. Hence, we take as the default case Title IV absent the bonus allowances.[4] (We assume the same level of scrubbing in Phase I as has occurred.)

For comparison, we constructed a scenario that was identical except that allowances could not be banked, so emissions in each period must be less than or equal to allowance allocations in that period. Also, we assume that no scrubbers are built in Phase I, based on estimates from Carlson, Burtraw, Cropper, and Palmer (1998) suggesting that, absent the bonus allowances, scrubbers were uneconomic, even with the opportunity to bank allowances at those facilities.

The result of this comparison is reported in Table 7.2. The first two columns of numbers in the table represent the change in SO$_2$ emissions at selected eastern states with substantive changes in 1995 and 2005 due to the opportunity to bank in the program. As expected, emissions fall or stay constant in 1995 compared to the default. However, in 2005 emissions increase in most states and in the total.

The columns on the right compare the change in total health benefits (mortality and morbidity) valued in the model for 1995 and 2005 that result from the opportunity to bank. All numbers are in 1995 dollars, but they are not present valued. There are about $4 billion more in health benefits in 1995; however, in 2005 there are about $2.1 billion in decreased benefits.

The pattern with respect to both emissions and benefits reveals that the harm is less in 2005 than the improvement in 1995. One should not be mislead by this comparison, because the draw down of the allowance bank is expected to occur over a longer horizon than did its buildup. However, what one can conclude is that there is a fairly straightforward trade-off between near term and longer term emissions when banking is allowed. In general, the effect is to shift emission reductions toward the present. Excluding other scientific or social considerations, this would seem to be a good thing, especially when it allows the emission reductions to be achieved at significantly less cost.

These results are illustrated in a qualitative way in Figures 7.1 through 7.4. Figure 7.1 displays the percent change in emissions attributable to banking in the year 1995, and Figure 7.2 displays the same information for the year 2005. These figures illustrate the intertemporal shift in emissions from 1995 to 2005.

Table 7.2   Contribution of Banking to Emissions and Health Benefits

	Change in SO$_2$ Emissions (Thousand Tons)		Change in Health Benefits (Million 1995 $)	
State	1995	2005	1995	2005
AL	0	11	68	-34
AR	0	0	22	-21
CT	0	0	83	-26
DE	0	0	23	-7
DC	0	0	22	-6
FL	0	0	110	-55
GA	0	0	133	-61
IA	0	5	15	-18
IL	0	93	182	-195
IN	-106	3	173	-133
KY	-1220	268	161	-112
LA	0	0	24	-22
ME	0	0	18	-7
MD	0	0	162	-51
MA	0	0	129	-42
MI	0	0	138	-96
MS	0	0	30	-18
MO	0	4	47	-49
NJ	-3	-4	260	-77
NY	-18	-1	493	-172
NC	0	0	199	-74
OH	-19	-1	377	-205
PA	-129	74	460	-159
RI	0	0	22	-7
SC	0	0	80	-32
TN	-299	-52	187	-76
TX	0	78	34	-78
VA	0	0	227	-79
WA	-164	-72	75	-27
WI	0	0	35	-37
Total	-860	455	4067	-2116

Source: Burtraw and Mansur, 1998.

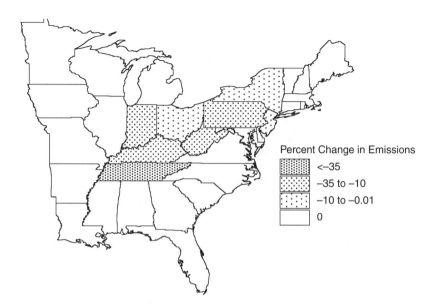

Figure 7.1   Percent change in Title IV Baseline Utility Emissions attributable to banking for 1995 (*Source:* Burtraw and Mansur, 1998).

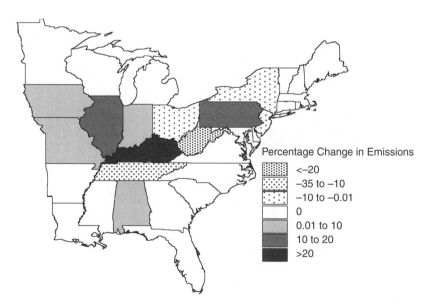

Figure 7.2   Percent change in Title IV Baseline Utility Emissions attributable to banking for 2005 (*Source:* Burtraw and Mansur, 1998).

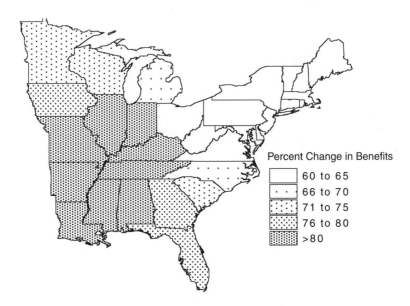

Figure 7.3   Percent change in Title IV Baseline Benefits attributable to banking for 1995 (*Source:* Burtraw and Mansur, 1998).

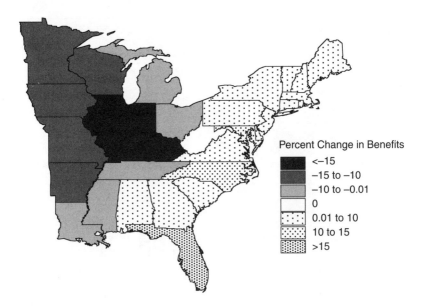

Figure 7.4   Percent change in Title IV Baseline Benefits attributable to banking for 2005 (*Source:* Burtraw and Mansur, 1998).

Figure 7.3 illustrates the changes in estimated health benefits attributable to banking in the year 1995, and Figure 7.4 illustrates the same information for the year 2005. Banking has
caused the realization of health benefits to be accelerated, but
the total health benefits are approximately neutral. The figures
also show that there is some minor geographic difference in how
states are affected.

REGIONAL EFFECTS OF TRADING

Legislative debates about acid rain in the 1980s had a sharp regional character. Since acid deposition typically occurs far from
the source of emissions, which were largely concentrated in the
Ohio Valley, many observers claimed that emissions from these
power plants were contributing to environmental degradation
in the Northeast. Long-range transport of emissions from the
Ohio Valley does have an important effect outside the region.
However, the regional decomposition of health benefits from
reduced emissions is less provincially divisive because atmospheric concentrations are affected closer to the source of emissions than where acid deposition occurs. Table 7.3 illustrates
that, expressed in per capita terms, those states providing 75
percent of the emission reductions accrue about 60 percent of
total health benefits.

To explore the regional effects of trading, we employed the
benefit-cost model without trading in order to calculate the distribution of benefits in the years 1995 and 2005. This comparison
could be constructed in a variety of ways.

One approach would be to define the No Trading case such
that individual facilities emit at less than or equal to the allowance allocation for that facility, absent the opportunity to
trade. This approach has the disadvantage that aggregate emissions would be less in the No Trading case. The reason is that,
absent the flexibility to trade allowances, plants are restricted to
a self-sufficient compliance strategy. Abatement activities are not
necessarily continuous because of the "lumpy" nature of capital
investments, especially scrubbers. Hence, in order to comply
with a facility-specific standard, some plants are likely to overcomply. In a trading program, such over-compliance creates

Table 7.3   Expected Total Health Benefits for 2010 and percentage of National SO$_2$ Emissions Reductions

State	Per Capita Health Benefits (1990$)	Percent of National Health Benefits (%)	Percent of National SO$_2$ Emission Reductions (%)
WV	170	1.8	12.0
OH	160	10.2	23.3
DC	160	0.5	0.0
PA	160	11.0	9.8
KY	150	3.3	11.0
VA	140	5.5	0.4
MD	130	4.1	0.4
IN	130	4.4	16.0
DE	130	0.6	0.0
NJ	130	6.2	0.4
NY	120	11.6	2.2
Other	40	40.8	24.5

Source: Burtraw et al., 1998.

marketable emission allowances enabling another facility to increase its emissions relative to the average emission rate, keeping aggregate emissions constant. However, absent the ability to trade, over-compliance at an individual facility leads to lower emissions in the aggregate (Oates, Portney, and McGartland, 1989).

A No Trading program such as that described above is considerably more expensive than the actual program. The ability to trade has reduced costs, and presumably these cost savings are reflected in a lower emissions cap than would otherwise have been considered economically affordable or politically feasible. Hence, we seek a comparison of trading and no trading that examines the environmental impact of trading while holding the aggregate level of emissions approximately constant.

To model this, we choose to constrain aggregate emissions in the No Trading scenario to equal those in the Baseline scenario.[5] In this experiment, the Baseline includes bonus allowances and associated emissions. To isolate the geographic effect of trading from the intertemporal effects of banking, we take as given in the No Trading scenario the Phase I retrofit scrubbing installations in the Baseline. As in the Baseline, other facilities solve the intertemporal investment algorithm to minimize the net present value of their compliance decisions. The result is that 15 additional facilities choose to scrub in the No Trading scenario in addition to those that scrub in the Baseline. At these facilities, scrubbing is less costly than fuel switching or blending, given their location and the transportation costs associated with alternative fuel choices. In the Baseline, these units were purchasers of allowances, but this option is not available in the No Trading scenario.

The results are reported in Table 7.4. The first two columns of numbers list changes in emissions as a result of the ability to trade. The total change is approximately 1 percent of aggregate emissions. The goal to hold aggregate emissions constant is difficult to achieve given the inter-temporal investment algorithm. However, the fact that emissions are slightly lower in the aggregate under trading is a bias against the benefits of trading that fails to undermine the qualitative results that are achieved. The second two columns of numbers list the changes in health benefits.

Figures 7.5 through 7.8 present these results in a qualitative manner. Figures 7.5 and 7.6 illustrate that the effect of trading is to increase emissions in the Ohio Valley, but not in a uniform way. For instance, in 1995 the effect of trading is to reduce emissions from Illinois, while they increase in 2005, in percentage terms. The effect of trading on most states outside the Ohio Valley is to reduce emissions.

The more important result may be the effect of trading on health benefits. Figures 7.7 and 7.8 illustrate that trading undermines the health benefits of the program in areas closest to where emissions increase. There has been significant concern that trading might serve to contribute to the transboundary effects of pollution, with the result that citizens in New England and along the eastern seaboard may suffer effects from emission increases in the Ohio Valley. However, those increases in the Ohio Valley imply decreases in other states that have an equal or greater impact on citizens in the east. As a consequence, it

Table 7.4   Contribution of Trading to Emissions and Health Benefits

	Change in SO$_2$ Emissions (Thousand Tons)		Change in Health Benefits (Million 1995 $)	
State	1995	2005	1995	2005
AL	-84	-55	37	13
AR	0	0	0	-10
CT	0	0	23	27
DE	0	0	7	10
DC	0	0	2	5
FL	-44	-44	103	88
GA	-101	-68	82	41
IA	-7	9	-2	-12
IL	-59	137	-21	-180
IN	-114	-16	-54	-110
KY	90	261	-32	-92
LA	0	0	5	-2
ME	0	0	4	5
MD	-25	-25	51	78
MA	-13	-13	44	51
MI	-46	-46	-5	-37
MS	12	-8	6	-1
MO	71	-5	-13	-32
NJ	-2	-2	74	84
NY	-19	-11	62	90
NC	0	-78	116	110
OH	120	-85	-95	-74
PA	-60	-7	46	92
RI	0	0	8	10
SC	-21	-21	46	32
TN	-18	54	10	-50
TX	-1	32	6	-26
VA	-8	-21	56	79
WV	14	-52	-7	0
WI	-8	1	0	-25
Total	-152	-53	566	124

Source: Burtraw and Mansur, 1998.

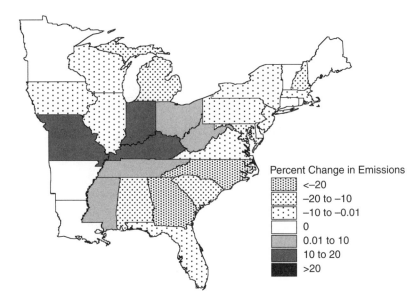

Figure 7.5   Percent change in Title IV Baseline Utility Emissions attributable to trading for 1995 (*Source:* Burtraw and Mansur, 1998).

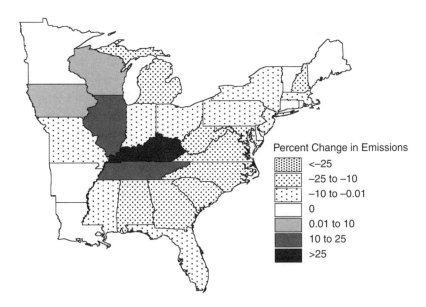

Figure 7.6   Percent change in Title IV Baseline Utility Emissions attributable to trading for 2005 (*Source:* Burtraw and Mansur, 1998).

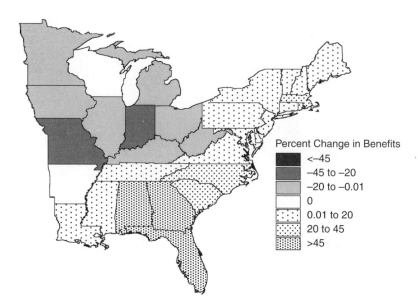

Figure 7.7   Percent change in Title IV Baseline Benefits attributable to trading for 1995 (*Source:* Burtraw and Mansur, 1998).

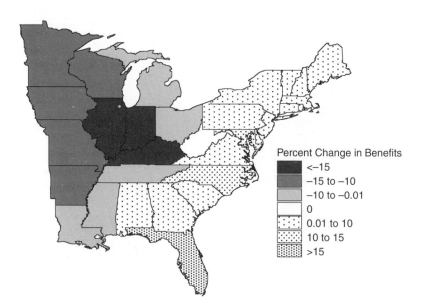

Figure 7.8   Percent change in Title IV Baseline Benefits attributable to trading for 2005 (*Source:* Burtraw and Mansur, 1998).

appears that trading actually leads to improvements in air quality in the east.

GAINS FROM TRADE IN THE FORMAL MARKET

Though they are substantial by any accounting, cost savings have been exaggerated in many accounts of the program. Advocates of ambitious climate change policies have suggested that SO_2 allowance prices are "so low" and that economists and engineers got it "so wrong" that policy makers should virtually ignore cost projections when developing new regulations such as a CO_2 or NO_x permit trading program. Some have claimed cost savings of nearly fifteen fold are attributable to the trading program based on a comparison of recent allowance prices just above $100 with projections of long-run marginal costs near $1500 per ton of abatement.[6]

This argument is flawed for several reasons (Bohi and Burtraw, 1997; Smith, Platt, and Ellerman, 1998). First, marginal costs may be a poor proxy for total costs (or cost savings). Even if allowance price were equal to marginal abatement cost in the least cost solution, it would not follow that all trading gains were realized. Price can equal marginal abatement cost even if many utilities fail to participate in the market. Second, historical estimates of marginal costs were generally made for the second phase of the program, and therefore cannot be compared with current allowance prices unless they are discounted to the present. The present discounted value is roughly just over one-third of the value of costs incurred around 2010, when the second phase is in full effect and the allowance bank is expected to be depleted. Third, analyses that took into account the ultimate design of the program suggested that long-run marginal costs would be about $700.

Together, these factors suggest that Phase I allowance prices in 1997 of about $125 should be compared to about $235, which is what EPA (1990) predicted would obtain as Phase I marginal abatement costs in 1997.[7] This comparison suggests that marginal costs have fallen by over half, compared to the vantage point in 1990. A critical question is: To what extent can this decline in cost be credited to the allowance trading program?

Marginal and Annual Costs

Carlson et al. (1998) offer an econometric model that can allow us to explore this and several other interesting questions. The model uses marginal abatement cost functions, derived from an estimated long-run cost function for electricity generation for over eight hundred generation units over the years 1985 to 1994, to predict the cost of emissions reductions at fuel-switching generators.[8] Scrubber costs estimates were based on observed capital and variable costs from retrofit scrubbers built for compliance in Phase I.

From an economic perspective, this study is a useful complement to engineering studies because it takes into account behavioral responses to changes in relative input prices. These behavioral responses include substitution among inputs to reduce jointly the costs of generating electricity and of complying with emission reduction requirements. The econometric approach affords a method for measuring the role of technological change in reducing the costs of SO_2 abatement over time. The approach also affords a method for developing forecasts of future compliance costs and gains from trade that implicitly incorporate future behavioral changes, including future responses to changes in technology.

To estimate potential gains from allowance trading in the long run, Carlson et al. compute the least cost solution to achieving the 8.95 million ton SO_2 cap in the year 2010. Several assumptions are critical to the calculation, and they are explored by sensitivity analysis. In the *preferred scenario*, electricity production averaged over all coal-fired units is assumed to increase at the rate of 1.49 percent per year. Output is assumed to increase more rapidly at scrubbed units, which are assumed to be utilized at 80 percent of capacity by 2010. Real prices of high- and low-sulfur coal are assumed to remain at 1995 levels while the rate of technical change experienced between 1985 and 1994 continues through 2010. An assumed 11 gigawatts of coal-fired capacity in place in 1995 will be retired by the year 2010 (about half of current Energy Information Administration (EIA, 1997) projections for retirement), and all of that coal-fired capacity will be replaced by natural gas plants. Baseline emissions—those that would have prevailed absent Title IV—are calculated using 1993 emissions *rates* applied to 2010 levels of electricity production. Finally, an important feature of the 1990 CAAA is that SO_2 emissions must be measured by a continuous emissions monitoring system (CEMS) rather than being estimated based on fuel consumption. Previous studies all use engineering estimates of SO_2 emissions based on fuel consumption. A comparison of the two measurement techniques reveals that, in 1995, CEMS emissions were about 7 percent higher than estimated emissions, implying that the SO_2 cap is, in effect, 7 percent below the cap based on engineering formulas. To be consistent with actual practice, the preferred scenario uses CEMS data.

Under the above preferred scenario, the total annual cost of achieving the SO_2 cap of 8.95 million tons in 2010 is estimated to be $1.01 billion (1995 dollars). Of this total, $380 million represents the cost incurred by plants that fuel switch, which account for about 60 percent of reductions from baseline emissions. The marginal cost of emissions reduction, which should approximate long run permit price, is $291 per ton of SO_2.

Annual compliance costs of $1 billion per year are less than half of the estimates of compliance costs originally predicted when the 1990 Clean Air Act Amendments were drafted (EPA 1989, 1990). This raises two questions: Are the Carlson et al. estimates of compliance costs biased downward? If not, why are they so much lower than EPA's original estimates of such costs?

Under various combinations of scenarios we used the Carlson et al. model to explore a number of the assumptions listed above. We find that holding technology constant at 1995 levels, compared with the preferred assumption of continuing trends in technology improvements, *increases* marginal abatement cost by about 50 percent. The assumption that setting fuel prices at 1989 levels, compared with the preferred assumption of 1995 levels, *increases* marginal abatement costs by nearly 20 percent.

EIA's assumption that 22 gigawatts of capacity retire by 2010, compared with the preferred assumption of half that amount, *lowers* marginal abatement cost by about 15 percent (because these units are replaced either by gas or scrubbed coal facilities, either of which result in lowered emissions). The assumption common to all previous studies that engineering formulas are the source of emission estimates, compared to the preferred assumption that CEMS data is used, *lowers* marginal abatement cost by nearly 20 percent (because CEMS data to date yields emissions that are higher at the average facility, forcing greater levels of abatement for compliance).

From these experiments, the characterization of technological change emerges as the most important assumption in explaining the difference between the econometric estimates and previous studies. Changing assumptions about other factors, such as fuel prices, retirement and monitoring each weigh in as significant but of much less importance.

Carlson et al. explore these assumptions in tandem in order to better understand the difference between their preferred estimates and previous ones. Table 7.5 summarizes this sensitivity analysis and comparison. The first row of the table reports the preferred estimate. The second row reports the preferred estimate with the assumption that trends in technological change stop in 1995. The third row represents the perspective from 1989 with respect to both fuel prices and (static) technology, and uses engineering estimates of emissions in place of CEMS.

These sensitivity scenarios largely close the gap with previous studies of the EPA at the time of adoption of the Amendments. Under the maintained assumption that fuel switching

Table 7.5   Long-Run (Phase II, year 2010) Cost Estimates

Scenario	Annual Cost (Billion 1995$)	Marginal Cost per Ton SO_2 (1995$)	Average Cost per Ton SO_2 (1995$)
Preferred estimate*	1.0	291	131
w/1995 Technology	1.6	436	
w/1989 Prices and 1989 Technology	1.9	560	
EPA (1990)	2.3–5.9	579–760	348–499
EPA (1989)	2.7–6.2		377–511
EPA (1995)	2.3	532	252
EPRI (1995)	1.4–2.9	543	286–334
EPRI (1997)		436	

Source: EPA (1989, 1990, 1995), EPRI (1995, 1997); *Carlson et al. (1998).

determines marginal abatement cost, the assumption of stable 1989 fuel prices and technology (the third row of the table) produces marginal cost estimates approximately as large as those predicted when Title IV was written (the fourth and fifth rows of the table).

Annual costs continue to differ significantly among these rows. A major factor explaining the difference in annual cost is the assumption by the EPA in 1990 that a greater number of scrubbers (37) would be built than were actually constructed in Phase I (28) or than are likely to be built under the preferred estimate. Also, EPA (1990) failed to anticipate the decline in the cost of scrubbers, improvement in performance of scrubbers, increased utilization of these units, and improvement in the utilization of nuclear units to meet baseload capacity. Since fuel switching is a marginal compliance option, the estimates of marginal cost remain close in the comparison, but differences in scrubber estimates help explain differences in inframarginal costs and total cost.

Also important to total (annual) cost are differences in the baseline from which emissions reductions are measured. In all of our calculations, we assume that the emission *rates* (lb. of SO₂/mmBtu) that would have prevailed absent the 1990 Clean Air Act Amendments are those that prevailed in 1993. These are much lower than 1989 emission rates, hence the reductions in emissions necessary to achieve the 8.95 million ton cap, by our calculations, are much lower than imagined in 1989 (specifically, about 2 million tons lower). Holding marginal abatement cost curves constant, lowering the necessary reduction in emissions will lower total compliance costs.

Subsequent studies have captured to some degree the changes in prices, the lower investment in scrubbers, and changes in technology over the period between 1989 and 1995. However, the studies listed in Table 7.5 are all engineering studies and do not endogenously account for expected changes in technology (or behavior) implicit in historical trends. This is revealed by comparing the second row of the table—the preferred estimate with 1995 technology—with the last three rows of the table, which shows estimates of marginal cost and total cost that are quite similar.

Potential Gains from Trade

To calculate the potential gains from trade, Carlson et al. compare the cost of meeting the SO_2 cap using a command-and-control approach with the least-cost (preferred) solution identified above. The command-and-control approach is modeled as an average emissions rate of 1.2 pounds of SO_2 per million Btus of heat input.[9] The estimated potential gains from trading are $784 million, or about 44 percent of the cost of command and control.

While these potential gains are significant, they are not as large in absolute terms as were originally predicted. The GAO (1994) estimated greater gains in both absolute and relative terms, suggesting that a no trading regulation would cost approximately $5.3 billion annually—140 percent more than the least-cost solution ($2.2 billion).

The explanation for relatively modest estimates of trading gains using Carlson et al. is that many of the factors that have caused marginal abatement costs to fall also would have lowered the costs of achieving the SO_2 emissions cap via command-and-control policies. These factors include the fall in the price of low-sulfur coal and technical improvements that have facilitated fuel switching. Burtraw (1996) suggests that incentives under the allowance trading program have accelerated the pace at which these changes have occurred. However, to the extent that these innovations would have emerged under a command-and-control approach, they lower the potential cost savings from trading compared to a command-and-control baseline.

In addition to *lowering* marginal abatement cost curves, the fall in low-sulfur coal prices has made marginal abatement cost curves *more homogenous*. This is because costs of transporting low sulfur coal to more distant locations, for example, the East and Southeast, has fallen, rendering differences in transportation cost a less important component of the overall cost of fuel switching. Since a major source of trading gains is differences in marginal abatement cost curves among units in the market, this increased homogeneity is also responsible for lowering gains from trade.

In summary, estimates of costs for both a command-and-control approach and allowance trading have fallen over time due to a number of factors. Allowance trading is expected to result in cost savings relative to a command-and-control approach, but the absolute magnitude of these savings is expected to be somewhat less than previously envisioned due to changes in fuel markets and technology. However, a more rigid approach that forced firms to adopt specified technologies would have precluded them from taking advantage of the full range of options in the industry. Compared to this, allowance trading could be argued to constitute a greater savings than we estimate.

Realized Gains from Trade in Phase I

One way to measure the performance of the market to date is to look at the allocation of compliance activities among firms in the current period. Economic theory suggests that the marginal cost of compliance activities should be the same at all facilities (except as may be constrained by local ambient air quality restrictions).

To investigate this, Carlson et al. evaluated estimated marginal abatement cost functions at the level of facility emissions in the industry in 1995 and 1996. These results are reported in Table 7.6. In 1995, the cost of efficient trading is projected to be $552 million, with a marginal cost for fuel switching activities of $101. This compares with a cost under a command-and-control emission rate standard of $796 million, representing a savings of 30 percent. Further, the projected marginal cost of $101 is remarkably close to allowance prices in this period (around $90 in 1995).

However, the second row of the table reports the estimated actual cost of compliance when the abatement cost functions are evaluated using observed emissions at individual facilities. The *actual* cost to the industry in 1995 is estimated to be $832 million, or 50 percent more expensive than a least-cost solution (reported in row 1) according to the model. The only other estimate for 1995 that we are aware of is Ellerman et al. (1997) who found costs in 1995 to be $726 million.

The notion of an industry marginal cost does not apply in this context, since costs presumably differed among firms. However, Carlson et al. calculate the marginal cost at each facility

Table 7.6   Cost Estimates for Compliance in 1995 and 1996

Study	Annual Cost (Million 1995 Dollars)	Marginal Cost per Ton SO_2 (Fuel Switching 1995 Dollars)	Average Cost per Ton SO_2* (1995 Dollars)
1995			
Carlson et al. (1998) *Efficient trading*	552	101	194
Carlson et al. (1998) *Actual emissions*	832	180 (weighted marginal cost)	291
Ellerman et al. (1997)	726	153 (average cost)	210
1996			
Carlson et al. (1998) *Efficient trading*	571	71	xxx
Carlson et al. (1998) *Actual emissions*	910	xxx	xxx

* Includes scrubbing costs.

weighted by that facility's portion of total generation. Summed for the industry this results in an estimate of $180. Ellerman et al. do not report marginal cost but they find an average cost from fuel switching activities of $153. Both of these figures compare poorly with observed allowance prices in 1995 (near $90). We consider the proximity of the Carlson et al. econometric estimates to the Ellerman et al. survey estimates of actual costs, and the distinction between these estimates and the estimated cost of efficient compliance as evidence that there were unrealized potential gains from trade in 1995.

In 1996, performance did not change dramatically. Carlson et al. estimate the least cost solution to achieving 1996 emissions to cost $571 million. The estimated *actual* cost increased slightly from the previous year, indicating that $339 million of potential cost savings were unrealized in the second year of the allowance market. In 1995 and 1996, it appears that different patterns of compliance behavior co-existed in the industry. Many utilities appear to have taken advantage of the flexibility afforded by the allowance program to find ways to reduce costs of compliance, including taking advantage of allowance trading per se. How-ever, many other utilities appear to have pursued a solitary strategy, rationalizing to some degree the cost of emission reductions within the firm, but not taking advantage of the allowance market to rationalize costs with other firms in the industry (Bohi and Burtraw, 1997).

This glance at the first years of performance in the market is disconcerting, but it may not accurately reflect the long-run prospects for the program. An industry that has heretofore been subject to cost recovery rules in a regulated setting will take some time in adjusting to a new incentive-based approach to environmental regulation. Indeed, numerous studies and surveys have found that cost recovery rules and regulatory oversight of utilities undermined their ability or incentive to minimize costs in the early years of the program (Bohi, 1994; Rose, 1997). However, due to the rapidly changing structure of the industry and the growth of competitive pressures to reduce costs, we can be relatively confident that the future holds better things in store for the program.

One reason for optimism is that trading activity is increasing. Trades can be recorded with the EPA at any time prior to the use of an allowance for compliance, and recorded trades are monitored in the EPA's electronic, on-line Allowance Tracking System (ATS). The EPA has developed an algorithm for classifying trades as "economically significant" if they are transfers between independent firms, but the majority of trades that are recorded have been transfers for accounting convenience or other reasons within firms. However, the number of economically significant trades has virtually doubled each year through 1997 (see Kruger, McLean, and Chen, this volume).

A second reason for optimism has to do with the part of the glass that is "half-full." Although there was little change between 1995 and 1996 with respect to the potential gains from trade that utilities "left on the table," there was sizable change in the magnitude of cost savings that were captured. Of the potential savings from fuel switching in 1995, one-quarter of a potential $443 million in potential savings were realized, or $106 million. Changes in relative fuel prices and an increase in the total level of emissions in the industry led to a greater amount of potential savings in 1996. In that year, the potential savings from fuel switching totaled $644 million, and about half of this sum was realized, or about $301 million, triple that of the previous year. This trend mirrors the trend in the volume of allowance trading activity, doubling over the first two years of the program.

A third reason for optimism has to do with over-arching trends in the electric utility industry in the United States. The industry is in a fundamental period of realignment as competition at the wholesale level, and ultimately at the retail level, is beginning to emerge. This type of competition is placing pressure on the industry to find ways to reduce costs in all segments of its business. One should not expect the industry to absorb $300 million in unnecessary costs in the future when allowance trading provides a fairly simple means of reducing those costs.

Although $300 million is small change to the industry as a whole, it is money that comes out of the hide of ratepayers, and this should be of concern to state regulators. There is evidence that many regulators have failed to play a proactive role, and in some cases in order to protect local economic interests they have obstructed the least cost implementation of the program.

The good news is the volume of trading has increased and utilities are waking up. With competition on the horizon, the opportunity to reduce costs is less likely to be overlooked and we can be optimistic about the performance of the program in the long-run.

Economic Costs Do Not Equal Compliance Costs

The economics literature recognizes that all types of regulation impose "hidden" costs on the economy stemming from the interaction of the regulation with pre-existing distortions. Compliance costs describe the out-of-pocket expenses by a firm or industry to comply with regulations. Economic costs describe the value of goods and services that were lost to the economy due to the regulation. This can include so-called hidden costs or benefits, such as costs incurred but not reported as compliance costs or indirect productivity changes that result from environmental compliance.

One type of important hidden cost stems from the interaction of the program with the pre-existing tax system. Important distortions away from economic efficiency stem from pre-existing taxes on factors of production, such as the labor income tax. Labor taxes impose a difference between the before-tax wage (or the value of the marginal product of labor to firms) and the after-tax wage (or the opportunity cost of labor from the worker's perspective). This difference causes workers to substitute away from labor to leisure compared to an efficient outcome.

Any regulation that raises product prices potentially imposes a hidden cost on the economy by lowering the real wage of workers. This can be viewed as a "virtual tax" magnifying the significance of previous taxes, with losses in productivity as a consequence. If there were no pre-existing distortions in the economy, the impact of regulatory costs would be of little concern. However, the cost of distortions associated with taxes grow more than proportionally with the size of the tax, and hence the hidden cost of regulation can be of great importance when pre-existing taxes are taken into account.

This hidden cost has been termed the tax-interaction effect (Parry, 1995), and it tends to erode the usual efficiency benefits identified with setting prices to include external costs. The tax-interaction effect is particularly important in the allowance trading system, relative to a command-and-control approach. In a competitive market, the price of the final product should reflect not only compliance cost for emission reductions but also the opportunity cost (or price) of allowances used for compliance. Though the trading program is expected to result in significant savings in compliance costs, it internalizes additional costs in the way of allowance prices into electricity prices.[10]

Goulder, Parry, and Burtraw (1997) have investigated the magnitude of the tax-interaction effect in the context of the SO_2 program using both analytical and numerical general equilibrium models. They find that this effect will cost the economy about $1.06 billion per year (1995 dollars) in Phase II of the program, adding an additional 70 percent to their estimated compliance costs for the program.

The cost of the tax-interaction effect can be largely (but not entirely) offset by policies that raise revenues for the government, because these revenues can (in principle) be used to offset pre-existing taxes and correct distortions in the labor market resulting from these taxes. The authors find that over half of the economic cost of the tax interaction effect, or $622 million, could be avoided if emission allowances were auctioned rather than grandfathered and the revenue was used to reduce the marginal tax rate on labor income. Unfortunately, the SO_2 program does not raise revenues since allowances are distributed for zero cost to the emitter. Consequently, the current program design imposes a hidden cost on the economy that could be avoided if allowances were auctioned instead of allocated without charge.

Economists have long argued for market-based approaches to environmental problems. The usual justification is the tremendous potential savings in compliance cost. The importance of the general equilibrium perspective should be appreciated in this context. We can ask what is the cost, in a general equilibrium context, of a command-and-control approach, and how does this compare to the use of nonauctioned tradable permits.

Table 7.7 illustrates the relative potential cost savings and hidden costs of the use of grandfathered emission allowances. The values in this table are expressed in percentage terms, normalized around the values in the first cell. This value in the first cell represents the least-cost estimate of compliance in 2010, or partial equilibrium cost, estimated by Carlson et al. (1998) and reported above. The second cell in the first row

Table 7.7   General Equilibrium Cost of SO_2 Allowance Trading as Percentage of Partial Equilibrium Least Cost Compliance

Percentage Values Normalized around First Cell	Least-Cost Compliance (%)	Command-and-Control Performance Standard (%)
Partial eqm measure	100	135
General eqm measure		
with revenue	129	n/a
without revenue	171	178
	(Title IV)	

represents the percentage of costs under the command-and-control scenario modeled in that study, about 135 percent of the least cost outcome.

The remaining rows reflect estimates of cost in a general equilibrium context. The first column summarizes the Goulder et al. (1997) finding that the general equilibrium costs of a market-based policy (emissions tax or auctioned permit system) to be about 129 percent of the partial equilibrium measure of costs in the least-cost solution. The bottom row indicates the cost of a permit system that fails to raise revenues is about 171 percent of the least-cost partial equilibrium estimate.

The last cell in the bottom row of the table yields an estimate of the relative cost of command-and-control policies in a general equilibrium setting. We find that the type of policies modeled in the context of the SO_2 program would result in general equilibrium costs that were 178 percent of those measured in the least-cost solution in a partial equilibrium framework.[11] In other words, the general equilibrium cost of the tradable permit program (171) is only slightly less than the general equilibrium cost of a command-and-control program (178). In this context, anyway, the evidence suggests that the failure to raise revenue squanders much of the cost savings in compliance costs that can be achieved by a flexible tradable permit system.

The recommendation that allowances be auctioned comes with significant political liability. The endowment of allowances without charge, so-called "grandfathering" of allowances, is an important form of compensation to the electric utility industry. The industry's attitude toward the SO_2 program would have been considerably more negative had this compensation not existed.

However, there is an equity aspect to this issue that counterbalances the concerns of industry. At the time legislators adopted the SO_2 program in 1990, state public utility commissions were regulating the industry and setting electricity prices, and they were the safeguard to ensure utilities could not charge customers for something the utilities received free. Hence, endowing allowances at zero cost was not controversial to the design of the SO_2 program. However, in the near future we expect regulators to exit the business of setting prices, at least with respect to electricity generation, and electricity prices will be set in a competitive market. In the textbook and presumably in the market, SO_2 allowances take on the value of their opportunity cost, and this will be passed on through marginal cost pricing in a competitive electricity market, regardless of how the utility acquired the allowances originally. The value of this endowment, coming out of the hides of electricity consumers and accruing to the industry, is potentially very large.

Under the assumption that the program works efficiently and firms value SO_2 allowances at their opportunity cost (the price of an allowance equal to the marginal abatement cost), the magnitude of the compensation under the program (the grandfathering of allowances valued at their opportunity cost) far outweighs the compliance cost incurred by firms. The present discounted value of this difference is between $10 and $20 billion (1995 dollars). This represents a tremendous transfer of wealth from electric utility customers to the industry.

There are important lessons here for the design of other environmental programs that may refer to the SO_2 program as a model. Goulder et al. (1997) find that the tax interaction effect is more significant, relative to the magnitude of compliance costs, for programs that are aimed at small emission reductions such as may describe possible policies for CO_2 reductions.[12] The design of a CO_2 permit program would involve smaller emission reductions in percentage terms and therefore a much greater transfer of wealth relative to the cost of compliance. However, both the equity and the efficiency aspects of the tax-interaction effect can be largely remedied by a carbon tax or auctioned carbon permits.

Recognizing that there may be political obstacles to a revenue-raising carbon policy, a hybrid system involving an auction of some portion of the permits and grandfathering the remaining may be a useful compromise. Regardless of the outcome in the specific case of CO_2 trading, the efficiency and equity aspects of allocating permits is a huge topic that will play a more prominent role in the design of trading programs in the future.

CONCLUSION

An important measure of success of the program from an economic perspective should be the comparison of benefits and costs, to the extent they can be measured. From this perspective, the SO_2 program is successful. Benefits that have been modeled appear to be an order of magnitude greater than costs, especially due to the effects on human health and visibility. Unmodeled environmental pathways may reinforce this finding in the future, but to date evidence suggests use values are relatively small. The important possible wildcard is the measure of nonuse values.

Costs of compliance are significantly less than were anticipated at and before the program's adoption. Several factors contribute to this success. Most important to date has been the role of changing fuel prices; while in the long run the role of technological change is likely to be more important. These factors combine to lower expected long-run costs by over half of what was anticipated at the outset of the program.

Most of the change in the cost of compliance has occurred outside the formal institution of the allowance trading program. Performance of the SO_2 market to date appears to have failed to capture significant potential gains from trade. Anecdotal evidence and incentives embedded in regulatory oversight of utilities during early compliance appear consistent with this statistical assessment.

However, from a broader perspective, there are two vantage points from which to view the trading program as an important success. One is from the vantage point of overall costs of compliance. The flexible approach embedded in the trading program has allowed many firms to capitalize on advantageous trends in fuel prices to date and on changes in the market structure of upstream supply industries to lower their compliance cost. These changes have occurred largely outside the formal market, but the flexibility of the market-based approach has helped make them a reality.

A second view of the success of the program stems from its contribution to the movement toward regulatory reform reaching from deregulation of the railroads in 1980 to the Energy Policy Act in 1992. These reforms unleashed incentives for reducing costs that are reinforced by the SO_2 program and will contribute to its long-run performance.

Finally, as scholars and policy analysts attempt to draw lessons from the SO_2 program, one area that should receive significant attention is the manner in which emission allowances are allocated to the industry. Evidence suggests that grand-fathering or free allocation of allowances can impose significant efficiency costs. Furthermore, this approach represents a tremendous transfer of wealth that raises equity issues as well. Rarely in economics do efficiency and equity issues point in the same direction, but in this case they do. The recommendation that follows is that emission allowances should be auctioned or allocated in ways that raise revenue for government that can be used to reduce other distortionary taxes. If the allocation of allowances is to serve as compensation for industry, this function should be weighed carefully against the benefits of raising revenue. A hybrid program, in which some portion of allowances are grandfathered and the rest auctioned by the government could offer a compromise that would improve programs of this type in future applications.

REFERENCES

Austin, David, Alan Krupnick, Terrell Stoessell, Dallas Burtraw, and Gar Ragland. 1998. "Report to Maryland Department of Natural Resources on the Development of the Maryland Externalities Screening and Valuation Model." Washington, DC: Resources for the Future.

Bohi, Douglas R. 1994. "Utilities and State Regulators Are Failing to Take Advantage of Emission Allowance Trading." *The Electricity Journal* 7 (2): 20–27.

Bohi, Douglas R., and Dallas Burtraw. 1997. "SO_2 Allowance Trading: How Do Expectations and Experience Measure Up?" *The Electricity Journal* 10 (7): 67–77.

Burtraw, Dallas, Alan J. Krupnick, Erin Mansur, David Austin, and Deirdre Farrell. 1998. "The Costs and Benefits of Reducing Acid Rain." *Contemporary Economic Policy*. Forthcoming. Available as Resources for the Future Discussion Paper 97-31 REV.

Burtraw, Dallas, and Erin Mansur. 1998. "The Effects of Banking and Trading in the SO_2 Allowance Market." Resources for the Future. Mimeographed.

Carlson, Curtis, Dallas Burtraw, Maureen Cropper, and Karen Palmer. July 1998. "SO_2 Control by Electric Utilities: What Are the Gains from Trade?" Resources for the Future Discussion Paper 98–44. Washington, DC.

Electric Power Research Institute (EPRI). September 1995. "The Emission Allowance Market and Electric Utility SO_2 Compliance in a Competitive and Uncertain Future." Prepared by Keith White, Energy Ventures Analysis, Inc., and Van Horn Consulting. TR-105490. Palo Alto, CA.

Electric Power Research Institute (EPRI). April 1997. "SO_2 Compliance and Allowance Trading: Developments and Outlook." Prepared by Keith White. EPRI TR-107897. Palo Alto, CA.

Ellerman, A., Denny, Richard Schmalensee, Paul L. Joskow, Juan Pablo Montero, and Elizabeth M. Bailey. 1997. "Emissions Trading under the U.S. Acid Rain Program: Evaluation of Compliance Costs and Allowance Market Performance." Center for Energy and Environmental Policy Research, MIT. Cambridge, MA.

Goulder, Lawrence H., Ian W.H. Parry, and Dallas Burtraw. 1997. "Revenue-Raising vs. Other Approaches to Environmental Protection: The Critical Significance of Preexisting Tax Distortions." *RAND Journal of Economics* 28 (4) (winter): 708–731.

Goulder, Lawrence H., Ian W.H. Parry, Roberton C. Williams III, and Dallas Burtraw. 1998. "The Cost-Effectiveness of Alternative Instruments for Environmental Protection in a Second-Best Setting." *Journal of Public Economics.* Forthcoming.

Johannesson, Magnus, and Per-Olov Johansson. 1997. "Quality of life and the WTP for an increased life expectancy at an advanced age." *Journal of Public Economics* 65: 219–228.

Oates, Wallace E., Paul R. Portney, and Albert M. McGartland. 1989. "The *Net* Benefits of Incentive-Based Regulation: A Case Study of Environmental Standard Setting." *American Economic Review 79:* 1233–1242.

Parry, Ian W.H. 1995. "Pollution Taxes and Revenue Recycling." *Journal of Environmental Economics and Management* 29 (3) (supplement): S-64-S-77.

Portney, Paul R. 1990. "Economics and the Clean Air Act." *Journal of Economic Perspectives 4* (4): 173–181.

Rose, Kenneth. 1997. "Implementing an Emissions Trading Program in an Economically Regulated Industry: Lessons from the SO$_2$ Trading Program." In *Market-Based Approaches to Environmental Policy: Regulatory Innovations to the Fore,* Richard F. Kosobud and Jennifer M. Zimmerman (eds.). New York: Van Nostrand Reinhold.

Smith, Anne E., Jeremy Platt, and A. Denny Ellerman. 1998. "The Cost of Reducing SO$_2$ (It's Higher Than You Think)." *Public Utility Fortnightly* (15 May): 22–29.

U.S. Energy Information Administration (EIA). December 1997. *Annual Energy Outlook 1998.* DOE/EIA-0383(98). Washington, DC.

U.S. Environmental Protection Agency (EPA). September 1989. "Economic Analysis of Title V (Acid Rain Provisions) of the Administration's Proposed Clean Air Act Amendments (H.R. 3030/S. 1490)." Prepared by ICF Resources, Inc.

U.S. Environmental Protection Agency (EPA). July 1990. "Comparison of the Economic Impacts of the Acid Rain Provisions of the Senate Bill (S. 1630) and the House Bill (S. 1630)." Prepared by ICF Resources, Inc.

U.S. Environmental Protection Agency (EPA). September 1995. "Economic Analysis of Title IV Requirements of the 1990 Clean Air Act Amendments." Prepared by ICF Resources, Inc.

U.S. Government Accounting Office (GAO). 1994. "Air Pollution: Allowance Trading Offers an Opportunity to Reduce Emissions at Less Cost." GAO/RCED-95-30. Washington, DC.

NOTES

1. Allowances are allocated to individual facilities in proportion to fuel consumption multiplied by an emission factor during the 1985–1987 period. About 2.8 percent of the annual allowance allocations are withheld by the EPA and distributed to buyers through an annual auction run by the Chicago Board of Trade. The revenues are returned to the utilities that were the original owners of the allowances.

2. The integrated assessment involved nearly thirty researchers at a dozen institutions. The assessment is based on reduced-form models that were calibrated to several larger models of utility emissions and costs, atmospheric transport of pollution, visibility impairment, effects on aquatic systems and human health, and valuation of effects. Economic assessment of costs are calculated with an engineering model constructed for the assessment. Economic valuation of damage to

aquatic systems relied on random utility models of recreational use. Health mortality valuation relied on compensating wage and contingent valuation studies, and morbidity valuation relied on a number of studies and methods. Valuation of visibility effects at national parks used contingent valuation methods, and valuation of visibility in residential areas used a combination of contingent valuation combined with hedonic property value studies.

3. Though lake recreation benefits are modeled only for the Adirondacks area, benefit values are expressed per dollar per affected capita (users of the resource). Hence, these estimates of use benefits may be an upper bound estimate of benefits per capita nationally. Austin et al. (1998) have recently completed modeling of environmental pathways affecting the Chesapeake Bay that are affected by SO_2 emissions.

4. More precisely, for the evaluation of the No Banking scenario, we reallocate the bonus allowances to the years in which they are used for compliance in the Baseline scenario that includes banking. This is accomplished by solving the intertemporal compliance algorithm in the model for the Baseline with and without the bonus allowances, and noting the difference in emissions on an annual basis. This difference is added to total allowance allocations each year for the No Banking scenario.

5. This is achieved by raising the allowance allocation for individual facilities in the No Trading scenario above the level corresponding to the allocation for each facility in the Baseline. We repeatedly solved the model to find the allocations that equate aggregate emissions in these two scenarios.

6. See for example, "Economists' Cold Forecast; Assumptions: Expect their dire predictions about the impact of the global warming treaty on the United States. Ig nore all of them," by Elaine Karmarck, *Baltimore Sun*, December 28, 1997.

7. EPA (1990) predicted $210 in 1995 dollars for the year 1995. Inflated at a 6 percent rate of interest, this is equivalent to $235 for the year 1997.

8. The cost function treats fuel type (high-sulfur and low-sulfur coal), labor and generating capital as fully variable inputs. The econometric model consists of the cost function plus two share equations that specify the share of total costs attributed to capital and labor, and an equation for the firm's mean annual emission rate. The study uses a translog form for the cost function, adding dummy variables for each plant in the database to measure fixed effects that vary among the plants. Costs for units with scrubbers are taken directly from reported data.

9. This approach already encompasses many of the beneficial incentives of the SO_2 trading program compared to a technology-forcing approach by providing individual facilities with flexibility in achieving the standard. Other command-and-control approaches that were seriously considered in the United States, such as forced scrubbing at larger facilities, could have cost substantially more.

The uniform emission rate standard does not take into account the fact that some units may face unrealized "economic" emission reductions beyond those mandated by the standard. Therefore, emissions are lower under the uniform standard than they are under a trading program, which provides firms with higher abatement costs the flexibility to capture the slack in the effective emission constraint at other firms (Oates, Portney, and McGartland, 1989).

10. The effect on product prices should occur without regard to how the firm acquired allowances originally, if prices reflect marginal costs and allowances are valued at their opportunity cost.

11. The number 1.78 (178%) is the product of 1.29 times 1.35 times 1.02. The number 1.29 (129%) is the ratio of general equilibrium to partial equilibrium cost from Goulder et al. (1997) for a policy that raises revenue such as an emissions tax. The

number 1.35 (135%) is the ratio of command and control to efficient least cost from Carlson et al. (1998). The number 1.02 (102%) is the ratio of general equilibrium costs for a performance standard relative to an emissions tax identified in Goulder et al. (1998).

12. Small emission reductions require small compliance expenditures, leaving a larger quantity of emissions to be included in a permit trading scheme. Allowance prices would be low, relative to a case with greater emission reductions, but they apply to a larger quantity of emissions. Hence, the portion of costs associated with permit use relative to the portion of costs associated with compliance cost is greater.

Development and Maturing of Environmental Control Technologies in the Power Industry

WILLIAM DEPRIEST

As a result of more stringent air quality regulations and increased awareness of air pollution, reduction of air pollutant emissions has become a high priority for many industrialized nations. Regulatory agencies in the United States have introduced a market-based compliance program for SO_2 control and are looking to fossil-fired power plants for a significant portion of the new emissions reduction requirements. As a result, private industry and government agencies have been pressing the development of new technologies to meet these more stringent requirements and to take advantage of the added flexibility of the market-based compliance approach. A good example of this effort in the United States is the changes the industry has made in the application of flue gas desulfurization (FGD) technology.

In this section, we will identify the current emission control retrofit options available for managers of coal-fired power plants for regulated pollutants such as particulates, SO_2, and NO_x. It will also identify retrofit options for potential future-regulated pollutants such as air toxics.

We will then track the progress made in the design and construction improvements of the various emission control retrofit options and the progress made in increasing the cost-effectiveness of emission controls. The various factors affecting cost will be discussed and the current dollar per kilowatt costs for different technologies will be presented.

Air pollution may be defined as any atmospheric condition in which substances are present at concentrations high enough above their normal ambient levels to produce a measurable effect on man, animals, vegetation, or materials. The ultimate aim of industrialized nations is to provide an answer to the question: What is the optimum method to control air pollution? It is quite clear that the abatement of air pollution in the large populated areas of the world will require a substantial economic investment, and perhaps changes in patterns of living and energy use as well. It is unrealistic to speak of no air pollution whatsoever as it is virtually impossible to eliminate entirely all manmade emissions of foreign substances into the atmosphere. It is much more sensible to aim toward the reduction of pollutant emissions to a point such that noticeable adverse effects associated with the presence of pollutants in the air are eliminated. Because of the great expenditure of money that will be required, it would be prudent to strive for the most cost-effective measures of control.

We will discuss the application of the various technologies commercially available to control these pollutants to the lowest regulated levels.

PARTICULATE CONTROL

The firing of pulverized coal in electric generating units has been a major contributor of particulate emissions in the industrialized world. There are several retrofit options available to electric generating units today for control of particulate emissions. These retrofit options include the electrostatic precipitator (ESP), the reverse air baghouse (RABH), the pulse jet baghouse (PJBH), and the hybrid baghouses such as the Compact Hybrid Particulate Collector (COHPAC). These different technologies have evolved through the years to address the ever increasing stringent emissions standards and also the market demand for more cost-effective controls. Note that future regulation of air toxics may result in further evolution of particulate control technology.

The cost ranges for the retrofit options presented in this study were developed using Sargent & Lundy's current market databases from recent retrofit projects and the Electric Power Research Institute (EPRI)/Sargent & Lundy (S&L) State-of-the-Art Power Plant (SOAPP) Technology Modules (1992). The SOAPP Modules were developed for inclusion in the SOAPP Workstation, which is a tool electric utilities can use to conceptualize new or retrofit power plants. The cost ranges generally represent the capital costs of around 95 percent of the retrofits performed. There will always be site-specific cases where a difficult retrofit will result in higher capital costs.

Electrostatic Precipitators

ESPs effectively remove particulate from flue gas by charging fly ash particles and collecting them on an opposite-charged collection plate. The level of control ESPs can provide is a function of the resistivity of the coal, the size of the unit, and the size and number of collection fields. The type of coal used in the boiler determines the amount of flue gas and fly ash generated and the chemical and physical characteristics of the fly ash. With the advent of stricter air pollution codes, efficiency requirements less than 99 percent are no longer adequate, and most current requirements are in the 99.5 percent to 99.9 percent range.

The advantages of ESPs over the other particulate control options include a capacity to handle large gas volumes, high collection efficiencies, low draft loss, ability to operate with relatively high-temperature gases, and, probably most important, the ability to withstand upsets in operating conditions with little impact on long term performance. Disadvantages of ESPs are the electric energy requirement and general poorer performance on small particles, which may be the focus of future regulation. These particles, less than ten thousandths of a millimeter in diameter ($10\mu m$), are associated with increased health risks and frequently have a higher concentration of air toxics contained in their fraction.

Figure 7.9 presents a total capital cost comparison of a typical rigid electrode ESP with a 12 inch plate spacing design versus a 16 inch plate spacing design. The 12 inch plate spacing is a standard design, which is well suited for retrofitting. The 16 inch plate spacing is a newer design employing fewer electrode

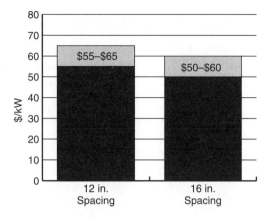

Figure 7.9   ESP capital costs (1997).

plates, reducing the weight and cost of the ESP. Consequently, the 16 inch plate spacing design has a lower capital cost, but slightly higher operating costs. Typically, these capital cost savings will more than offset the cost of additional auxiliary power required for the larger distance between the electrode and the plate. The control costs presented are for a nominal 600 MW unit burning a high ash (10.97 percent), high sulfur (3.28 percent) coal while attaining a 0.005 lb/MBtu particulate emission limit (approximately 99.9 percent efficiency).

Note that the capital costs provided are based on U.S. retrofit installations and actual costs outside the United States may vary greatly. However, the relative cost savings expected within should closely represent the relative cost savings expected outside the United States.

Reverse Air Baghouse

Fabric filters such as RABHs are one of the most efficient devices for the removal of particulates. Fabric filters have the capability of maintaining collection efficiencies above 99.9 percent. The basic features of a fabric filter unit consist of woven or felted fabric, usually in the form of tubes (bags) that are suspended in a housing structure (baghouse). The gas stream is distributed by means of specially designed entry and exit plenum chambers providing equal gas flow though the filtration medium. RABHs use a form of reverse airflow cleaning to clean the filters. A large volume of low-pressure cleaned gas is directed countercurrent to the normal gas stream flow during the cleaning cycle. The reversal of gas flow causes the caked dust to break loose from the bag and fall into the dust hopper. Conversely, the pulse jet baghouse (PJBH) uses a high pressure pulse of air into the bags to dislodge the filter cakes and allow them to fall into the ash hopper system.

The advantages of RABHs include a high collection efficiency over a broad range of particle sizes, high volumetric capacities, and relatively low power requirements. Disadvantages of RABHs compared to PJBH include the relatively high capital cost and the large amount of plant space required for installation. A disadvantage of the RABH compared to the ESP are the relatively high draft losses (resistance to the flow of gas through the system).

Pulse Jet Baghouse

PJBHs are another type of fabric filter which employ a different method of cleaning the filters. The process involves the application of a high-pressure pulse of compressed air inside of the top of the collector for a short time, a fraction of a second. This action tends to form a wave action down the collector while rapidly expanding the fabric and quickly dislodging all collected dust. Vibration from the wave action and fabric flexing from the pressure increase are the primary cleaning mechanisms.

PJBHs have been used for many years in industrial applications, but are relatively new to the power industry. The advantages of PJBHs when compared to RGBHs include the lower space requirements and lower capital cost requirements. A primary disadvantage of PJBHs is that it is relatively new to the power industry.

Figure 7.10 presents a total capital cost comparison of the two types of baghouses, RABH and PJBH, and an ESP at a unit burning low sulfur coal (1%). Due to the influence that sulfur oxides has on ash resistivity, it is apparent that the baghouse has some advantages over the ESP in low sulfur coal applications.

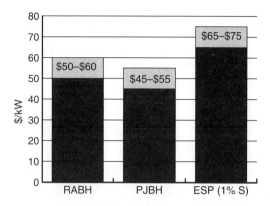

Figure 7.10   Baghouse and ESP capital costs (1997).

Although not shown here, the ESP has advantages for higher sulfur coals (> 2%). The PJBH has a significant capital cost advantage over either the ESP or the RABH. Application of this technology in the power industry may result in higher actual costs due to unforeseen problems. The costs presented for the baghouses are for a nominal 600 MW unit burning either a high sulfur coal (3.28%) or a low sulfur coal (1%) while attaining a 0.005 lb/MBtu particulate emission limit. For comparison purposes, the costs presented for the ESP retrofit are for a unit burning low sulfur coal (1%).

Compact Hybrid Particulate Collector

COHPAC is a novel, low cost, retrofit particulate control concept developed by EPRI. As a retrofit application, the technology is especially appealing for units that have undersized ESPs or at installations where ESP performance has been affected by the implementation of other pollution control measures, such as fuel switching.

In the COHPAC configuration, an ESP and PJBH are in operation together. The dirty flue gas enters the ESP where 85 percent to 95 percent of the inlet loading is removed. This limits the inlet loading into the PJBH downstream to 0.6 to 0.7 lb/MBtu. The flue gas is further cleaned by the PJBH, often attaining outlet emissions of 0.01 lb/MBtu or lower and opacity of 5 percent or less.

The primary advantages of COHPAC are the ultra low emissions it offers and the fact that it can be an ideal retrofit option for an underperforming ESP. A COHPAC type PJBH can offer economic advantages compared to upgrading or replacing an existing inadequate particulate collector. Figures 7.9 and 7.10 indicate capital costs in the $60/kW range for retrofitting a new ESP or RABH.

The capital costs for COHPAC retrofit installations are very site specific. If new booster fans, large quantities of ductwork, or additional auxiliary power transformers are needed, then the $/kW cost can easily double. For a medium-difficulty retrofit application, it has been shown that capital costs (in 1997 dollars) have ranged from $25 to $50 per kW. These costs are for a nominal 600 MW unit burning a high sulfur coal (3.28%) while attaining a 0.005 lb/MBtu particulate emission limit.

NO_x CONTROL

There are several retrofit options available to electric generating units today for control of NO_x emissions. These retrofit options include combustion controls such as low NO_x burners (LNB) and reburning and post-combustion controls such as selective catalytic reduction (SCR) and selective noncatalytic reduction (SNCR). These different technologies have evolved significantly in the recent past to address more stringent emissions standards and the market demand for more cost-effective controls.

The costs for the combustion and post-combustion retrofit options presented were developed using S&L's recent experience as well as the U.S. Environmental Protection Agency (U.S. EPA) report evaluating NO_x control costs for utility boilers in the northeast U.S. ozone transport region and the SOAPP Technology Modules referenced earlier.

Combustion Controls: Low NO_x Burners

Retrofit low NO_x burners (LNB) can reduce NO_x emissions 40 percent to 60 percent and are commercially available. LNBs can be teamed with other technologies for even further NO$_x$ reductions. While LNBs can be installed on many pulverized-coal boilers, they cannot be adapted to wet-bottom furnaces such as cyclone-fired boilers.

LNBs control NO$_x$ by maintaining conditions unfavorable to NO$_x$ formation. They restrict the air and fuel mixing in the combustion zone nearest the burners. Minimizing the mixing reduces the amount of fuel nitrogen that is oxidized and minimizes NO$_x$ formation in the early stages of combustion. LNBs are designed to create a longer, cooler flame so that the air and combustion gases thoroughly mix in the latter part of the flame. The formation of NO$_x$ from nitrogen in the combustion air is controlled by limiting temperatures to less than 2700 degrees F, approximately.

There are numerous types of LNBs available including LNBs with overfire air (OFA) and without OFA. LNBs with OFA allow for a more distinct separation in the furnace of a fuel-rich primary combustion zone and a slightly air-rich (but lower temperature) burnout zone. This arrangement generally results in lower NO$_x$ emissions from the boiler.

Combustion Controls: Reburning

Reburning is an NO$_x$ control technology that can potentially reduce NO$_x$ emissions by 60 percent. In reburning, a second combustion (reburning) zone is created above the main coal combustion zone. The reburning zone is created by diverting 10 percent to 20 percent of the unit's heat input to this zone and operating the zone to create an oxygen-deficient environment that encourages reduction of NO and NO$_2$ to N$_2$. Overfire air is added above the reburning zone to complete combustion of the main and reburning fuels.

The reburning fuel can be natural gas, oil, or pulverized coal. Natural gas reburning (NGR) has been tested on pilot and demonstration scale to a greater extent than coal or oil. Therefore, the technical risk is probably less with NGR than with oil or coal. Also, NGR has the lowest capital requirement if gas is available at the site.

Reburning is primarily a retrofit technology. Cyclone units are prime candidates for reburning applications since most

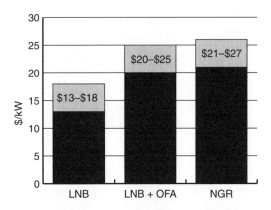

Figure 7.11   Wall-fired NO_x combustion control capital costs (1997).

other less expensive means of controlling NO_x require furnace
or combustion modifications that are not readily available with
cyclones. The balance-of-plant impact on the unit would be the
reburning fuel handling and storage equipment. Pipeline costs
for NGR are not taken into account in the capital cost breakdown since they are very site-specific.

Figures 7.11 and 7.12 provide a comparison of capital costs for
retrofitting combustion controls on wall-fired boilers and tan-
gentially fired boilers. The cost data is presented for nominal
660 MW wall-fired units and 375 MW tangentially-fired units.

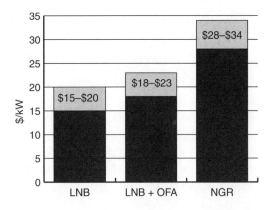

Figure 7.12   T-fired NO_x combustion control capital costs (1997).

The different burner arrangements in these two types of boilers account for the different capital costs and controlled NO$_x$ emission rates. For wall-fired units, the following controlled NO$_x$ emission rates are typical: 0.45–0.50 lb/MBtu for LNB only, 0.35–0.45 lb/MBtu for LNB with OFA, and 0.35–0.45 lb/MBtu for NGR. Similarly, for tangentially-fired units, the following controlled NO$_x$ emission rates are typical: 0.40–0.45 lb/MBtu for LNB only, 0.30–0.35 lb/MBtu for LNB with OFA, and 0.25–0.35 lb/MBtu for NGR. Note that these estimates are very dependent on fuel type and may vary significantly between different grades of bituminous and sub-bituminous coals.

Post-Combustion Controls: Selective Catalytic Reduction

Selective catalytic reduction (SCR) with ammonia injection can reduce NO$_x$ emissions as much as 85 percent, and higher under favorable conditions. SCR has been commercially demonstrated in Japan, Western Europe, and the United States. The catalytic reduction of NO$_x$ with ammonia (NH$_3$) occurs at temperatures between 570°F and 750°F. The process requires a titanium/vanadium based catalyst and ammonia addition at an NH$_3$/NO$_x$ molar ratio of 1.0–1.1. Care must be taken in design and operation to limit residual ammonia. Excessive residual can react with sulfur oxides and form solids of ammonium sulfate or bisulfate. Both of these compounds can contribute to air heater plugging. In some cases, it may be prudent to desulfurize the gas first, reheat the gas and then use an SCR to reduce NO$_x$ emissions.

Retrofitting SCR will require ductwork modifications in the section between the economizer and the air heater to accommodate the catalyst. An economizer bypass may also be needed in order to control the flue gas temperature at the catalyst. The catalyst will likely be a parallel flow-through arrangement to minimize fly ash impaction on the catalyst's surface. Regenerative air heaters may require redesign to minimize plugging problems.

The primary advantage of SCR is its high NO$_x$ removal potential (> 80% removal). Disadvantages of SCR include a decrease in boiler efficiency as well as a capital cost associated with retrofitting a large system in a typically tight conditions. Also the potential ammonia slip may foul and plug downstream equipment.

Post-Combustion Controls: Selective Noncatalytic Reduction

Selective noncatalytic reduction (SNCR) can achieve approximately a 50 percent NO_x reduction. SNCR follows the same principles of SCR except that a catalyst is not used. SNCR takes place at temperatures of 1600°F to 2200°F, so the NH_3 must be injected into the furnace in this temperature window. The process is very sensitive to temperature, and if the NH_3 is injected above the 2200°F limit some of the NH_3 may be oxidized to NO_x. Conversely, if the NH_3 is injected below the 1600°F limit, then excessive ammonia slip may occur.

There are several different forms of ammonia which can be injected, such as urea injection, anhydrous ammonia injection, and aqueous ammonia injection. The most common form is urea injection due to its ease of handling. SNCR requires little retrofit equipment and no catalyst, resulting in a capital cost much lower than SCR.

Advantages of SNCR when compared to SCR include its lower capital cost and a broader temperature window for NO_x removal. As with SCR, a primary disadvantage is the potential for ammonium bisulfate/sulfate deposition on downstream equipment, especially the air heater.

Figure 7.13 presents a total capital cost comparison of SCR and SNCR. The costs are for a nominal 600 MW unit burning a high sulfur coal (3.28%) while attaining a 0.15 lb/ MBtu emission limit for SCR and a 0.30 lb/MBtu NO_x emission limit for SNCR. The range provided for SCR retrofits is a broader range ($60–$100 per kW) since SCR installation is a very site-specific process which could potentially result in significant ductwork modifications. As the figure indicates, SCR is significantly more expensive than SNCR. However, the NO_x removal efficiency of SCR is much greater than that of SNCR. In most cases, retrofitting with SNCR is the optimum choice for units with a low capacity factor where moderate NO_x reduction is needed.

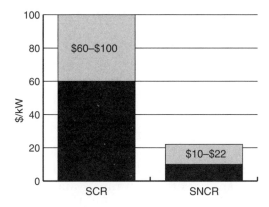

Figure 7.13 SCR vs. SNCR capital costs (1997).

SO$_2$ Control

There are several retrofit options available to electric generating units today for control of SO$_2$ emissions. These retrofit options include commercially available wet flue gas desulfurization (FGD) technologies such as forced oxidation FGD and inhibited oxidation FGD processes and dry FGD technologies such as lime spray dryer FGD. Also, use of furnace and duct sorbent injection are commercially available options.

The costs for the retrofit options presented were developed using S&L's recent experience retrofitting generating units totaling 4000 MW of capacity.

Wet Flue Gas Desulfurization

Wet FGD systems have been applied to a wide range of fuels providing SO$_2$ removal efficiencies approaching 99 percent. Wet FGD systems have been predominantly lime or limestone systems along with a few dual alkali, once-through sodium, magnesium oxide, and Wellman-Lord systems. The most common wet FGDs commercially employed is the limestone FGD with forced oxidation.

Wet FGD systems generally remove SO$_2$ from the flue gas stream by contacting limestone with SO$_2$ in a co-current or countercurrent absorber. In a limestone FGD with forced oxidation, the absorbed SO_2 present as a sulfite in the liquid phase is oxidized within the SO_2 removal system, and calcium sulfate dihydrate, $CaSO_4 \cdot 2H_2O$ (gypsum), is formed.

Figure 7.14 shows the progression of the capital cost requirements for wet linestone FGD systems over the last 25 years. Costs in 1970 represented a fledging technology just realizing its first commercial applications and thus the relatively high costs. By 1980 these growing pains were over and a more mature technology emerged. With 1990 came the new regulatory requirement of annual emission limits making instantaneous emission rates of less importance. Total annual emission rates are a less capital intensive design criteria and the cost of FGD dropped again. The lower costs of the mid-1990s represent an increased comfort level with the technology allowing it to be applied to a more relaxed emissions accounting system. Specifically, the emissions trading program for SO_2 created by the Clean Air Act Amendments of 1990 has allowed flue gas desulfurixation designers to apply improved FGD technology saving as much as 25 percent of capital costs.

Dry Flue Gas Desulfurization

Dry FGD systems have shown the capability of 95 percent SO_2 removal efficiency, predominantly on lower sulfur coals. The

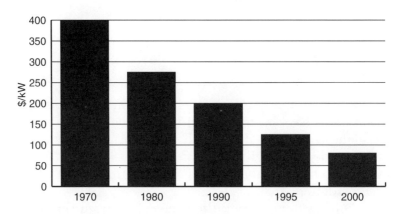

Figure 7.14   Wet FGD capital costs (1997).

most common form of dry FGD is the lime spray dryer process. In this process, slaked lime slurry is sprayed into flue gas in a spray dryer vessel downstream of the air heater and upstream of a particulate control device. SO_2 reacts with the lime to form primarily calcium sulfite and some calcium sulfate.

The advantage of dry FGD include when compared to wet FGD is the lower capital cost requirement. The major disadvantages of dry FGD when compared to wet FGD is its relative inefficiency with high sulfur coal, the higher reagent feed ratio required, and most importantly, that fact that the lime reagent is more expensive than limestone.

Figure 7.15 provides a cost comparison of wet FGD and dry FGD installations. The process and equipment required for dry FGD systems are less complex than for wet FGD systems. Therefore, the capital costs for dry FGD systems are lower than for wet FGD systems. However, the cost of lime is considerably more than limestone and therefore, much (if not all) of the capital advantages of dry FGD is eroded by the higher operating cost.

Sorbent Injection

Sorbent injection is a commercially available technology that has an SO_2 removal efficiency of between 40 to 50 percent. Two common types of sorbent injection are in-duct sorbent injection and

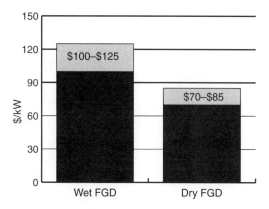

Figure 7.15 Wet FGD vs. dry FGD capital costs (1997).

in-furnace sorbent injection. In-duct sorbent injection involves the injection of sorbent into flue gas in the existing ductwork between the air heater and the particulate control device. Types of sorbent used include dry hydrated lime, slaked lime slurry, and sodium compounds such as sodium bicarbonate or sodium sesquicarbonate.

In-furnace sorbent injection involves the injection of limestone or hydrated lime into the furnace cavity of the boiler to react with SO_2. In conjunction with furnace sorbent injection, water is also sometimes injected into the ductwork between the air heater and the particulate control device for flue gas and particulate conditioning to enhance SO_2 collection and to maintain particulate emission compliance.

The primary advantage of sorbent injection is its minimal capital cost. Also, the waste product produced as a result of the process is a dry, powdered solid which is easily handled by conventional fly ash handling systems. Disadvantages of sorbent injection include its low SO_2 removal efficiency (40 to 50 percent) and the potential for solids deposition in the ductwork. Also, performance of the ESP may be affected by sorbent injection. Particulate loading will increase in the particulate collection device and the humidified gas may cause corrosion in the downstream ductwork and the particulate collection device.

Figure 7.16 provides a total capital cost comparison for in-duct sorbent injection and for in-furnace sorbent injection.

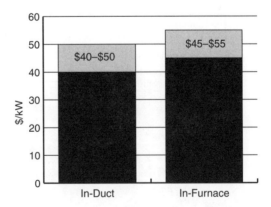

Figure 7.16   Sorbent injection capital costs (1997).

Capital costs for in-furnace injection are slightly higher due to the more extensive modifications required in the boiler. Due to its low removal efficiency, sorbent injection has no practical application with high sulfur coals. Therefore, the costs provided are for a nominal 600 MW unit burning a medium sulfur coal (1.28%) while attaining a 0.80 lb/MBtu SO_2 emission limit.

AIR TOXICS CONTROL

Several studies are underway in the United States to determine if electric generating units are a significant source of air toxics and are to be regulated as such. These studies have been focusing on probable air toxics which include inorganics such as mercury and other metals as well as organics such as benzene and toluene. Based on preliminary results from these studies, it appears that mercury and other metals such as beryllium, cadmium, and manganese may be air toxics of concern from power plants.

Based on this information, a preliminary investigation of retrofit technologies can be made for the control of air toxics. Some conventional control technologies discussed previously have shown some capabilities of controlling air toxics to varying extents. The air toxics control capabilities of traditional particulate and SO_2 control technologies will be discussed next.

Air Toxics/Particulate Controls

Many trace metals in coal are volatilized at the high temperatures in the furnace. As the flue gas is cooled in the backend of the boiler, these vaporous metals can condense in various forms and at various temperatures. The trace metals may condense to form either very small particles or they may be absorbed or adsorbed onto the smaller fly ash particles. In either case, the majority of the trace metals inventory is present as the smallest particulate matter in the flue gas stream. Therefore, collection efficiency for the very small (< 5 μm) diameter particulate is very important.

For plants that have upgraded precipitators to meet increasingly stringent opacity limits, some of the very small particulates may have already been captured. Baghouses provide an additional capture mechanism for trace metal vapors through the dust cake that covers the bags. The dust cake provides a surface on which the air toxics may condense or react with constituents of the dust cake and be removed with the fly ash. COHPAC provides a very compact, yet highly effective, method of removing the smaller particulate. This technology may offer a very cost-competitive option for trace element emission control.

Air Toxics/SO₂ Controls

The most widely implemented SO_2 reduction technologies for coal-fired power plants are the wet lime/limestone FGD system and the dry lime FGD systems. Both of these technologies offer varying degrees of air toxics control. Most of the mercury control data for dry FGD systems has been developed from municipal solid waste (MSW) and hazardous waste incinerators. These applications tend to have higher flue gas mercury concentrations than coal-fired power plants. The dry FGD systems are particularly effective for coals with moderate to high chlorine levels—0.1 percent to 0.3 percent because the vaporous mercury reacts with the chlorine to form a solid particle and is, therefore, easier to collect in a baghouse. The injection of activated carbon into dry FGD systems can further reduce mercury emissions from MSW incinerators through adsorption of mercury on the activated carbon particles. Since dry FGD systems are generally followed by fabric filter baghouses, the addition of and subsequent collection of activated carbon is relatively easy.

Wet FGD systems have also been shown to aid in the removal of air toxics such as mercury and hydrochloric acid. Oxidized mercury compounds leave the flue gas stream by condensing in the low-temperature environment of the absorber. The removal of mercury and other hazardous air pollutants can be optimized by increasing the mass transfer characteristics of the absorber. Mass transfer characteristics can be improved by a number of methods, including increasing the liquid-gas surface area, adding gas to liquid contactors, and optimizing the slurry chemistry to increase the solubility of the mercury compounds.

Other Emerging Retrofit Control Technologies for Air Toxics

Activated carbon and activated coke have been demonstrated in Europe and Japan as combined desulfurization, denitrification, and air toxics removal processes. The major benefit of the activated carbon process is that it combines the control of SO_2 and NO_x with air toxics in one system. Activated carbon processes are expected to be very effective in the removal of vaporous compounds, and there is some evidence to show that some of the semivolatile organic compounds may also be reduced. The removal of trace metals condensed on the surface of particulate would be done by a fabric filter baghouse in conjunction with the activated carbon system.

Catalytic incineration has been demonstrated in industrial applications to be effective in controlling VOCs in gaseous waste streams. Such a catalytic system could conceivably be retrofit on the backend of an existing boiler. However, due to the capital and operating costs of this technology, care in the combustion process to prevent formation of VOCs would appear to be a more cost-effective control mechanism.

REFERENCES

DePriest, W., W.R. Bullock, and J.M. Mazurek. April 1994. "CO_2 and Air Toxics: Planning for Future Regulatory Uncertainties." Typescript.

Electric Power Research Institute/Sargent & Lundy. December 1992. "State-of-the-Art Power Plant (SOAPP) Workstation Technology Modules." Palo Alto, CA.

U.S. Environmental Protection Agency. December 1992. "Evolution and Costing of NO_x Controls for Existing Utility Boilers in the NESCAUM Region." EPA-453/R-92-010.

More Clean Air for the Buck: Lessons from the U.S. Acid Rain Emissions Trading Program

SARAH WADE

Although the SO_2 market experienced many of the same characteristics of any startup market, it is blossoming into a full-fledged commodities market. Over the past years, there has been a steady increase in the number of allowance transfers. It is notable that initially the vast bulk of these transfers were between and among individual boiler units (the level at which the emission source is defined under the program) within single operating systems, although many such systems cross several state borders. This type of transaction is sometimes referred to as internal optimization. It indicates that a company, when given the flexibility to determine the best means of reducing total emissions, will review the operations of its entire physical plant and phase in control measures at the location and of a size that makes economic sense, within the constraints of the environmental program. Since the first year of the program, we have seen a further increase in the number of transactions that are between, rather than within, companies.

General economic performance during the first years was excellent throughout the United States. Notwithstanding the investment in the reduction and overcontrol of SO_2 emissions, overall U.S. electric power generation continued to increase, as did electricity generation in the regions specifically affected by the requirements of the SO_2 program—a result that flatly refutes the claims made by opponents of acid rain legislation throughout the 1980s. The program also provided a workable policy solution to a regionally divisive issue—namely there were concerns about the impact of emissions requirements on various utilities' ability to compete in the marketplace. Through allowance trading, utilities were able to manage their environmental decisions in the manner that best suited their needs.

That emissions trading is instrumental in this economic response is suggested by the path that prices have followed since active trading began, first in anticipation of the program and then continuing into the present. At the time the legislation was enacted, predictions of marginal compliance costs and allowance prices ranged from \$350 to \$1000 per ton; however, allowances have traded at much lower levels.

The two-years' experience with the SO_2 program amply demonstrates the spectacular success of an emissions budget and trading program in delivering substantial and early reductions and substantial cost-savings. Equally striking is the effect these emissions reductions are having on the physical environment they are intended to protect. Significant drops in SO_2 levels are now being recorded. Acid deposition is not the only environmental problem in the United States to which the long-distance transport of pollution is critical. The EPA and states throughout the eastern U.S. are grappling with the effect of NO_x transport on ozone smog formation in urban areas. In the SO_2 program, they can find a model for addressing this problem.

Similarly, both the economic and environmental challenges of climate change demand the use, in any international agreement on climate change and greenhouse gas (GHG) emissions, of an emissions budget and trading approach. Nowhere is the need for cost-effectiveness and the benefit of early reductions more critical. The economic dynamic of a GHG emissions budget implemented through a competitive global market for GHG emissions reductions could produce the kind of cost-savings and investment in early emissions control already seen in the United States SO_2 emissions budget and trading program.

Although an international trading mechanism may take some time to secure fully the cooperation of developed and developing countries, there are significant developments occurring at the private and national levels. A prime example is the effort being undertaken by British Petroleum Amoco (BP). In the fall of 1998, BP took the unprecedented step of committing to reduce its GHG emissions by 10 percent below 1990 levels by 2010. It is important to note that BP's target is not contingent upon the outcome of international negotiations. BP provides an excellent example for other companies that are interested in making voluntary early GHG emissions. There are at least four important features of the BP program which should be highlighted.

Perhaps one of the most important steps being taken by BP is to implement a system to accurately report and track their greenhouse gas emissions. This has involved developing and improving an emissions inventory to estimate the GHG emissions from all sources controlled by BP. To date, BP has focused on measuring and building a CO_2 inventory and is now working on a similar effort to measure methane. This work includes developing and testing estimation and measurement methods as well as formalizing a reporting and data collection process. This process is the critical step in developing an effective GHG reduction strategy. As Sir John Browne, CEO of BP, points out, "that which you measure, you manage." Many companies do not have a good estimate of their GHG emissions and thus they do not have a sense of their exposure to reduction requirements.

BP has also adopted a voluntary emissions cap. BP has agreed to limit its total amount of GHG emissions to a level that is 10 percent below the company's best estimate of its 1990 emissions levels. This goal is twice as stringent as the goal established in the Kyoto Protocol. By adopting an emissions cap, BP has established a clear and quantifiable performance target. They will be able to easily demonstrate both to the public and to themselves, their success or failure in achieving this target. In choosing this performance standard rather than a detailed technology-based plan, BP has established a challenge for its employees and business units to figure out how to reduce emissions in the most cost-effective ways possible.

BP is implementing a GHG emissions trading program to facilitate its effort to achieve these significant emissions reductions. BP has identified 12 business units located around the globe and representing a diverse array of operational functions. One purpose of the trading program is to give BP both experience and information about emissions trading. For example, they will develop a trading desk that has experience in pricing and structuring transactions involving GHG emissions. The trading program will also provide direct incentives for the business unit managers to find the most cost-effective ways of making emissions reductions. BP believes this will encourage employees—the people who are most intimately familiar with the business processes at BP—to find innovative control methods. This information will better enable BP to assess its options for reducing emissions and to understand the costs involved with this effort. As BP gains experience with this trading program, they have the option to expand it to include the entire company and the opportunity to trade emissions reductions with external companies. The Environmental Defense Fund (EDF) is helping BP to establish and evaluate its emissions trading program.

Finally, BP has committed to sharing with others the information it develops in the course of implementing this program. BP recognizes that in order for its efforts to be truly credible, they must withstand the scrutiny of third parties and the general public. To this end, BP is investing resources in developing a comprehensive reporting system and in working with various third parties, including EDF, to ensure that its effort is transparent.

BP has indicated many reasons for its GHG commitment; EDF would like to note two of them. First, BP has stated its view that the preponderance of evidence points toward the conclusion that human activity is adversely impacting climate and therefore it makes sense to begin managing those activities. Second, BP has expressed a belief that in order for it to remain competitive in the future, it needs to build in the effort to reduce GHG emissions in a manner that is cost-effective and productive. It believes that it can accomplish this objective while also making significant emissions reductions. EDF applauds BP both for its courage in taking this step and for the leadership it is showing.

8

From Autarkic to Market-Based Compliance

A. Denny Ellerman

Learning from Our Mistakes

Allowances have been a central feature of Title IV from the beginning; and it is appropriate to assess how electric utilities have made use of this novel instrument for achieving environmental goals. Given the basic requirement that every ton of emissions be covered by an allowance and that allowances are allocated to every affected unit, utilities have no choice but to use allowances, although there is no requirement to trade them. If they wished to do so, utilities could treat allowances simply as nontradable permits and reduce emissions to match the number of allowances allocated to each unit. In fact, they have not done so.

Electric utility use of allowances has changed significantly from the early years of Phase I compliance to the present. The central feature of this change is the relation of internal compliance decisions to the allowance market, and the change can be characterized as a movement from autarkic to market-based compliance. Like all attempts to categorize human activity, there are exceptions and the change is uneven, but the main outlines persist. This evolution in electric utilities' use of allowances helps to explain what are otherwise puzzling phenomena in Phase I, and it also reveals what may be viewed as one of the most attractive features of allowances, the ability to mitigate the cost of mistakes.

The year 1995 was a pivotal one in the evolution of the electric utility use of allowances. It was the first year in which emissions had to be covered by an allowance, but it was also a year of surprise dominated by the fact that the market price for allowances, which was believed already too low, fell even lower. The experience was to change utility attitudes toward the allowance market and to lead to an integration of the market price for allowances into compliance decisions. Accordingly, the discussion in this chapter proceeds in three sections before concluding: the pre-1995 years of compliance planning in which autarkic compliance prevailed, the 1995 revelation of over-investment in compliance, and the post-1995 change to market-based compliance.

AUTARKIC COMPLIANCE

Autarky denotes a self-sufficient disregard for the benefits of trade. In this context, the word describes the distinct tendency of utilities to plan for compliance in Phase I without much regard to emissions trading possibilities outside of the utility. The word does not imply that utilities ignored emissions trading possibilities within the utility. To the contrary, utilities have shown little hesitation in trading internally, both in space and through time; and there can be little doubt that internal trading yielded significant cost savings. In planning for Phase I compliance, utilities acted as if they faced a utility-specific cap, within which they created their own implicit market for allowances. What made the planning autarkic was that the price implicit in this internal market bore little relation to the outside market price for allowances.

The results of compliance planning became evident in 1995 as the planned Phase I emission reductions were implemented. Two basic patterns in the use of allowances can be observed. A frequent pattern was to reduce emissions more than required at one or a few units and to use a portion of that overcompliance to avoid reductions at other units. TVA is a good example of this pattern. Over 90 percent of the emission reduction effected by TVA in 1995 was accomplished at the two scrubbed units at the Cumberland plant, while half of TVA's 26 affected units required additional allowances to cover 1995 emissions. It's evident that TVA and other utilities were not taking allowance allocations at the unit level as given, and that they were trading within the utility to avoid abatement cost at units where emissions exceeded the allowance allocation.

The other pattern was to reduce emissions at almost all units but by far more than required. The Southern Company provides a particularly good illustration of this pattern. The reduction of emissions is not as concentrated at a few units as was the case for TVA: the two units making the largest emission reductions account for only 27 percent of the total. Moreover, only 4 of Southern's 50 affected units needed allowances from other units to cover 1995 emissions; the other 46 units banked allowances. Perhaps most surprising, but also revealing of compliance planning, the Southern Company received more allowances in 1995 than were needed to cover emissions in the counterfactual; and only 13 of Southern's 50 affected units were constrained.[1] Nevertheless, SO_2 emissions were reduced by 40 percent. There is no other explanation for this utility's compliance behavior in 1995 than purposeful overcompliance in order to bank allowances for later use in Phase II.

These two examples are repeated and mixed at a number of other utilities. A total of 203 units were constrained by the allowance allocation in 1995, but 95 of these benefited from allowance transfers from other units within the same utility to cover emissions in excess of their own allowance allocation. These 95 units were operated by 27 different utilities, about three-quarters of the 37 utilities with multiple affected units with at least one unit constrained by the allowance allocation.[2]

The second pattern is also observed, not so much among utilities like Southern, which were unconstrained in the aggregate, but among those that were. Most of the 1995 emission reduction—3.2 million out of the total 3.9 million tons—was made by 24 utilities for which the utility-level cap was constraining. These utilities were constrained to reduce emissions by only 1.5 million tons, but they reduced emissions far more than necessary to meet the 1995 utility caps, even allowing for some margin for error. Further evidence of inter-temporal banking can be observed in the 33 utilities, like Southern, that were not constrained by the utility cap. These utilities received 0.85 million allowances in excess of the counterfactual emissions, mostly at Table A units, as the result of emission reductions effected before 1993. These utilities also made further reductions totaling 0.77 million tons to bank a total of 1.62 million allowances for Phase II.

Although autarkic compliance characterized Phase I planning for most utilities, a few did take advantage of the allowance market. The most well known instances are Carolina Power and Light and Illinois Power. Carolina Power and Light did not have any Phase I units, but it swept the 1993 allowance auction, obviously for use in Phase II. Illinois Power had Phase I units, and it relied heavily on allowance purchases on the open market; but its use of the allowance market for compliance came only after an initial proposal to build a scrubber at one of the Baldwin units was frustrated. In addition to Illinois Power, five other operating entities acquired small numbers of allowances from the open market to cover emissions in excess of the 1995 allocation to these utilities.

Autarkic compliance implies higher cost for a given amount of abatement, but it is hard to imagine an alternative. The lead times for some compliance decisions required action sooner rather than later, and the market for allowances was nascent at best in 1993 and early 1994, when many of these decisions were being made. An executive needed little imagination to realize that the consequences of not having enough allowances to cover emissions in Phase I were more serious than the consequences of having spent a little more (and reduced emissions more) from not having relied on the allowance market. Moreover, the recovery of costs for environmentally mandated expenditures was virtually assured. It is not surprising then that most utilities planned to go it alone.

OVER-INVESTMENT IN PHASE I COMPLIANCE

The year 1995 marked the start of Phase I and as a result allowances had an operational reality that they did not possess before. No one doubted the requirement to cover emissions with an allowance. Moreover, the price of an allowance was readily discernible, and open market trading in allowances had risen steadily in volume from virtually nothing in 1993 to about 5 million allowances in 1995 (Ellerman et al., 1997a). Immediate, real time comparisons could be made between allowance prices and the cost of using more or less sulfur in operational decisions such as spot purchases of coal.

A significant revision of expectations concerning allowance prices also occurred during this year. Although the nascent allowance market of 1993 and early 1994 indicated values from $130 to $150, experts were almost unanimous in affirming that the market price of allowances was "too low" and that allowances would be worth more once Title IV got under way. According to this argument, prices were low because utilities were not buying due to utility conservatism and public utility commission regulation. Moreover, it was argued that defects in the design of EPA's mandatory auction led to a downward bias in the clearing price.[3] More realistic prices would appear in 1995 when allowances would have to be surrendered and actual compliance costs were compared with open market allowance prices. As shown in Figure 8.1, allowance prices did not rise with the start of Phase I. They remained steady at about $130 for the first half the year and then fell precipitously in the latter half of the year to reach an all-time low of $67 in early 1996.

The first sign that things were not what they were expected to be was the collapse of the low sulfur coal premium in Central Appalachia in early 1995. This region is the largest coal producing area in the United States and a principal supplier of low sulfur coal. In Figure 8.2, the top two lines are the prices of low and mid-sulfur coals and the bottom line is the difference, or the low sulfur premium. All coal prices declined in early 1995, but low sulfur prices declined more than mid-sulfur prices. This was not what had been expected: Title IV was supposed to result in higher premiums of low sulfur coal. In fact, the pre-1995 premium of $4 a ton of coal—approximately equal to $200 an allowance—incorporated the expectation that allowance prices would rise when Title IV became effective in 1995. When allowance prices did not increase, the coal premium had to fall, the start of Title IV notwithstanding. It fell because coal buyers were making comparisons between coal premiums

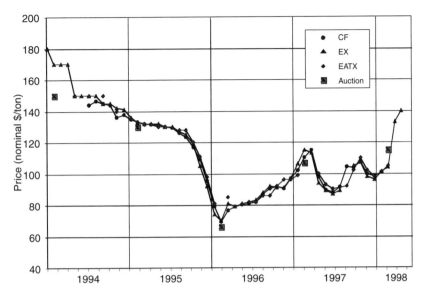

Figure 8.1   Allowance prices, 1992–1998 (1995 or current vintage) (*Source:* CF: Cantor Fitzgerald; EX: Emissions Exchange; EATX: Fieldston Publications, Inc.; and Auction: CBOT/Auction Clearing Price).

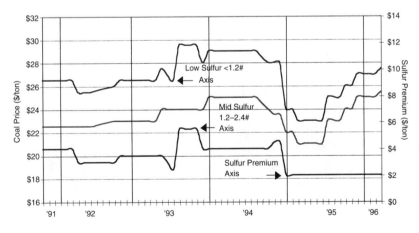

Figure 8.2   Central Appalachian coal prices (12,500 Btu/lb., spot).

and open market allowance prices and purchasing the higher sulfur product.

The second sign that the earlier expectations were mistaken appeared with the release of the U.S. EPA's quarterly continuous emissions monitoring reports, which gave actual emissions at all Phase I affected units.[4] It was easy to calculate the difference between the unit's required allowances and allocated allowances and to project for the year a cumulative Phase I bank of more allowances than had been expected. Consultants and other analysts by the fall of 1995 were led on this basis to estimate that the bank would reach 12 million tons.[5] This was much more than had been previously predicted, and a little more than will likely occur, but the point was made: the number of allowances required to cover emissions was less than had been expected. Instead of a utility scramble for allowances and low sulfur coal, more allowances were going to be available than had been expected. The implications for allowance prices were obvious, and it was at this time that allowance prices began the sharp, downward adjustment that marked the latter half of 1995.

In retrospect, the situation is clear. Far less abatement was required in the aggregate to get below the 1995 cap; and far more allowances would be banked for use in Phase II. Figure 8.3

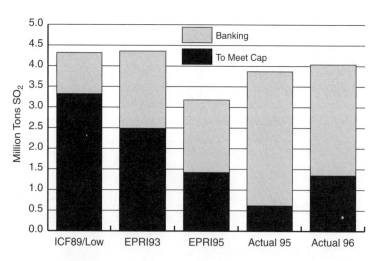

Figure 8.3 Mandatory reduction and banking components of 1995 Title IV abatement.

presents a comparison of earlier predictions of compliance in early Phase I by ICF and the Electric Power Research Institute with the MIT Center for Energy and Environmental Research estimate of what actually happened in 1995 and 1996 (ICF, 1989; EPRI, 1993; EPRI, 1995; Ellerman et al., 1997). The height of the columns indicates the reduction of emissions attributable to Title IV, which is then split into two parts: that required to reduce emissions to the aggregate cap and the extra amount attributable to banking. From the very beginning, it was expected that allowances would be banked. In 1989, ICF's estimate for low electricity growth (which is what happened) was a 3.3 million ton reduction of emissions to meet the cap and an additional 1.0 million tons banked. EPRI's later and more informed studies in 1993 and late 1994 predicted more banking, 1.8 million tons in both, but less of a required reduction to meet the cap: 2.5 million tons in 1993 and then 1.4 million tons in the later study. In reality, the aggregate reduction required to meet the cap was only 0.6 million tons in 1995 and 1.3 million tons in 1996. This comparison indicates that expectations about the amount of emission reduction that would be required to meet the cap were being revised as Phase I approached. Still, the amount actually required in 1995 and the amount banked appears to have been a surprise.

Everything indicates over-investment in compliance in Phase I, or if you wish, too much compliance.[6] This overinvestment resulted from the expectation of higher allowance prices in Phase I and the underlying failure to appreciate the extent to which aggregate abatement requirements had become less over time. The compliance actions taken in 1995 were for the most part decided earlier. They did depend on allowance price assumptions, and some of the most significant actions were irreversible for some period of time. As a result, these compliance actions continued impervious to changes in the current price of allowances. Scrubbers and multiyear contracts for low sulfur coal are two salient examples.

Scrubbers are complicated pieces of equipment that require several years from construction contract to operation. The decision to retrofit a scrubber depended on many considerations, some site-specific, others regulatory, but a very important factor was the expected value of allowances. Whether the utility was considering the one-time bonus allowances associated with most scrubbers or the ongoing stream of unused allowances generated by the scrubber's over-compliance, higher allowance values translated into a greater offset of the capital and operating costs of the scrubber. Thus, higher expected allowance prices led to more investment in scrubbers and more irreversible Phase I compliance. Since the on-going operating cost of a scrubber is much lower than the total cost, including amortized capital, these devices continued to operate even with lower allowance prices.

Multiyear contracts need not have such long lead times, and they are irreversible only for the length of the contract. Nevertheless, any utility planning to switch to low-sulfur coal to meet Title IV requirements faced the decision of whether to contract early for Phase I supplies and for what duration. The alternative was to depend on the spot market for low-sulfur coal during Phase I. Expectations of higher allowance prices and higher premiums for low-sulfur coal prompted many utilities to sign multiyear contracts for low-sulfur coal in 1993 and 1994, some for the entirety of Phase I, based on the price expectations prevailing in those years. Since the whole purpose of the contract is to insulate the purchase and sale from the vagaries of the market for the length of the contract, the compliance so determined did not respond to current allowance prices.

In retrospect, it is evident that the pre-1995 argument for higher allowance prices was badly flawed. The argument was lent some credibility by the novelty of allowances, the thinness of the early allowance market, and the internal costs observed by many utilities planning for more or less autarkic compliance. Nevertheless, the nascent allowance market, including the auction, was providing a more accurate signal of what was to come.

Some utilities did cancel decisions about scrubbers in response to these early prices.[7] As previously noted, others, such as Carolina Power & Light or Illinois Power, did not let arguments about the defects of the early allowance market dissuade them from taking advantage of the opportunity presented. Why more did not pay attention to these early price signals, and whether compliance decisions could have been changed, may be an enduring topic of academic discussion about Title IV. There should be little debate, however, about the consequences of over-investment in Phase I compliance.

A one-time adjustment in allowance prices occurred as new and increasingly irrefutable information appeared about the abatement required and the abatement already committed. Elements of irreversibility in compliance decisions meant that the planned reductions would occur anyway, and that the error would be banked. The subsequent adjustment of allowance prices set the stage for integrating the allowance market more fully into compliance decisions.

MARKET-BASED COMPLIANCE

The dominant feature of compliance decisions after 1995 is adjustment to the overinvestment that became evident in that year. The response took two forms. One was the short-term adjustment to the really low allowance prices after mid-1995, and the second was the long-term adjustment of Phase II compliance plans.

Lower allowance prices justify less current abatement. The convergence of the Central Appalachian low-sulfur coal premium to the allowance price in early 1995 indicated that coal buyers were prepared to use more allowances and to buy higher-sulfur coal rather than to purchase low-sulfur coal at a premium equivalent to a $200 allowance value. Another indication of this short-term adjustment is provided by the comparison of 1996 compliance with 1995.[8] A number of utilities were taking advantage of the significantly lower allowance prices in late 1995 and in 1996 to shift to higher-sulfur coals. The average SO_2 emission rate for the 386 nonscrubbed units that were subject to Phase I in both 1995 and 1996 increased by 4.6 percent, from 1.85 to 1.94 lb./mmBtu.

This switching back to higher-sulfur coal, and the concomitant use of more allowances, provide clear evidence that utilities were willing to base compliance decisions on the allowance market. Utilities that continued to adhere to an autarkic compliance plan, without regard to outside prices, would not have increased emissions in the second year of Phase I. If anything they would have reduced emissions even more as Phase II approached. Not all utilities responded to lower allowance prices in this manner. Some probably were keeping to previous plans, but such behavior can equally be explained by irreversible coal contracts.

The more important adjustment to overinvestment in compliance during Phase I is the long-term response. Banked allowances permit the deferral of compliance with the Phase II emission limits for a few years, and the extent of deferral depends on the amount of banking. If the pre-1995 expectations for banking had been correct, the cumulative bank at the end of Phase I would have been about 6 million allowances.[9] As a result of over-investment in Phase I compliance, current estimates for the Phase I bank lie in the range of 10 to 12 million tons. Obviously, costs that would have been incurred in say 2003, when the smaller bank ran out, can now be put off for a few more years.

If electric utilities are arbitraging between current Phase I and future Phase II compliance costs, then a deferral of the time when the bank runs out will affect current allowance prices. The value of an allowance not used today will be the present value or the discounted cost of that future abatement. Thus, if the time of the future abatement is pushed off several years, because of an unexpected access of allowances for instance, the present value will fall, not because the expected expenditure is any less, but because it is later. Any utilities that were buying allowances before would do so now only at a lower price.[10]

The same considerations that led to the one-time adjustment also define the floor for that adjustment and for a new equilibrium to be found. The current demand for allowances will increase as some utilities shift to higher-sulfur coals. Also, there is a price at which utilities participating in the market would begin to purchase allowances for Phase II compliance: the present value of the marginal cost expected to be incurred when the utility's augmented bank runs out. Furthermore, once that floor has been found, allowance prices could be expected to increase as the future expenditure approaches and the discounted value rises.

These adjustments will also become increasingly attractive for utilities that have not been allowance market participants.

Autarkic utilities, who found themselves with more allowances than expected in 1995, would be tempted to sell into the current market. The cash could be invested in the interim and the savings pocketed when the expenditure is made. Similarly, utilities expecting a higher present value for Phase II compliance than the current allowance price will be tempted to purchase in the current market. Doing so would permit the interest on the deferred expenditure to be pocketed.

The behavior of allowance prices since mid-1995 is consistent with arbitrage between Phase I and Phase II costs. The price of allowances did fall as the over-investment in Phase I compliance was revealed; a floor was established; and prices have risen steadily, if irregularly, since. Such a pattern would not have emerged if utilities had kept to earlier autarkic compliance plans. The evolution of allowance prices suggests that utilities were willing to adjust compliance, both currently in Phase I and prospectively in Phase II, as market values indicated and to participate in this market as appropriate opportunities arose.

CONCLUSION

The post-1995 adjustment to over-investment in Phase I compliance reveals a new dimension of the cost-saving characteristics of allowance trading: the ability to reduce the cost of mistakes. The word "mistake" carries a pejorative connotation, but it is only the recognition of the reality of decision-making in an uncertain world. Mistakes are inevitably made; the issue is always what people learn from mistakes and how they respond. The opportunity to mitigate the cost of error is an attribute that is not indicated by the usual analyses of emissions trading which assume perfect foresight, nor is it an attribute shared by regulatory mechanisms that operate by other means than the use of allowances.

In the case of Title IV, pre-1995 compliance planning was characterized by what turned out to be erroneous expectations of allowance prices and a tendency to disregard allowance market signals, such as they were in these early years. When combined with lead times and irreversibility, utilities invested too heavily in Phase I compliance. The result is higher cost of compliance in

Phase I than would have been incurred if, magically, there had been better foresight. But the story does not end here, as it would if the regulatory mechanism were command-and-control, or even a credit-based form of emissions trading. Utilities who were not committed by irreversible decisions in early Phase I found themselves in the pleasant situation of facing lower current compliance costs than they had expected. And the ability to bank the unused allowances meant that future abatement expenditure could be deferred for a few more years with consequent, further cost savings. These savings partially offset the higher Phase I cost associated with over-investment.

Allowances make it possible to act on what is learned: in this instance, to make the cost-reducing responses to the inevitable mistakes of decision-making in an uncertain world. The market in allowances transmits the true value of current abatement to agents and allows them to adapt to the extent that they can. And the ability to bank makes the rigidities of investment and contract less irreversible. Not surprisingly, given the opportunity to benefit from learning, electric utilities are abandoning autarkic compliance and embracing market-based compliance. This ability to learn and to act on what is learned is one of the most important attributes of the use of allowances for meeting environmental goals.

References

Bailey, Elizabeth M. March 1998. "Intertemporal Pricing of Sulfur Dioxide Allowances." Working paper 98-006, Center for Energy and Environmental Policy Research, Massachusetts Institute of Technology (MIT), Cambridge, MA.

Cason, T.N. 1993. "Seller Incentive Properties of EPA's Emissions Trading Auction." *Journal of Environmental Economics and Management* 25 (September): 177–195.

Cason, T.N. 1995. "An Experimental Investigation of the Seller Incentives in EPA's Emissions Trading Auction." *American Economic Review* 85 (September): 905–922.

Cason, T.N., and Charles R. Plott. 1996. "EPA's New Emissions Trading Mechanism: A Laboratory Evaluation." *Journal of Environmental Economics and Management* 30 (March): 133–160.

Ellerman, A. Denny, Richard Schmalensee, and Paul L. Joskow. 1997a. "November 1996 Update on Compliance and Emissions Trading under the U.S. Acid Rain Program." Working paper 97-005, Center for Energy and Environmental Policy Research, MIT, Cambridge, MA.

Ellerman, A. Denny, Richard Schmalensee, Paul L. Joskow, Juan Pablo Montero, and Elizabeth M. Bailey. October 1997b. "Emissions Trading under the U.S.

Acid Rain Program: Evaluation of Compliance Costs and Allowance Market Performance." Center for Energy and Environmental Policy Research, MIT, Cambridge, MA.

Electric Power Research Institute. 1993. "Integrated analysis of fuel, technology and emission allowance markets: electric utility responses to the Clean Air Act Amendments of 1990." EPRI TR-102510. Palo Alto, CA.

Electric Power Research Institute. 1995. "The emission allowance market and electric utility SO$_2$ compliance in a competitive and uncertain future." EPRI TR-105490S. Palo Alto, CA.

ICF Resources Incorporated. September 1989. "Economic Analysis of Title IV (Acid Rain Provisions) of the Administration's Proposed Clean Air Act Amendments." H.R. 3030/S. 1490. Washington, DC.

Joskow, Paul L., Richard Schmalensee, and Elizabeth M. Bailey. 1998. "The Development of the Sulfur Dioxide Emissions Market." *American Economic Review 88* (4): 669–685.

Myers, Todd A. and Pamela Custode. 1995. "CAAA Phase I Performance: Overcompliance." *Coal* 100 (10) (October): 25–26. Chicago: Intertec Publishing.

Schennach, Susanne M. May 1998. "The Economics of Pollution Permit Banking in the Context of Title IV of the 1990 Clean Air Act Amendments." Working paper 98-007, Center for Energy and Environmental Policy Research, MIT, Cambridge, MA.

NOTES

1. In keeping with Ellerman et al. (1997), counterfactual emissions are estimated as 1996 heat input times the 1993 emission rate. The word "constrained" as used in this sentence and elsewhere means that the allocation of allowances to the unit or to the utility was less than counterfactual emissions for the corresponding entity.

2. For 13 utilities, every affected unit in 1995 received more allowances than the estimate of counterfactual emissions. Another 7 utilities had only a single affected unit, and therefore no opportunity to trade internally in the current year.

3. See Cason (1993), Cason (1995), Cason and Plott (1995) for the argument and Joskow et al. (1998) and Ellerman et al. (pp. 17–33) for the counter-argument.

4. See for instance, Myers and Custode (1995).

5. See for instance, Myers and Custode (1995).

6. See Ellerman et al., 1997, pp. 18–53 for a more extensive presentation of this argument.

7. The amount of retrofitted scrubber capacity, 13 GW^e, is less than initially predicted. Also, a number of respondents to the MIT/CEEPR survey of Phase I compliance cost indicated deferrals and cancellations as a result of lower allowance prices. See the footnote on p. 50 in Ellerman et al. (1997).

8. See Ellerman, Schmalensee, and Joskow (1997) for a more complete discussion of compliance in 1996.

9. This number is based on an extrapolation of the estimate in EPRI (1995) of 1.8 million allowances banked in each of 1995 and 1996, assuming a million fewer allowances per year for the last three years of Phase I.

10. See Bailey (1998) for evidence concerning effective arbitrage and Schennach (1998) for a discussion and illustration of the theory of banking.

Southern Company's BUBA Strategy in the SO_2 Allowance Market

GARY R. HART

Southern Company (Southern) is one of the largest electric utility holding companies in the United States. In 1997, Southern generated more than 160 million MWh of energy, 78 percent of this was with coal-fired generation. To meet these generation requirements, Southern spent over $2.1 billion to purchase approximately 58 million tons of coal in 1997 from sources throughout the United States.

As a result of the implementation of Title IV of the Clean Air Act Amendments of 1990, Southern had 28 of its 73 coal-fired units named as affected units under Phase I (1995 through 1999). This was the greatest number of "affected" units of any utility operating system in the United States. Using the substitution provisions of the Act, Southern chose also to bring into Phase I an additional 22 coal-fired units as substitution units. Under the Act, the EPA allocated to each affected unit the right to emit a limited number of tons of SO_2 for each year during Phase I. This annual right to emit a ton of SO_2 is known as an allowance. Southern had the largest EPA allocation of SO_2 allowances in the United States during Phase I.

When President Bush signed the Clean Air Act Amendments of 1990 on November 15th, 1990, the basic rules of the legislation had been available for some time. In our opinion, this bill was considered a "market-based" approach to environmental compliance and did not mandate any SO_2 control devices to be installed, but allowed utilities the flexibility to chose their least-cost option or options for compliance with the Act.

PHASE I COMPLIANCE

After running numerous compliance simulation models, the cost of inputs such as scrubbers (flue gas desulfurization), natural gas, low-sulfur coal (1%), NSPS coal (approximately .7%), high-sulfur coal, SO_2 allowance values and other control options were evaluated by Southern to determine the best least-cost strategy.

These simulations pointed to a least-cost strategy of *fuel switching* to a low sulfur or 1 percent sulfur coal during Phase I of the Act. A 1 percent sulfur coal at 1 lb./12,000 mmBtus emits SO_2 at a rate of approximately 1.67 lb./mmBtu. The cap established for each affected unit during Phase I was calculated using a 2.5 lb./mmBtu SO_2 emission rate (see Table 8.1 showing a sample calculation for Alabama Power Company's Gaston unit #5). Our plan was to procure a substantial supply of this low-sulfur coal for our affected units during Phase I while at the same time paying little or no premium for this 1 percent coal as opposed to a coal that emitted the 2.5 lb./mmBtu SO_2 rate. As an example, in the Gaston unit #5 calculation, the total annual tons emitted from using a lower sulfur 1 percent type coal were 33,819 tons of SO_2 for 1996 as compared to the EPA allocation of 59,840 using a 2.5 lb./mmBtu SO_2 rate. Hence this excess or differential of 26,021 tons (or SO_2 allowances) did not have to be returned to the EPA but instead could be sold, banked, or traded as we deemed most beneficial to the company.

Table 8.1   Phase I SO_2 Allowance Calculations, Alabama Power Company Gaston Unit #5

Type of Emission	1996 Emissions (Tons SO_2)
Actual SO_2 emissions (low-sulfur coal at 1.67 lb./mmBtu)	33,819
Allowance of SO_2 emissions* (cap at 2.5lb./mmBtu)	59,842
Surplus emissions (to be traded or banked)	26,021

* Based on 1985–87 average generation of 47,874,093 mmbtu multiplied by the Phase I allowed SO_2 rate of 2.5 lb./mmBtu.

This plan or strategy became known internally as the *BUBA Strategy* an acronym, which stands for *Bank, Use,* and *Buy Allowances.* Conceptually, we would buy and burn the lower sulfur 1 percent coal at our facilities during Phase I of the Act. This in turn would mean that we would emit lower levels of SO_2 than we were allowed (i.e., *overcomply*) and we could then "bank" the differential. This same procedure would take place for each year during Phase I and by the end of the 5-year period in Phase I Southern would have banked a substantial quantity of SO_2 allowances.

Phase II Compliance

During Phase II, Southern would continue its least-cost strategy and continue to procure the 1 percent type sulfur coal (1.67 lb./mmBtu SO_2 emission rate), even though the Phase II cap is calculated at a 1.2 lb./mmBtu SO_2 emission rate. The implication to Southern is that it will have to now "trade in" some of its banked Phase I allowances in order to be in compliance with the Title IV requirements. Our simulation model predicted that this bank should last well into Phase II before Southern depletes its allowance bank and is then confronted with the dilemma of either going into the market for additional allowances or spending large sums of capital dollars for the installation of scrubbers.

SO_2 Allowance Market

With many of the large utilities following a similar banking strategy during Phase I, the initial SO_2 market has been characterized by a relatively small number of players; a market that at times has lacked "depth" and has generated prices that are subject to some degree of manipulation by the actions of a small number of players. Also due to utility regulatory and tax disincentives, many of the large holders of allowances had to find other creative instruments to leverage their allowance holdings for future use in Phase II. Two major disincentives that kept most utilities from being aggressive players in the market are the tax treatment of allowance sales and the regulatory treatment of the net proceeds from such sales. Since allowances granted by the EPA are put on the books at a zero-dollar value, any sales are therefore fully taxable as capital gains. To compound matters further, in many cases the net proceeds from any allowance sales (after taxes) would flow directly through fuel adjustment clauses as a credit and thus provide near-term fuel cost savings to the electricity consumer with no affect on profits. The asset management problem for Southern or any other utility is whether to liquidate an asset now for $150 or hold it and use this same asset when it will be needed for compliance purposes in five years. At that future date the allowance would also command a value in excess of the prior $150 spot price.

In response to these disincentives, many utility allowance holders have turned to alternative instruments to grow their allowance banks (see Table 8.2). Using section 1031 of the tax code, many have turned to the 180-day loan as a vehicle to increase their allowance holdings. This vehicle has allowed utilities to "loan out" their excess holdings and put them in the hands of brokers, traders, and so on who in turn repay the utilities with interest but all in the form of allowances. Another successful instrument has been the use of a swap transaction. For those holding excess Phase I allowances but in need of a stream of Phase II allowances, many have taken advantage of the "vintage" aspect of the allowance trading program and have swapped a block of Phase I allowances for a stream of Phase II allowances. The returned stream of future allowances in total is greater than the block of Phase I allowances because of discounting and helps meet the needs of both parties.

Table 8.2 Unique Trading Instruments Developed in the SO_2 Allowance Market

---

180-day tax-free loans of SO_2 allowances that earn interest (permitted under section 1031 of the tax code).

Forward swaps of one vintage allowance for another.

Forward purchase agreements.

Swap of SO_2 allowances for coal.

Swap of SO_2 allowances for future CO_2 offset credits.

Table 8.3   Selected Institutions in the SO$_2$ Allowance Market

Environmental brokerage firms.

Nonprofit public interest groups.

Environmental desks of energy and trading at electric utilities.

Emissions Marketing Association.
  Independent nonprofit trade association (under section 501 (c) 6).
  Formed January 1997.
  Currently over 100 members both in the United States and abroad.
  Membership includes utilities consultants, independent power
  providers, regulators, environmentalists, and academics.

Additionally, many other typical financial type options have developed in this market as well as other unique opportunities to swap SO$_2$ allowances for coal or for future CO$_2$ offset credits. Many "environmental" brokerage firms or new "environmental desks" have been created as a result of this legislation as well as a new professional organization known as the Emissions Marketing Association to assist in the education and interaction of those active in this market (see Table 8.3).

SUMMARY

We believe that the market-based compliance concept utilizing emission credits or allowances has been successful due in large part to the EPA by allowing a free market to develop and function and by not placing restrictive caps on the amount of banking allowed or limits on the utilization of the bank. The EPA has acted as a type of clearinghouse for this system and through their annual auction and their compliance verification process has assured those participating in the market that the allowances that they buy, sell, or trade are valid and fungible. In summary, it has also allowed those being regulated to be creative and choose the least-cost compliance strategy for their specific situation.

Electric Industry Restructuring and the SO_2 Emissions Trading Program: A Look Ahead by Looking Back

KENNETH J. ROSE JR.

In the middle of the first phase of the first national venture into an emissions trading program, states have begun to explore electric generation retail competition. What impact will electric industry restructuring have on the SO_2 emissions trading program or any future trading program? To answer this question, we have to consider what happened just after passage of the Clean Air Act Amendments of 1990 (CAAA) and the nature of the changes that are occurring today in the electric supply industry.

Some of the same attributes that made the electric utility industry a suitable candidate for an emissions trading program also provided reasons for concern that it may not be the best industry to try first on such a large scale. On the favorable side, electric power production is highly concentrated in large power plants across the country. Also, since most of these plants are investor-owned utilities with customer rates and environmental constraints determined by federal and state regulators, a great deal of information has been collected on data essential for monitoring and enforcing emissions trading. These data include operating costs, costs of various pollution control technologies, fuel usage, and emissions.

Given this wealth of information and the concentrated nature of the industry, what could possibly be a problem? In a word—regulation is the problem. More specifically, the style of regulation that has been used for decades to determine the rates firms can charge their customers. This cost-based method of regulation involved the review of investment and operating costs incurred by the regulated company. If deemed appropriate, these costs are allowed to be passed through to customers along with a "fair" return on investment. The main weakness of such a system is that regulators, no matter how vigilant or careful, will never be able to acquire the same level of information about the firm's past and future cost management as the company has or can obtain, that is, not without incurring very high and unreasonable information costs. Because of this asymmetry of information, cost-regulated firms can pass along costs that a competitive firm could not.

The result is that cost-based regulation provided poor incentives to minimize investment and operation costs. Partly in an effort to shore-up the weakness of the process of rate setting, additional procedures and processes were added over the years. This was somewhat counterproductive and added to making the overall process cumbersome and litigious. As if all this was not bad enough, regulatory decisions are often tainted by political influence and the result is a system that can be arbitrary and at times easy to manipulate by the regulated companies themselves, as well as by others. Under these conditions, no one should be surprised when a price-regulated utility does not behave like a firm in a competitive market.

Given this, how effective would a market-based environmental program be when it is superimposed on an industry that is cost-based regulated? The answer is that suboptimal decisions should be expected by regulated firms when complying with the CAAA. The next question is: What was actually observed early on in the SO_2 trading program?

Before discussing what occurred, however, it should first be said that, despite the obstacles, there is little doubt that the trading program has successfully met two goals. First, emission targets have been met and exceeded. EPA reports that in 1997, SO_2 emissions from Phase I units were 23 percent below the allowable level and were below allowable levels in 1995 and 1996 as well (U.S. EPA, 1998). Second this has been done at a lower cost than if a command-and-control program had been used. The question that remains is: Did the affected utilities take full advantage of the opportunities that the new trading program presented? The answer to this last question is simply, no, they did not.

Ideally, it should be expected that a firm that is interested in minimizing its costs would integrate the price of allowances into its decision making process to determine a least-cost strategy. If the firm had compliance options with an expected marginal cost below the price of allowances, then those options should be undertaken. If this results in over compliance, then any excess allowances can be sold. Conversely, if further compliance is required to meet the requirements of the law, then allowances should be purchased, foregoing any other further compliance options that the firm had where the marginal cost was higher than the allowance price. At least, this is the way economists believe compliance should be integrated with the firm's decision-making process.

Given the lead time needed to prepare for Phase I of Title IV, most affected utilities had finalized their Phase I compliance plans by mid-1993. In this first stage of compliance, most affected utilities chose switching to lower sulfur coal or blending low-sulfur coal with higher sulfur coals. Allowances were used primarily by shifting them internally from other units within the same utility's operating system or within the holding company. Scrubbing, expected to be a common compliance option, was used far less than expected before the CAAA was passed. Significantly, only one Phase I affected utility purchased allowances in large numbers for compliance. Clearly, at this time, most utilities were choosing a self-sufficient compliance strategy and eschewing allowance purchases from others as a means of compliance. The result was that further cost saving opportunities that interutility trading offered were simply missed.

From anecdotal evidence of the time, two factors seem to help explain this self-sufficiency early in the program. First, it is clear that affected utilities did not consider allowance purchases as a compliance option in the same way other options that actually reduce emissions were considered. From early accounts (from compliance plans or "Integrated Resource Plans" filed with state utility commissions), allowance purchases was considered an inferior option if considered at all. From these filings, it can be seen that the purchase of allowances was rarely considered side-by-side with other more "established" compliance options such as fuel switching or scrubbing.

Examples include testimony before the U.S. House of Representatives in October of 1994 where a utility representative, when confronted with the fact that few utilities were using allowances for compliance, testified that it was his belief that to comply with the law it was his duty to reduce emissions, not buy allowances. In another instance, an executive from a Midwestern utility was heard to argue that it should be a policy of a state commission that a utility cannot hold too many allowances. Another Midwestern utility filed its plan with its utility commission, concluding in the plan that switching was believed to be the best option and stated, as an aside, that if allowance purchases were considered, it would be the lowest cost option. It did not elaborate on why allowance purchases were not chosen. Finally, when asked why a utility chose scrubbing (at a very high cost) over allowance purchases, the author was told by a staff member of the utility commission that regulated the utility that they (the commission staff) did not believe that enough allowances were available for purchase to bring the plant into compliance, despite the fact that such purchases had been made at another Phase I affected plant of a similar size.

Another factor that may explain sub-optimal decisions was political pressure to continue to use in-state coal. Several states passed laws to mandate or encourage continued use of in-state coal (two of these were later declared by a court to be unconstitutional). This clearly had an influence on several scrubbing decisions, but did not have much of an overall impact on the market.

Given the prevailing regulatory procedures at the time and from what some utility commissions stated in orders, it is not hard to see why fuel switching, when politically feasible, would be an attractive option to a utility. Most states at the time had in place (and many still have) "automatic fuel adjustment clauses" that allow higher fuel prices to be passed through to customers without the need for a detailed and time consuming rate case. All that is required is a filing and review by the utility commission. Also, in general, costs incurred to comply with federal environmental laws are usually allowed to be recovered from customers. As a result, any higher fuel costs that arise from switching to lower sulfur coal plus any additional incidental costs, such as fuel handling, had a reasonably high probability of being recovered.

Allowances, on the other hand, had no precedent and it was uncertain how they would be treated when cost recovery was sought. Utilities feared that if they purchased allowances and it turned out to be the wrong decision, say because the market price for allowances later fell below what they had paid, they would be subject to an unfavorable review by the utility commission. Conversely, if they made the correct decision in hindsight, it would not translate into any benefit to the company. Any savings would simply be passed through to their customers. In short, many companies could see only drawbacks from venturing into the allowance market and few, if any, benefits. This was likely a contributing factor to a thin allowance market in the early years and explains, at least in part, why allowance prices drifted lower through 1997.[1]

That, in sum, was the state of the world in the early 1990s on this issue. Then the industry and the way it has been regulated for 90 years began to change significantly. In late 1992, Congress passed and the President signed into law the Energy Policy Act of 1992. This was the first passage of federal legislation to begin the process of opening up wholesale electric markets (sales for resale to end-use customers and sales by utilities to other utilities) to competition. Shortly after, states began the process of considering retail competition (i.e., allowing end-use retail customers to choose their electric supplier). In 1996, the first four states passed restructuring legislation; these were New Hampshire, Rhode Island, California, and Pennsylvania. Since then, more than a dozen states have enacted legislation with the remaining states in various stages of movement toward legislation or consideration of restructuring. Federal legislation is also being discussed by Congress that would mandate retail access across the country.

The idea of allowing competition at both the wholesale and retail level has been discussed for many years as a theoretical possibility, however, the legislative and regulatory process necessary to make it a reality did not begin in earnest until the mid-1990s. This has had a profound affect on the industry. Utilities across the country, including those in states that have not yet passed legislation to opened up their retail electric markets to competition, are taking action to reduce their operating costs and increase their competitiveness.

This regulatory restructuring has resulted in considerable restructuring of the companies themselves as well. There have been numerous consolidations and mergers in the industry in the past few years with others pending approval and more, perhaps many more, expected in the near future. Also, either as a requirement of state regulatory restructuring or through voluntary action by the utility, generation assets are being spun-off into separate entities (either affiliated or not affiliated with the original utility) or sold to new owners. Thus far, over 30 thousand megawatts of generating capacity are currently in the process of changing to new owners in deals that exceed $12 billion. This means that many of the annual allocation of allowances are already being transferred to new owners either through mergers and acquisitions or from regulated utilities to unregulated (that is, not price regulated) non-utility generators through asset sales. This may only be the beginning of a process that may end with most allowances in the hands of generation owners that are no longer price-regulated.

It is too early to tell just how successful electric industry restructuring will be. It is not known at this time, for example, if market power will be a significant problem in the developing competitive generation markets. However, if restructuring has the intended result of encouraging price competition among power suppliers, then better cost control by electric suppliers should be the result. This should encourage more trading by generating companies and a more robust market for allowances. EPA reports that trading activity between "economically distinct" companies that are financially unrelated to each other has picked up considerably, with nearly 8 million allowances being transferred in 1997. This was more than the previous three years *combined*.[2] This may be a signal that self-sufficiency is no longer the guiding strategy that it was early on for affected companies. Not surprisingly, allowance prices are at the highest level since 1993, which should be expected with an increase in trading activity.

The increase in trading activity may be due to many other factors besides industry restructuring, such as more familiarity with the program by Phase I participants and the availability of better information from trade associations and market facilitators. An important factor is the imminent arrival of Phase II that will bring in more utilities and result in reduced allowances for Phase I utilities. It is safe to assume, however, that at least some of the increased activity is due to industry preparation for a competitive generation market.

What lessons can we draw from all this so far on the usefulness of trading programs? The good news is that trading mechanisms appear to be robust enough to allow substantial savings (over command-and-control mechanisms) to occur even when faced with less than ideal conditions. In addition, the national limit or cap on allowances and emissions ensures that environmental goals will be met or exceeded. This suggests that trading programs can be used in a variety of settings and be successful. Will the experiences of the early SO_2 program be repeated in other emission reduction/trading programs if applied to electric generation? It is probably unlikely that some of the early problems encountered with the SO_2 will be repeated in a future trading program since in many ways the electric utility industry of 1990, when the CAAA was passed, is simply fading from existence.

REFERENCES

U.S. Environmental Protection Agency. August 1998. *1997 Compliance Report, Acid Rain Program.* EPA-430-R-98-012. Washington, DC.

NOTES

1. The debate continues on the relative importance of this and other factors on the price of allowances. See Dallas Burtraw, "Appraisal of the SO_2 Cap-and-Trade Market" and A. Denny Ellerman, "From Autarkic to Market-Based Compliance: Learning from Our Mistakes," this volume.

2. EPA reported that the transfers of allowances between "economically distinct parties" was 0.9 million in 1994, 1.9 million in 1995, 4.4 million in 1996, and 7.9 million in 1997. U.S. Environmental Protection Agency, "Acid Rain Program Update No. 4, The Next Generation," EPA-430-R-98–006, May 1997.

PART FIVE

AN APPLICATION AT CENTER STAGE

THE PIONEERING REGIONAL
CAP-AND-TRADE MARKET TO
REDUCE URBAN SMOG

9

The RECLAIM Program (Los Angeles' Market-Based Emissions Reduction Program) at Three Years

James M. Lents

The Southern California Regional Clean Air Incentives Market (RECLAIM) program was the first market-based program designed to be applied to a diverse group of sources. This is a cap-and-trade program—an emissions cap is set for each facility for each year of the program, and facilities are required to meet their cap or trade emission credits with other facilities to increase their caps. The program was adopted in October 1993 with business and government support and some limited business and government opposition, and almost universal opposition from the local environmental community. During the adoption of the program, many issues were raised about the program by supporters and foes alike. Since there was no other pre-existing program of this type, the answers to many of the questions were not well defined at the time of adoption.

Actual program information is now available for the first three years of the program to help answer many of the early questions. On the one hand, the program has proved enforceable, companies did not abuse their initial allocations, trading has been active without emissions concentrating in certain areas of the Basin, and credit prices are well below what was predicted for this point in the program. On the other hand, environmental justice issues are being raised about the program, and the real emissions reductions expected to begin in 1997 are not expected until about 2000. Thus, some important questions about emissions trading in this market cannot be answered at this point in time.

Angered over delays in cleaning up the air in the Los Angeles region, air pollution activists in the Legislature in 1987 changed state law revamping the South Coast Air Quality Management District (California State Legislature AB2595, 1987). A new budget, a tough mandate for reducing pollution, and a new political structure for the governing board resulted. The accelerated effort continued into the 1990s, when the recession in the Basin led to rising unemployment and the falling of housing prices (Shirley and Meral, 1992, pp. 1–4). Concern was being voiced about the impact of ever-tighter air quality regulations on economic development in the South Coast Basin. New, more conservative legislators in Sacramento were proposing laws to slow down the air pollution control effort that had been steadily marching ahead.

In this atmosphere, the South Coast Air Quality Management District (SCAQMD) began a series of meetings in 1990 with a moderate, business-sponsored organization, Californians for Economic and Environmental Balance, to discuss an alternative, market-based air quality improvement program. This program would eliminate the traditional emission point regulations used almost universally in the United States and instead set an emissions cap and emissions reduction budget for a whole facility. Businesses would be free to reduce emissions anyway they wanted; and if successful beyond minimum requirements, they could sell their excess emission reduction credits to businesses that found it uneconomical to meet their emissions reduction targets. Two ground rules were agreed to at the initial meetings. One, the District would make the program as straightforward and usable by business as feasible; and two, business would support a program that met national clean air requirements.

By 1991, the Environmental Defense Fund was actively embracing the concept of market-based environmental improvement programs; although, it maintained no significant representation in Southern California. The feelings of other environmental groups were mixed. The Natural Resources Defense Council (NRDC), the local Coalition for Clean Air (CCA), and the American Lung Association (ALA) were willing to remain neutral and work on the concept (based on conversations with Mary Nichols of NRDC, Linda Waade of CCA, and Gladys Meade of ALA, 1990). The Citizens for a Better Environment (CBE) opposed the effort from the beginning (based on a conversation with Jim Jenal of CBE, 1990).

Some of the state and federal regulatory groups were slow to warm to the concept. The EPA Region IX office and the California Air Resources Board (CARB) questioned the need for such a program (based on conversations with David Howekamp of EPA Region IX and James Boyd of CARB, 1991). The Executive Secretary of the State and Territorial Air Pollution Programs and Association of Local Air Pollution Control Organizations (STAPPA/ALAPCO) was also initially cool to the idea (based on a conversation with Bill Becker, 1992).

In the end, the NRDC, CCA, ALA, and CBE opposed the program that was finally adopted[1] while the EPA and CARB supported it.[2] STAPPA/ALAPCO never took an official position.

The program as initially conceived was to include NO_x, SO_x, and VOC emissions. However, the issues surrounding VOC became contentious and complex. The key difficulty with business was the SCAQMD's proposed enforcement (i.e., monitoring) program (based on a conversation with Robert Wyman of the law firm Latham and Watkins, 1992). The proposed program called for bar-coded labels on every container that included VOCs.[3] Business contended that the proposed program was too invasive and expensive. EPA and CARB thought the proposed program was too weak to ensure enforcement (based on conversations with Howekamp and Boyd, 1992). Environmentalists were greatly concerned about the toxics aspect of VOCs (based on a conversation with Waade, 1992). Faced with attack from all sides, the SCAQMD postponed its consideration of VOC to a later date and moved ahead to address NO_x and SO_x. The combined NO_x and SO_x market-based program adopted for the Los Angeles region was designated as the Regional Clean Air Incentives Market (RECLAIM).

After adoption of the NO_x and SO_x market program, consideration of the VOC program was revived in 1994. This time 22 large and medium-sized businesses carried out a 90-day field test of the proposed enforcement program using bar-coded labels. The results were generally positive. However, the economic recovery in the region was now underway and companies worried that the VOC cap associated with the program would impede their growth. EPA also raised significant concerns over allowing any VOC trading between companies subject to the new federal air toxic regulations (Title III). Once again the effort was dropped in the fall of 1995 (based on a conversation with Pat Leyden, former director of stationary source programs for SCAQMD, in May 1998).

Credits in the RECLAIM program were allocated for a 12-month period in terms of pounds per year. The RECLAIM program did not allow banking of credits for several years into the future as some programs do. Future banking of credits was not allowed in order to ensure that allowed emissions in any given future year stayed in conformance with the State Implementation Plan (SIP) commitments. Subsequent to adoption of the RECLAIM program, the issue of future banking of credits has been discussed, but not implemented to date.

Facilities under different ownership were divided into two different annual cycles six months apart. The two groups are allowed to trade with one another, however. This division was created to provide for a six-month trading period between the two groups to help smooth out the trading process. If this had not been done, all credits associated with a single year would die simultaneously. It was feared that this abrupt loss of credits could result in panic on the part of facilities that needed credits and thus lead to large distortions in credit prices.

PROGRAM COMPONENTS AND
INITIAL CONCERNS

The RECLAIM program today is called a cap-and-trade program. As described earlier, it is based on a declining emissions cap for each facility, and facilities are allowed to buy credits to increase their emissions allowance or sell them if they are not needed.

Universe of Sources

The adopted program applies to all facilities that emit four or more tons of NO_x or SO_x per year with a few exceptions. Sewage treatment plants and landfills, for example, were excluded from the program. Some participants raised concerns about including sources as small as four tons per year in the program because there was a feeling that smaller sources might be unable to effectively participate in the program (SCAQMD, 1993a, p. 22 Comment 22). Concerns were also raised that larger businesses, to avoid control, might simply buy smaller businesses and close them down to get their emission credits (SCAQMD, 1993b, Appendix H, Letter #17, p. H-17-13). Others thought companies might want to enter the program at a later date, and provisions were made for sources to enter the program after the start (SCAQMD, 1993c, Rule 2001 (c)(1)(E)). As the RECLAIM program was initially designed, it included 390 facilities in the NO_x market and 65 facilities in the SO_x market (SCAQMD, 1993a, p. 2-4).

Allocation of Emissions

The allocation of emissions to the various RECLAIM sources was one of the most contested issues. Business representatives argued that recession impacted facilities should not be locked into their lower (1991–1992) production emissions (based on a conversation with Wyman, 1992). Some environmentalists argued, on the other hand, that to allow overall greater emissions than were actually occurring would be wrong and possibly illegal (SCAQMD, 1993b, Appendix H, Letter #16, p. H-16-1). In the end, businesses were allocated starting emissions based on their highest year of production in the most recent four years (1989–1992) with emissions calculated using existing rules and Reasonably Available Control Technology (RACT) requirements. Since all businesses will not operate at their peak production in any given year, the RECLAIM allocation procedure did over-allocate NO_x and SO_x emissions. Comparing allocated NO_x emissions with actual NO_x emissions from the same sources demonstrates that initial allocated emissions were 51 percent higher than actual 1994 emissions (SCAQMD, 1998, p. 3-3). This large discrepancy resulted from a combination of the use of multiple years and the ongoing recession.

Future year allocations were determined in an interesting and innovative manner. The local Air Quality Management Plan (AQMP) includes a general indication of expected emissions reductions from the proposed sources (SCAQMD, 1991, Appendix IV). Thus there was an established emissions amount that the RECLAIM sources, overall, were expected to conform to. However, there was not an established emissions reduction amount for individual facilities. Thus, a mechanism was needed to set ending emission allocations. If emissions were simply prorated off of their initial allocations, then some businesses that had moved ahead of others to add control early argued that they would have been penalized for doing the right thing (SCAQMD, 1993a, p. II-Z-28). In addition, some businesses that had been in a slump for more than three years, such as some members of the aerospace industry, argued that the initial allocation scheme was already unfair since it only looked back four years. They argued that corrections should be made in setting up final allocations to recognize this long-term problem (based on a conversation with Wyman, 1992).

The ultimate compromise devised for the ending points had four elements. The first element in determining a company's ending allocation was to identify the facilities highest production in the most recent six years before the start of the program (as opposed to the four years for the starting allocation). Then the facility's year 2000 emissions were calculated assuming the control measures defined in the 1991 AQMP were applied to the source operating at its peak production year. The use of these three elements unfortunately resulted in overall emissions greater than the AQMP attainment allocation.[4] Thus, element four of the process was to proportionally reduce each facilities emission allocations by 26 percent for NO_x and 14 percent for SO_x to achieve allocations in conformance with those set out in the AQMP.[5]

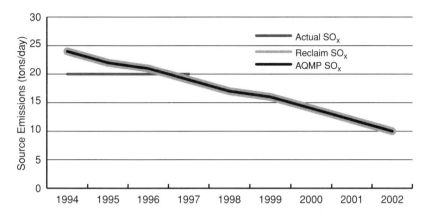

Figure 9.1a   Overall allocation of initial RECLAIM SO$_x$ emissions compared with AQMP target SO$_x$ emissions and actual SO$_x$ emissions from the sources in 1993. Note that the AQMP SO$_x$ and the RECLAIM SO$_x$ superimpose.

Interim year allocations were calculated by making a linear fit between the starting and ending points for each source. Some sources ended up with no reduction requirements while others had significant reductions (SCAQMD 1993a, p. I-B-2). Figures 9.1a and 9.1b illustrate the overall allocation scheme along with the

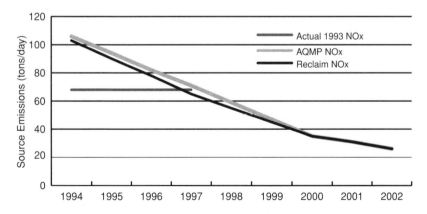

Figure 9.1b   Overall allocation of initial RECLAIM NO$_x$ emissions compared with AQMP target NO$_x$ emissions and actual NO$_x$ emissions from the sources in 1993.

1990 AQMP emissions reduction plan for the RECLAIM sources and actual 1993 emissions.

As can be seen in Figures 9.1a and 9.1b, there is a three-year period (1994–1997) where allocations were in excess of actual 1993 measured emissions. Environmentalists raised concerns that companies might actually increase emissions resulting in a worsening of air quality in the first few years of the program if this scheme were adopted (based on conversations with Waade and Jenal). Business arguments mainly revolved about disagreements over their individual allocations. In the adoption of the program, SCAQMD staff was directed to address some of the business allocation concerns as a follow-up to the rule adoption (SCAQMD, 1993d).

Tracking and Enforcement

In order to provide businesses as much flexibility as possible, emissions allocations were made on a facilitywide basis. This form of allocation made the tracking and enforcement of emissions difficult. A government inspector could not look at a single piece of equipment and determine whether that piece of equipment was in conformance with emissions allocations since another piece of equipment at that moment might be emitting under its allocation. In the traditional command-and-control regulatory format, inspectors enforce at the equipment level. There was considerable debate on how to properly address this issue. The SCAQMD wanted as much automated emissions monitoring as feasible so all emissions points could be tracked simultaneously. The industry raised concerns that the extensive monitoring requirements might increase operational costs to such a degree that command and control would be preferable (based on a conversation with Wyman, 1993). The compromise was a combination of automated emissions monitoring for large emission points and record keeping requirements for small emission points. An additional debate surrounded the need for stripchart recorders to backup the automated digital recorders in order to "enhance" enforcement. The SCAQMD's and EPA's lawyers insisted on this backup based on their concern about the potential for manipulating digital data and the value of stripchart data in court proceedings (conversation with Diana Love, SCAQMD chief prosecutor, 1993).

Trading

There was little debate on the trading format. The SCAQMD wanted this aspect of the program to stay in the private sector, and the other stakeholders agreed. In the adopted program, the SCAQMD does have to certify the validity of emissions credits being traded. The contentious issue was the timing of the certification. If the certification (approval) had to occur before a trade, businesses argued that the SCAQMD's review process might bog down, as the permit program often does, and this would hamper trading (based on a conversation with Wyman, 1993). The environmental community argued equally vociferously that there should be a stringent pre-approval process (based on a conversation with Waade, 1993). The program ultimately included a simplified notification process where the trading partners were required to inform the SCAQMD about a trade and how near-term credits were generated. No pre-approvals were required, but SCAQMD checks the accuracy of each trade between accounts before the trade is recorded. Errors have been detected in a few cases and were corrected before the trade was finalized (based on a conversation with Leyden, 1998).

Federal LAER and Offset Requirements

The RECLAIM program was required to conform to federal Lowest Achievable Emissions Rate (LAER) and offset requirements. EPA did determine that the federal offset requirements would not have to be met on a trade-by-trade basis, but LAER was required to be set and applied at the individual equipment level (based on a conversation with Ken Bigos, U.S. EPA, 1998). A different offset ruling would have likely made the program unworkable. The SCAQMD was required to demonstrate that overall, federal offset requirements were being met.

THE RECLAIM PROGRAM AT THREE YEARS

The actual universe of sources in the RECLAIM program has evolved over time. Table 9.1 illustrates the changes in participants in the program between 1994 and 1997. The number of facilities in RECLAIM has decreased by 16 percent since the start of the program. The prime reason for this decrease in the number of facilities is the determination that many had fewer emissions than originally thought or were found to be in an exempt category. Five percent of the decrease over the three years is due to facility shutdowns.

The facility shut-downs are of special interest since one of the initial concerns was that larger companies might buy up smaller companies and put them out of business to get their emissions credits. Twenty RECLAIM companies were shut down from 1994 to 1996. On an annual basis, this represents less than 2 percent of the RECLAIM facilities per year. This rate of shut-down is consistent with the normal SCAQMD shut-down rate for sources outside of RECLAIM (based on a conversation with Anopom Gangul, SCAQMD Engineering Manager, April 1998). The SCAQMD contacted persons representing nineteen of the twenty facilities that were shut down. The results of the contacts are presented in the three-year RECLAIM audit (SCAQMD, 1998, Appendix C). None of the shut-downs to date appear to be purchases by another company to get RECLAIM credits.

Sixteen facilities were added to the RECLAIM universe in the first three years. With the exception of four of the facilities, the additions were due to determinations that they met the criteria for inclusion and must be included. Four of the facilities,

Table 9.1   Universe of Sources for RECLAIM Program

Sources	At Start	1994	1995	1996	Total
Added	—	14	2	0	16
Excluded	—	55	6	0	61
Shut down	—	5	9	6	20
Net participants	392	346	335	329	

Source: SCAQMD, 1998, Table 1-1, p. 1-3.

however, opted into the program (SCAQMD, 1998, pp. 1-5 to 1-6). These latter four are of the most interest because of the voluntary nature of their participation. These four cited the administrative efficiency, flexibility, and potential value of the emissions credits as the reason for entering the program. The addition of only four facilities in three years does not indicate a landslide of interest by smaller emitters to get into the program. It would be of value to determine what aspect(s) of the program are keeping these facility owners from coming into the program at this time.

Allocation of Emissions and Actual Emissions

Table 9.2 shows the AQMP emissions goals along with total RECLAIM NO_x plus SO_x adjusted emissions. The present RECLAIM allocations are equal to the 1997 AQMP, but 9 percent above the approved 1994 AQMP. In the overall scheme of things, the adjusted allocations are within reasonable bounds of even the 1994 AQMP. Assuming no further significant increases to RECLAIM allocations, the program continues in line with the basin's clean-up plan.

As discussed earlier, the environmental community raised concerns that companies might increase emissions in the beginning since starting allocations exceeded actual emissions.

Table 9.2 Total RECLAIM Emissions Allocations Compared with AQMP Goals

| | Planned Emissions Allocations | | | | |
Year	1991 AQMP	1994 AQMP	1997 AQMP	Original Allocations	Adjusted Allocations
1994	130			128	137.8
2000	49	52	59.7	49	59.9
2003	36	39.7	43.2	36	43.1

Notes: Emission allocations are shown in average tons/day. Allocations were actually made in tons/year. The1994 AQMP is the only EPA-approved plan. Adjusted Allocations are net adjustments made as of the end of 1997. These allocations include ERCs that were converted to RECLAIM credits.
Source: SCAQMD, 1998, Table 3-1, p. 3-3.

Figure 9.2 illustrates the allocated emissions compared with the actual emissions for the first three years of the program.

There was not a wholesale increase in emissions from RECLAIM sources as some worried. There was a gradual rise in actual emissions. The SCAQMD indicated that 45 percent of the emissions rise is due to an artifact growing out of missing data requirements.[6] The economy was improving during this period of time and accounted for 8 percent of the increase (SCAQMD, 1998, pp. 3-13 and 3-14). The unaudited 1996 data shows a slight decrease compared to 1993. The SCAQMD suggested that this decrease could simply be better reporting with less missing data (SCAQMD, 1998, p. 3-3). It is clear from Figure 9.2 that the RECLAIM allocations are not yet starting to suppress NO_x and SO_x emissions in the South Coast Basin and, as a result, RECLAIM companies on the whole are not significantly reducing their NO_x and SO_x emissions.

A key goal of RECLAIM is to reduce emissions. Thus, the time when RECLAIM starts to force emissions reductions is important. As noted earlier, at the beginning of the program, it was thought that the actual forced emissions reduction would begin in 1996–1997 depending upon the size and form of economic growth in the region. Based on data collected by the SCAQMD for the three-year audit, the SCAQMD now projects

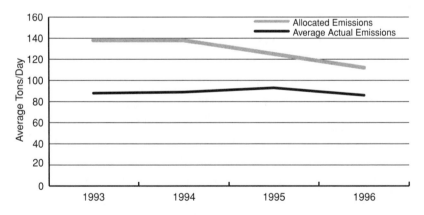

Figure 9.2   A comparison of the sum of actual NO_x and SO_x emissions with RECLAIM allocated emissions (*Source:* SCAQMD, 1998, Table 3-1, p. 3-3).

that emissions credit demand will start to exceed supply in 1999 for NO_x and 2001 for SO_x (SCAQMD, 1998, p. 3-6). This is much later than was originally anticipated when the program was adopted. Studies to date have not given a reason for this retarded emissions credit demand especially in light of the strong economic growth of the region in recent years.

Tracking and Enforcement in Practice

As would be expected, the major tracking and enforcement issues occurred early in the program with continuing improvement over the past three years. However, the overall quality of the emissions reporting system is not where it was expected to be at three years into the program. Table 9.3 indicates the status of continuous emissions monitors over the first three years of the program. The program has moved from having only 69 percent of monitors approved in late 1995 (two years into the program) to 93 percent approved by 1998 (four years into the program).

Getting approved monitors at major emission points, albeit two years later than planned, was an important achievement for developing an enforceable market-based program. A second important enforcement goal of the program was to get real-time emissions data reported to the SCAQMD for compliance analysis. It was originally hoped that computers at the SCAQMD could do "intelligent" analysis of the reported data suggesting locations where emissions violations might be developing and

Table 9.3   Status of Continuous Emissions Monitor Certifications for 1995–1998

CEM Status	Late 1995	Late 1996	January 1, 1998
Certified or provisionally approved	69%	86%	93%
Under variance	27%	6%	1%
Super-compliant	4%	5%	5%
Newly submitted	0%	3%	1%

Source: SCAQMD, 1998, Table 5-3, p. 5-19.

where inspections should be directed. Table 9.4 shows data transmitted to SCAQMD by RECLAIM monitors for similar time frames as Table 9.3.

As can be seen in Table 9.4, the electronic reporting program has a long way to go. Thirty to 80 percent of data that should be electronically reported is not reaching the SCAQMD. The most disconcerting aspect of Table 9.4 is the lack of progress over the three-year period. The late 1997 compliance data are little different to worse than the late 1995 data. In all fairness, it should be pointed out that the SCAQMD reported good compliance with actual emission caps which are the bottom line for the program (SCAQMD, 1998, p. 5-5). Thus the lack of electronically transmitted data is fortunately not translating into noncompliance with emission limits.

The debate about the need for stripchart recorders continued after their installation due to the large volume of paper that had to be dealt with. A bill was introduced in the state legislature to modify the stripchart requirements. The bill as adopted calls on the SCAQMD to "endeavor to provide sources the option to keep records by way of electronic or computer data storage systems" (California State Legislature 5B 2170, 1997). The Western States Petroleum Association (WSPA) and the SCAQMD will soon release a joint contract to look for alternates (conversation with John Higuchi, SCAQMD, 1998).

Trading

RECLAIM trading has been robust through the first three years of the program and exhibits the typical characteristics of a

Table 9.4   Compliance with Electronic Reporting Rules

Source	Late 1995	Late 1996	Late 1997
Large	76%	74%	68%
Major	48%	63%	62%
Process unit	30%	32%	20%

Source: SCAQMD, 1998, Fig. 5-3, p. 5-19.

market-based program. As of December 31, 1997, 1,200 trades had been accomplished involving 244,000 tons of NO_x and SO_x. This is an average of 203 tons per trade. The total dollar value of all of the trades is $42 million (SCAQMD, 1998, p. 4-3). Only 17 percent of the tons traded represented actual sales. The other 83 percent of trades represent no-cost trades between commonly owned facilities or no-cost trades between other facilities or brokers to achieve some other company purpose (SCAQMD, 1998, Fig. 4-1, p. 4-3). Figure 9.3 illustrates year-by-year trades from 1994 through 1997.

Referring to Figure 9.2, in 1995 facilities were allocated a total of 32 tons/day more than they needed. To get rid of these unwanted credits, a facility would have to trade away about 11,700 tons of emission credits. In reality, 60,800 tons were traded. Thus, there were 49,100 tons of emissions credits traded for some reason other than to simply get them off of company books. Similarly, in 1997, extrapolating from Figure 9.2, there should have been only about 5,000 tons of excess credits yet 54,300 tons were actually traded at no cost. Clearly, the holders of credits are finding it easy to move credits around and are acting to do so.

The trades for cost represent more valuable data for evaluating the market. Figures 9.4 and 9.5 illustrate the cost of different year credits as they sold in 1995, 1996, and 1997 along with the

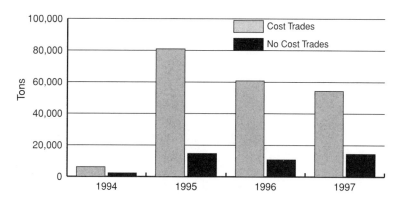

Figure 9.3 Total RECLAIM trades from 1994 through 1997 (*Source:* SCAQMD, 1998, Figures 4-2 and 4-3, p. 4-5).

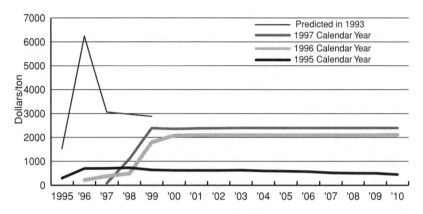

Figure 9.4   Actual and predicted trading price of RECLAIM
SO$_x$ credits during the first three years of the program
(*Source:* SCAQMD, 1998, Figure 4-5 and Table 4-3, p. 4-11).

originally projected price of credits in the 1993 socioeconomic
study.

The early peak in credit prices predicted in the original socioeconomic evaluation obviously did not occur. The long term
prediction of prices for SO$_x$ credits was in the ballpark, however.
The original economic evaluation predicted a long-term value
for SO$_x$ credits of $3,000 per ton. The actual trading value in the

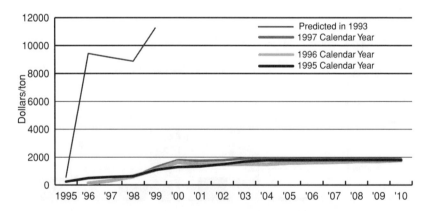

Figure 9.5   Actual and predicted trading price of RECLAIM NO$_x$
credits during the first three years of the program (*Source:*
SCAQMD, 1998, Figure 4-4 and Table 4-3, p. 4-11).

first three years was about $2,200 per ton if the first year sales are ignored. The difference between the predicted and actual credit prices for NO_x is large. The original evaluation predicted a long-term value for NO_x credits of more than $11,000 per ton. The actual price during the first three years is closer to $2,000 per ton.

The lower than expected NO_x prices could be due to several factors. There are likely continuing concerns about the viability of trading programs several years into the future. Will they continue to exist over the next decade? Will political concerns result in the addition of credits to the market if demand and thus prices increase? In addition to these confidence concerns, the actual cost of NO_x control in some instances has come down since 1993. Will control costs continue to decrease thus making credits less expensive? Whatever the reason, the availability of both NO_x and SO_x credits out to 2010 has exceeded demand during the first three years of the RECLAIM program keeping prices lower than anticipated.

The sales price of RECLAIM credits also clearly points out when the industry expects the credit supply to get tight. This is demonstrated by the sudden increase in the actual price of credits from 1998 to 1999. Thus, credit purchasers indicate through their purchases that they anticipate that the RECLAIM program credit surplus will not fully evaporate until 1999 or shortly thereafter. This is considerably later than was originally anticipated when the program was developed.

Federal LAER and Offset Requirements

In keeping with federal requirements, new sources and source expansions must apply Lowest Achievable Emissions Rate (LAER) in the South Coast Basin. The SCAQMD was allowed to demonstrate that the federally mandated 1.2:1 offset ratio was being achieved on the whole rather than on a case-by-case basis. The SCAQMD argues that it is meeting the federal offset mandate by demonstrating that actual emissions from RECLAIM sources, including new sources, are considerably under the 1994 emissions allocations at the beginning of the program.[7] The SCAQMD argues that the 1994 emissions represent potential to emit with RACT. Since the RECLAIM program is a closed universe with a total emissions cap where new sources must buy into the system, then in reality it ensures offset of emissions better than the open, command-and-control system. In fact, the SCAQMD demonstrates using 1994 as a baseline that an offset ratio between 37:1 and 168:1 is being achieved. EPA has accepted this argument to date (based on a conversation with Bigos, 1998).

Environmental Justice

One of the most difficult issues associated with market-based programs is distribution of emissions reductions. With command and control, specific pieces of equipment at specific locations are controlled. With RECLAIM, the market determines where the control will occur. This leaves citizens in the region of major sources sometimes feeling disadvantaged if the source opts to buy credits instead of control. An example of this occurred in association with a non-RECLAIM market-based program in the South Coast Basin. Union Oil of California (UNOCAL) decided to purchase mobile source credits based on car scrapping in lieu of adding vapor recovery at its petroleum shipping and receiving terminal. The net emissions reductions in the Basin from the proposed mobile source reductions exceeded the emissions reductions planned for the shipping terminal, but the reductions are spread out over the Basin. CBE has filed a civil rights complaint with the EPA asking them to disapprove the SCAQMD's car scrapping market program (EPA Hearing No. 10-R-977, 1997). They state in their complaint: "Rule 1610 allows industrial facilities in the Los Angeles air basin to avoid reducing their emissions, as would otherwise be required by the Clean Air Act, by obtaining emission credits for purchasing and destroying pre-1982 cars and trucks. Rule 1610's operation has had the effect of concentrating in communities of color pollution that was formerly widely dispersed across the District by mobile sources . . ." EPA has not ruled on this complaint. CBE has also filed suit directly against UNOCAL asking the court to block the use of automobile credits in lieu of control (based on a conversation with Peter Greenwald, SCAQMD counsel, May 1992).

The issue of the distribution of emissions reductions was raised by environmental groups during the development of

RECLAIM. The SCAQMD committed to track emissions assignments in the Basin to determine if significant emissions
imbalances occur. RECLAIM emissions are reported on a geographic basis in the Three-Year RECLAIM Audit report for each
quarter of the program to date (SCAQMD, 1998, Appendices J
and K, p. J-1 and K-1). There does not appear to be any long-
standing trend to indicate that emissions are accumulating in
certain sectors to this point in time. However, as pointed out before, the emissions reduction crunch has yet to begin. This question can be better answered at the next audit.

Technology Implementation

One of the goals of RECLAIM is to stimulate innovative control
options to reduce NO_x and SO_x emissions. Command-and-
control regulatory approaches with emission limitations established for specific pieces of equipment tend to drive businesses
toward certain predetermined control processes. The RECLAIM
program has no specific equipment requirements. Thus, a business can group and control equipment or processes as it chooses.
There is some anecdotal information that the RECLAIM approach is leading to innovation in the marketplace. The cost of
credits, already discussed, is potentially one indication that
businesses are reducing pollutants at a lower cost than achievable under command and control. Prior to RECLAIM the
SCAQMD was adopting rules that cost over $11,000 per ton of
NO_x.[8] Additional NO_x control regulations in the old system were
expected to have similar price tags. This is the reason for the
high price projections in Figure 9.5.

The best demonstrable example of innovation coming out of
the RECLAIM program comes from the Atlantic Richfield Company (ARCO) refinery in Carson, California (based on a conversation with Abe Johnson, refinery manager, ARCO Carson
Refinery, 1997). ARCO, in order to meet RECLAIM NO_x reduction mandates, directed plant engineers to search for inexpensive NO_x reduction options. It was found that the removal of
certain constituents from waste refinery fuels significantly reduced NO_x and SO_x emissions. The problem was what to do
with the leftover petroleum byproducts once removed. ARCO
determined that the leftover products could be used to make

polypropylene. ARCO has set up a polypropylene plant at its refinery and will supply much of Southern California's polypropylene needs. Thus, ARCO reduced emissions and found a way to increase profits with the flexibility allowed by the RECLAIM program.

RECLAIM is young and emission reduction demands are not yet significantly impacting the market. It will be easier to tell if significant innovation has been stimulated by RECLAIM in the next few years.

CONCLUSIONS

The first three years of the RECLAIM program have been a success. The market appears to be working well. Companies are adapting to the concept, and emissions are holding steady to slightly declining in a growing economy. There have clearly been a few problems as well. Electronic emissions reporting still needs considerable improvement, and credit prices need to be better understood.

The low credit prices could offer a great story or be a harbinger of a problem in the making. On the positive side, the low prices are consistent with the lack of demand for credits in the short term. As noted earlier, the demand for credits is staying well under supply even though the RECLAIM program is by design reducing the supply of credits. It is possible that the RECLAIM program is leading to innovative, low-cost emission reductions that are quietly reducing demand and keeping prices low. If this is true then the RECLAIM program is proving clearly to be the best regulatory way to achieve urban emissions reductions.

On the other hand, the low credit prices could represent a lack of confidence in the market since the low credit prices include low prices for post-2000 credits as well. Maybe more confidence needs to be developed in the long-term market to stimulate credit prices. It has been suggested that the low future credit prices result from the fact that most credits have been sold as a package or "stream" of present and future credits such that higher future credit prices are masked in the overall cost of the trade.

Low-cost credits are not a problem unless they are inappropriately low. Inappropriately low-credit prices will not stimulate the needed emissions control innovation to achieve future emissions reductions. If control options are not developed, shortages in credits will develop with attendant higher costs. Companies could not afford to expand, which would put considerable pressure on government to allow faux credits of some sort or to simply arbitrarily increase the supply.

Finally, the issue of the distribution of emissions reductions must also be dealt with. If a market-based system is to work up to its potential then there will have to be acceptance of some limited emission reduction inequities over a region. In some early cases, this acceptance has not occurred, at least in parts of the community.

REFERENCES

EPA Hearing No. 10-R-977 R9. Filed July, 1997. Citizens for a Better Environment vs. South Coast Air Quality Management District.

SCAQMD. October 1993a. "The Regional Clean Air Incentives Market, Final." Volume 1. Diamond Bar, CA.

SCAQMD. 1993b. "Socioeconomic and Environmental Assessments." Volume 3. Diamond Bar, CA.

SCAQMD. February 1993c. "Regulation XX, Regional Clean Air Incentives Market." Diamond Bar, CA.

SCAQMD. October 1993d. Directive from Board Chairman Hank Weeda to the Executive Officer James Lents.

SCAQMD. May 1998. "Program Three-Year Progress Report and Third Annual Audit."

Shirley, Jill, and Gerald H. Meral. August 1992. "Jobs and the Environment." Planning and Conservation League. Sacramento, CA.

South Coast Air Quality Management District (SCAQMD). July 1991. "Final: 1990 Air Quality Management Plan, South Coast Air Basin."

NOTES

1. Testimony of the Coalition for Clean Air presented by Dennis Zane, Executive Director, Diamond Bar, CA, October 15, 1993. Testimony of the Citizens for a Better Environment presented by Richard Toshiyuki Drury, Staff Attorney, Diamond Bar, CA, October 15, 1993.

2. Letter from Governor Pete Wilson to Mr. Henry Wedaa, Chairman of Board, SCAQMD, September 9, 1993. And testimony of the EPA presented by David Howekamp, Director of Air and Toxics Division, Diamond Bar, CA, October 15, 1993.

3. The bar codes on the label would be required to include a unique number for each individual can and information about the contents of the can. When a facility supply operation turned over a VOC-releasing product to a user at the facility, they would scan the bar code as is done in most retail outlets today. The bar code reader would store the container information in a facility database, which the SCAQMD could access. An inspector could check the bar coded number on any can in use for enforcement purposes and simply collect the information in the scanned database to calculate emissions.

4. Because different operations at a facility operate at different production rates in different years, a facilities "highest" production year was not always clearly defined. In the end, the SCAQMD allowed facilities to choose the year that they wanted designated as their highest production year. Facilities selected the production year that maximized their emissions cap.

5. The final "squeeze" amount was calculated by taking the year 2000 total allocation for all RECLAIM sources shown in Figure 9.1 and calculating the reduction percentage needed to reduce the allocation in year 2003 to the AQMP designated amount for the RECLAIM sources. This squeeze percentage was applied to each individual facility's year 2000 allocation to get its year 2003 allocation.

6. If a facility's emissions monitoring equipment fails to operate properly resulting in missing emissions data, the RECLAIM rule calls for the substitution of data that are biased high as a means of insuring that equipment is promptly fixed and that a facility definitely meets its emissions limitations.

7. As previously shown in Figures 9.1a and 9.1b, actual emissions were lower than allocated (allowed) emissions in 1994. The SCAQMD successfully argued to the U.S. EPA that due to the pre-RECLAIM regulatory program, the 1994 allocated (allowed) emissions met the national RACT requirements. Thus, by federal law, the 1994 allocated (allowed) emissions level would have been the starting point for a federal emissions offset program without RECLAIM. In the non-RECLAIM case, the SCAQMD would have only had to provide offsets for larger sources at a 1.2:1 ratio. Smaller sources would have been allowed into the system with no offset requirements. The likely impact then of continuing without a RECLAIM program would have resulted in permitted emissions in the Basin dropping only slightly from 1994 levels. In fact, if most of the growth had actually occurred within the smaller non-offset sources, emissions could have increased from 1994 using the federal offset program. With the RECLAIM caps in place emissions from all significant sources in the South Coast Basin significantly decreased. It would have required an offset ratio of 37:1 up to 168:1 in the non-RECLAIM federal offset program to have achieved the same emissions reduction results as RECLAIM.

8. The SCAQMD projected that the control cost to meet the electric utility rule, adopted in 1990 would be over $20,000 per ton. The industry predicted higher costs. The actual installed cost ended up being in the $14,000 per ton range due to improved technology following rule adoption.

Assessing Market Performance and Firm Trading Behavior in the NO_x RECLAIM Program

Thomas H. Klier[1]

In this section I complement this prior comprehensive overview of the RECLAIM program and its market activity through 1996 by presenting a closer look at market activities and firm trading behavior of the RECLAIM NO_x market.

WHAT TYPE OF TRANSACTIONS HAVE TAKEN PLACE?

First, I would like to examine more closely the number and types of trades observed to date.[2] In order to do that I suggest a distinction of three main categories of trades in the RECLAIM program (see Figure 9.6): (1) intercompany trades, (2) trades between RECLAIM and non-RECLAIM facilities, and (3) intracompany trades. Intercompany trades as well as trades between RECLAIM and non-RECLAIM facilities can be either individually negotiated or facilitated through a broker. Intracompany trades refer to transactions between facilities owned by one company as well as adjustments within a facility's bubble.

Table 9.5 reports a detailed list of transaction activity by type of trade for all vintages traded in the NO_x RECLAIM market through April 20, 1998. Twelve and one-tenth of one percent of the 1,155 transactions represent directly negotiated intercompany trades between two RECLAIM facilities; 19.4 percent of the transactions were trades between different facilities owned

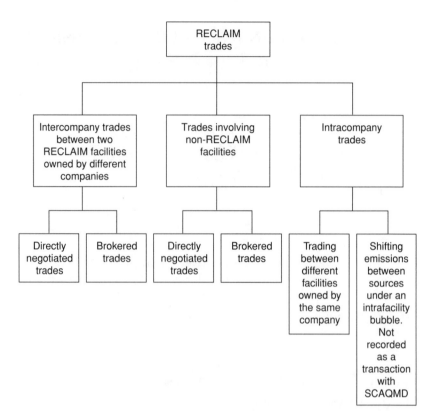

Figure 9.6   Types of RECLAIM trading activity.

by the same company. In addition to RECLAIM Trading Credits (RTCs) transactions posted by SCAQMD, many facilities have most likely engaged in intrafacility trading whereby they can shift emissions between sources within their facilitywide bubble; however, these transactions need not be recorded with the SCAQMD. A considerable amount of transactions have been through brokers. Table 9.5 identifies transactions with the two largest brokers; 40.5 percent of the 1,155 transactions listed have involved either Cantor Fitzgerald or the Pacific Stock Exchange as the seller or buyer.[3] These transactions represent mostly intercompany trades.

What can we learn from these numbers about market behavior? They speak to the importance of transaction costs. The secondary importance of directly negotiated intercompany

Table 9.5 All NO$_x$ Transaction Activity from January 1, 1994 to April 20, 1998: All Vintages

	Number of Transactions	%	Number of No-Price Transactions
Directly negotiated intercompany transactions.[a]	140	12.1	29[b]
Intracompany transactions: Trading between facilities owned by same company.[c]	224[d]	19.4	224
Brokered transactions with PSE of CF.[e]	468	40.5	257[f]
Other transactions.[g]	323	28.0	199
All transactions.	1,155	100.0	709

[a] Intercompany transactions represent non-brokered trades between two RECLAIM facilities that are not owned by the same parent company.

[b] Some of the no-price transactions that appear to be intercompany transactions may be interfacility transactions. Some facilities may be owned by the same parent company although their names are different. In addition, some no-price transactions between unrelated facilities may represent cases where RTCs were given to a facility as part of a package deal involving other environmental assets.

[c] Intracompany transactions are, by definition, transactions for which the seller and the buyer are two RECLAIM facilities with the same company name; no prices are recorded for these.

[d] There may be more than 224 intracompany transactions, see note *b*.

[e] These are the two largest brokerages: Pacific Stock Exchange and Cantor Fitzgerald.

[f] Broker as seller: 210 transactions at price > 0, 59 transactions at price = 0. Broker as buyer: 1 transaction at price > 0, 198 transactions at price = 0.

[g] Other transactions represent trades with facilities that were once but are no longer RECLAIM facilities, non-RECLAIM facilities who converted ERCs to RTCs and participate in the market, brokered trades with brokers other than Pacific Stock Exchange and Cantor Fitzgerald, trades between CF and PSE, changes of facility ownership, and other miscellaneous transactions. It also includes 5 transactions that took place prior to February 26, 1996 but were posted afterward and therefore couldn't be traced by the author.

Source: Compiled from SCAQMD RECLAIM Bulletin Board.

transactions is consistent with the high transaction costs generally attributed to this trading channel (Hahn and Hester, 1989). On the other hand, internal trading was a more attractive option. This type of trade is available at relatively low transaction costs. Finally, brokerage fees represent only a minor barrier toward entering the market. Accordingly, the majority of firms wanting to trade outside their firm's boundaries opted to enlist the services of a broker.

Table 9.6 breaks the first 51 months of transaction data into halves. We notice that brokers represent the dominant way to access the market in both time periods. In addition, other trades represent a considerably smaller share during the more recent time period, while intracompany transactions have increased. One can find evidence for a falling degree of uncertainty about the market and its rules by tracing the incidence of so-called reconciliation trades (see Table 9.7). RECLAIM allows facilities to reconcile their books for a period of 60 days after a certain vintage of RTCs has expired. While 65.6 percent of all transactions in the first period analyzed involved reconciliation trades, that percentage has since fallen to 39.6 percent. More specifically: among single-vintage trades, the percentage of reconciliation trades fell from 80.7 percent in the first period to 46.9 percent in

Table 9.6   All NO_x Transaction Activity from January 1, 1994 to April 20, 1998: All Vintages

	Percent of Transactions Jan. 1994–Feb. 1996	Percent of Transactions Feb. 1996–April 1998
Directly negotiated inter-company transactions.	10.3	13.5
Intracompany transactions: Trading between facilities owned by same company.	15.2	22.4
Brokered transactions with PSE or CF.	41.7	39.7
Other transactions.	32.9	24.4
Total transactions.	480.0	675.0

For notes see Table 9.5. As the number of RECLAIM facilities has changed since the inception of trading, the first 26 months of data for the first two categories of transactions correspond to 351 RECLAIM facilities (as measured February 26, 1996), while the second 25 months correspond to 329 RECLAIM facilities (as measured April 20, 1998).

Source: Compiled from SCAQMD RECLAIM Bulletin Board.

Table 9.7 The Incidence of NO$_x$ Reconciliation Transactions

	Jan. 1994– April 1998	Jan. 1994– Feb. 1996	Feb. 1996– April 1998
Multiple vintage transactions	353 (26.6)	149 (32.2)	204 (22.5)
Single vintage transactions	802 (60.8)	331 (80.7)	471 (46.9)
Total	1,155 (50.4)	480 (65.6)	675 (39.6)

A multiple vintage transaction is counted as a reconciliation transaction if it trades at least one vintage after its expiration date. Numbers in parentheses indicate percent of transactions that included reconciliation activity.
Source: Compiled from SCAQMD RECLAIM Bulletin Board.

the second. This demonstrates how facilities have been learning to use the market in a forward-looking manner.

PRICE TRENDS FOR NO$_x$ RTC

Table 9.5 also provides evidence for the prevalence of no-price transactions. Two main factors explain their incidence: (1) Because the staff at the SCAQMD need to know at any time who is holding RTCs, they require facilities intending to sell RTCs through a broker to transfer them to the broker's account. Once a buyer is found, the RTCs are transferred again, this time from the broker to the buyer. In turn, SCAQMD records a successful sale via broker as two transactions: one from seller to broker (usually recorded as a no-price transaction); and another from broker to buyer (usually recorded for a price). (2) If a company transfers RTCs from one of its facilities to another, it is always recorded as a no-price transaction.

What do we know about the prices RTCs have been trading for? Figure 9.7 indicates price trends as recorded in Cantor Fitzgerald auction data.[4] It shows the following: (1) the prices of RTCs are significantly lower than they were expected to be before RECLAIM began. (2) RTC prices are consistently increasing for later vintages. In addition, prices for specific vintages have been increasing over time. That is not surprising as the emissions cap is shrinking and marginal costs of control are rising over time. (3) Finally, Figure 9.7 shows transaction prices to remain low over the entire vintage range. Assuming the

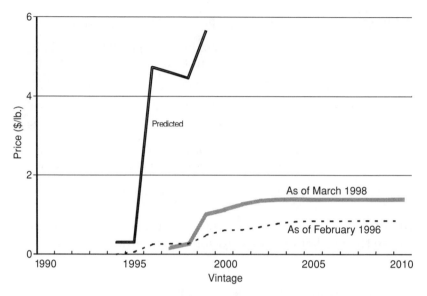

Figure 9.7   Price trends for NO_x RTC (*Source:* Cantor Fitzgerald auction data).

information on prices reflects marginal costs of controlling for NO_x, it seems that the additional flexibility in how to meet emission targets resulted in lower than expected control costs. This is similar to what has been observed in the SO_2 market (Burtraw, 1996).

VINTAGE-SPECIFIC TRADING ACTIVITY

Tables 9.5 and 9.6 analyzed the overall market activity in NO_x RTCs. However, as vintages can be traded well before their expiration date, there is merit in studying RTC vintage-specific trading information to complement the aggregate market data. Therefore, I present evidence on a subset of the overall market activity—analysis of RTCs that have already expired. This is done by way of a rolling time frame; I tabulate trades in cycle 1 and cycle 2 RTCs for 1995, 1996, and 1997 in turn (see Tables 9.8–9.10). That way one can compare market performance over time. Each table distinguishes categories of market participation by RECLAIM facilities based solely on the basis of a specific RTC

Table 9.8 Trading in NO$_x$ RTCs That Expired in 1995:
All RECLAIM Facilities

	Number of Facilities	% of Facilities	Pounds of NO$_x$ Sold	Pounds of NO$_x$ Bought
Sellers	73	20.8	10,586,780	
Buyers	67	19.1		3,634,693
Both buyers and sellers	28	8.0	33,658,926	26,375,631
No activity	183	52.1	—	—
Total	351[a]	100.0	44,245,706[b]	30,010,324[b]

[a] The number of RECLAIM facilities as of February 26, 1996.

[b] Quantities bought and sold are not equal as this table only represents the amount of RTCs traded by RECLAIM facilities and does not include RTCs bought or sold by other parties.

Source: Compiled from SCAQMD RECLAIM Bulletin Board.

vintage.[5] Facilities are counted as "no activity" if they neither bought nor sold RTCs of the vintage of interest. In turn, sellers (buyers; and sellers and buyers) refer to facilities who only sold (bought; or bought and sold) RTCs of that vintage. In addition, the tables report on the volume of RTCs traded.

Table 9.9 Trading in NO$_x$ RTCs That Expired in 1996:
All RECLAIM Facilities

	Number of Facilities	% of Facilities	Pounds of NO$_x$ Sold	Pounds of NO$_x$ Bought
Sellers	39	11.9	6,838,320	
Buyers	104	31.6		8,040,424
Both buyers and sellers	39	11.9	34,581,690	39,004,609
No activity	147	44.6	—	—
Total	329[a]	100.0	41,420,010[b]	47,045,033[b]

[a] The number of RECLAIM facilities as of April 20, 1998.

[b] Quantity bought and sold are not equal as this table only represents the amount of RTCs traded by RECLAIM facilities and does not include RTCs bought or sold by other parties.

Source: Compiled from SCAQMD RECLAIM Bulletin Board.

Table 9.10   Trading in NO_x RTCs That Expired in 1997: All RECLAIM Facilities

	Number of Facilities	% of Facilities	Pounds of NO_x Sold	Pounds of NO_x Bought
Sellers	43	13.1	5,673,973	
Buyers	95	28.9		6,736,957
Both buyers and sellers	37	11.2	32,429,462	40,138,646
No activity	154	46.8	—	—
Total	329[a]	100.0	38,103,435[b]	46,875,603[b]

[a] The number of RECLAIM facilities as of April 20, 1998.

[b] Quantity bought and sold are not equal as this table only represents the amount of RTCs traded by RECLAIM facilities and does not include RTCs bought or sold by other parties.

Source: Compiled from SCAQMD RECLAIM Bulletin Board.

Only for transactions in 1995 RTCs is there evidence of excess allowances: more pounds of NO_x were sold than bought by RECLAIM facilities. This trend turned around for both the 1996 and 1997 vintages. Furthermore, for the RTC vintages analyzed the percentage of RECLAIM facilities not participating ranges from 41 to 51. However, this tends to overstate nonparticipation, as it does not factor in possible activity in other vintages.[6]

Facility-Specific Evidence

Tables 9.11 and 9.12 provide information on facility-specific responses to the incentives provided by RECLAIM. Whenever RTCs are traded, the SCAQMD requires the parties to a transaction to report how the RTCs are going to be used as well as how they were generated. The two tables refine the classification system used by renaming and combining some of the categories to facilitate interpretation. Both tables show the percentage breakdown of code nominations for all transactions through April 20, 1998, as well as a comparison of the activity from January through February 26, 1996, and from then until April 20, 1998.

Table 9.11   Generation of RTCs sold from Januay 1, 1994 to
April 20, 1998: All Vintages

	Percent of Generation Codes		
	Jan. 1994– April 1998	Jan. 1994– Feb. 1996	Feb. 1996 April 199
Sold by third party, such as broker.	45.6	34.2	54.2
Process change resulting in lower emissions.	12.2	13.4	11.2
Use of new or additional equipment to reduce emissions.	5.5	9.5	2.5
Decrease in production.	24.1	32.2	18.1
Equipment of facility shutdown.	7.4	7.2	7.6
Conversion of ERCs to RTCs.	0.2	0.4	0.1
Facility acquisition.	4.2	2.3	5.5
Other.	0.8	0.8	0.7
Total	100.0	100.0	100.0

The percentages are based on code nominations per transaction and allow for multiple nominations per transaction or vintage, in the case of bundled trades. Due to rounding, the percentages may not total to 100.

Source: Compiled from SCAQMD RECLAIM Bulletin Board.

Let's start with the generation codes presented in Table 9.11. First, they show the large role intermediaries play in the market. In fact, the data in the table suggests that this role has gained importance over time. The second most frequent category overall is represented by a reduction in production at the facility level. That is noteworthy in particular, as the literature on emissions trading generally does not consider the adjustability of output levels. It is unclear, however, if the RECLAIM program led these facilities to decrease production or if the changes in output were a reaction to non-RECLAIM influences. In comparing the importance of a reduction in output across the two time periods, one can clearly see a significant cutback of that effect. The timing of that reduction coincides with the economy of Southern California picking up steam in the mid-1990s after going through a severe recession earlier in the

Table 9.12   Use of RTCs Bought from January 1, 1994 to April 20, 1998: All Vintages

	Percent of Use Codes		
	Jan. 1994– April 1998	Jan. 1994– Feb. 1996	Feb. 1996– April 1998
Meet annual compliance.	54.5	42.7	62.9
New source begins operation (within new or existing facility).	0.7	1.2	0.3
Third party, such as broker, is buying RTCs with intent to sell.	37.3	46.7	30.6
Environmental group, RECLAIM facility, or other intends to retire RTCs.	4.5	8.7	1.5
Facility acquisition.	3.0	0.6	4.7
Total	100.0	100.0	100.0

The percentages are based on code nominations per transaction and allow for multiple nominations per transaction or vintage, in the case of bundled trades. Due to rounding, the percentages may not total.
Source: Compiled from SCAQMD RECLAIM Bulletin Board.

decade. Finally, 12.2 percent of all generation code nominations represent facilities changing production processes and 5.5 percent using additional control equipment. The share of both of these generation activities has come down since the first 26 months of trading.

Table 9.12 reports on the uses of purchased RTCs. More than half of all use codes indicated RTCs were used to meet facility-specific annual compliance levels of NO_x emissions. In fact, the relative importance of that factor has been increasing substantially since the beginning of trading in RECLAIM. Second, brokers also have a large influence on the use side of RTCs, as they often acquire RTCs prior to selling them again.

CONCLUSION

Breaking out aggregate market behavior by type of trade as well as analyzing RTC vintage-specific trades has provided useful information to assess the performance of this environmental market. The data show that brokers play an important role in offering a relatively low-cost way of facilitating exchanges of RTCs.[7] While only a very small percentage of RECLAIM facilities has not participated at all in the market to date, breaking out activity in expired vintages shows that between 40 percent–50 percent of RECLAIM facilities remained on the sidelines in trading RTCs of a given vintage. It is important, however, not to overemphasize the actual market participation as a measure of success of RECLAIM, as transactions recorded by SCAQMD do not include adjustments within a facility's bubble. Yet these adjustments are responses to the flexibility in achieving compliance that is provided by RECLAIM. In comparing the first 26 with the second 25 months of market activity, I find the level of uncertainty in the market to have been reduced noticeably. The percentage of reconciliation trades has fallen substantially while overall trading activity has picked up. Looking ahead, a growing California economy in combination with a shrinking emissions cap for RECLAIM facilities are expected to further stimulate market activity.

REFERENCES

Dallas Burtraw. 1996. "The SO_2 Emissions Trading Program: Cost Savings without Allowance Trades." *Contemporary Economic Policy* 14 (April): 79–94.

Hahn, R.W. and G.L. Hester. 1989. "Where Did All the Markets Go? An Analysis of EPA's Emissions Trading Program." *The Yale Journal on Regulation* 6: 109–153.

Klier, Thomas, Richard Matoon, and Michael Prager, "A Mixed Bag: Assessment of Market Performance and Firm Trading Behavior in the NO_x RECLAIM Programme," *Journal of Environmental Planning and Manangement* 40(6) (1997): 751–774.

NOTES

1. Federal Reserve Bank of Chicago. The views presented are those of the author and not necessarily those of the Federal Reserve Bank of Chicago or the Federal Reserve System. The author would like to thank George Simler for excellent research assistance and Michael Prager for helpful comments.

2. The analysis includes data through April 20, 1998. This brief overview is an extension of: Klier, Thomas, Richard Mattoon, and Michael Prager, "A Mixed Bag: Assessment of Market Performance and Firm Trading Behavior in the NO_x

RECLAIM Programme," *Journal of Environmental Planning and Management* 40(6) (1997): 751–774.

3. Yet these numbers underestimate the role of brokers, as they also facilitate auctions and in doing so routinely execute trades through the auction, possibly holding transacted RTCs in custodial accounts until the buyer elects to take delivery.

4. Cantor Fitzgerald data are used since they represent true vintage-specific prices. SCAQMD's bulletin board includes prices that are averaged across vintages for some of the transactions representing RTCs of multiple vintages.

5. Of course, any of the facilities in Tables 9.7–9.9 could also have been trading RTCs of different vintages; in that sense, Tables 9.7–9.9 do not reflect the overall market activity of a specific facility.

6. Of the 329 facilities in RECLAIM as of April 1998, to date only 54 (16%) have *not* participated in the market *at all*.

7. See Klier et al. (1997), Endnote 27, page 771.

Environmental Justice: Time Boundaries and the Nature of Pollution Markets

KEVIN F. SNAPE

As we begin on the process of responding to the recent NO_x SIP call (11/07/97), most likely with the creation of 22 statewide pollution markets, there is much we can learn from the pioneering work done by Jim Lents and the RECLAIM market.

I would also like to preface my comments with three observations. First, The Clean Air Conservancy doesn't represent all environmental groups. The Conservancy was formed with the express task of finding market solutions to air pollution problems, and, as such, we often find ourselves outside the current mainstream of environmentalism. Our comments must be understood in that limited context.

Second, the SO_2 market has been a success by most fiscal measures and it shares a common trait with RECLAIM, they both have very forgiving compliance curves making them slow to dictate major shifts in polluter behavior. The compliance curves make the market politically palatable, but only at the cost of depressing the market price during the initial phase of each of these markets. The result being a slow pace of meaningful pollution reduction. While this delay in significant reductions may be vital to the long-term acceptance of the market, it ensures serious departures from an efficient market and as such needs acknowledgment.

Finally, the market is but one of a range of possible pollution reducing market tools; one with a relatively short history, meaning we have not yet emerged from the simple and inexpensive forms of "pollution substitution." Given that we have yet to watch this marketplace function within a set of "tight" constraints, it is premature to claim great success for any existing air pollution market. While the evidence to date has been impressive, we should temper our enthusiasm until these markets are fully tested. Moreover, there are a range of alternative market devices (green taxes for example) to be explored for efficacy in various phases of the pollution markets' life cycle. In other words, markets have proven effective for SO_2 in the early life of a market but there is no evidence yet that this is the most effective tool over the entire lifecycle of the market.

ENVIRONMENTAL JUSTICE AND MARKETS

If environmental justice is defined as a condition where one group disproportionately benefits from an economic function while some other group bears the disproportionate costs of that function, then SO_2, NO_x, and other forms of air pollution have historically qualified as unjust. For example, utilities in the Ohio Valley have reaped great benefit from the burning of low cost, high-sulfur coal while communities hundreds of miles downwind have borne the cost in terms of diminished human and environmental health outcomes while gaining none of the value associated with low electricity rates that accrue to coal burning states. I would argue that market-based pollution control systems encourage this type of benefit transfer.

The air pollution market is based on the principle of maximizing business flexibility as a means of achieving lowest possible cost compliance with a societal goal. The rationale for the market as a preference over regulation is to increase the likelihood of compliance with the pollution reduction targets by allowing business to decide how and when to comply. As a result, one of the strategies typically employed is to purchase allowances on the open market to meet annual compliance targets until the marginal cost of the allowance purchases exceeds the marginal cost of technology investment/process change needed to meet the emissions target. The end result of this "efficient" decision making is that two seemingly contradictory outcomes emerge.

First, by maximizing the range of compliance options available to business there will be a corresponding range of responses ranging from delayed pollution reduction to early over-compliance. Market incentives lead firms to choose those options, including trading, that minimize compliance costs. Society as a whole benefits from the increasing economic efficiency and the social benefit of decreasing air pollution levels.

Second, as firms exercise the increased flexibility in compliance there are trends toward an increase in inequality in short-term air pollution outcomes. In the case of firms exercising their rational choice to delay a capital intensive compliance strategy, their purchase of pollution allowances results in the downwind communities experiencing comparatively worse air pollution outcomes. While this strategy will only occasionally lead to worsening air quality in absolute terms, it will very likely lead to a growing disparity between the air quality between communities. In other words, the global air pollution outcomes can improve significantly while at the same time "hot spots" emerge in highly localized areas.

The question is not whether the inequality exists, it demonstrably does from even the most cursory reading of the SO_2 data. Instead, the question is whether the inequality matters as more than a theoretical issue. For example, in the case of NO_x reductions it is arguable that while NO_x is related to dramatic human and ecological health impacts, these impacts arise with NO_x as a precursor not as the active harmful agent. As a result, differential NO_x emissions, within the territory of a given market structure, would not seem particularly pernicious as NO_x emissions, in and of themselves, are fairly benign. The nature of the pollutant (toxic product versus precursor) then would constitute a clearly defining question as to whether or not this constituted an actionable justice question.

A second defining question could well be the nature of the exposure to the pollutant. Under what conditions will this pollutant interact with the impacted population? For example, in the RECLAIM market the population is living in an area that is dominated by an air inversion that traps pollutants for extended periods of time. Under these conditions, many firms can all be meeting their compliance levels, yet the overall effect can still be to exceed health safety thresholds. If a market encourages firms to comply with a "buy-and-burn" policy and it is located in areas that lead to increased long-term exposures, then we may also be moving into an environmental justice concern due to the potential of detrimental localized health impacts.

An additional concern over the nature of exposure deals with the nature of the compounds the population is exposed to. All federal and state regulatory standards are based on the assumption that there is a simple dose response curve relating exposure to a substance to impact on an organism. This makes sense as a theoretical approach for "pure" science but has questionable applications for the real world. As someone who lives in an intensely industrial area, I know I never breathe pure anything. Instead, I am continually inhaling a soup of industrial by-products that each may impact my health, an effect that might not be caught by the current regulatory approach. In addition to the individual impact, these various compounds interact with each other causing new compounds with their own separate health impacts that current models are incapable of dealing with. While this concern is often dismissed as unproven, it has never been adequately tested. Therefore, justice concerns require a knowledge of what constitutes the pollution mix.

From the discussion above, it seems clear that it is theoretically possible that market incentives can maintain and potentially intensify environmental justice concerns by differential speeds of air quality improvement within a market. A real world example of this can be seen in the proposed RECLAIM VOC market. In this market, a refinery took advantage of the flexibility available by removing VOC emissions from the air stream away from the refinery. They claimed, with some justification, that they were making legitimate reductions of VOCs in the airshed. However, the community around the refinery responded that the general airshed reduction merely exacerbated the difference between their continued poor air quality and the improvements seen in other neighborhoods, thus constituting an environmental justice concern. From their perspective, they felt that the broader community benefited from the product of the refinery, but the market system allowed the refinery to continue to pollute at a constant level by acquiring tradable credits. Pollution reduction benefits accrued to other areas. The community's interpretation is that they are being asked to bear a comparatively growing pollution disparity so that others can enjoy the economic benefits of low cost pollution reduction.

The most positive spin on all of this is that while justice concerns may emerge in a market setting, many of them will not constitute a sufficient threat to actually cause the emergence of the justice problem. Better still will be the realization that the root of the elimination of the inequality is inherent in the market. Not only is the market addressing marketwide low cost reductions, but also market forces are building that should lead to an eventual transition in behavior. That is, as pollution targets are tightened, the market will provide increasing fiscal pressure to engage in real pollution reductions. Given this type of behavior, education of communities that feel themselves aggrieved may be the most effective policy. By making sure that these communities are aware of the temporal limitations of market-based inequalities, they are less likely to object and more likely to perceive the benefits of rapid improvements in air quality inherent in the market system.

PART SIX

AN APPLICATION AT CENTER STAGE

VOLUNTARY DISCRETE EMISSION REDUCTIONS

10

Discrete Emission Reductions Trading

Joseph A. Belanger | Practical Application in the Connecticut
Regulatory Environment

The Clean Air Act Amendments of 1990 (CAAA'90) established new schedules by which states with air quality problems were expected to achieve attainment of the National Ambient Quality Standards (NAAQS). At that time, Connecticut was experiencing violations of several requirements of the NAAQS: namely, the particulate matter and carbon monoxide standards on a local basis in a few areas of the state, and the ozone standard on a statewide basis. The latter problem was the combined result of the highly urbanized nature of the state and its location just downwind of the Washington, DC–Pennsylvania–New Jersey–New York urban area.

It appeared that practical solutions to the particulate matter and carbon monoxide problems existed in the form of minor local controls and federally mandated activities, such as an enhanced inspection and maintenance for motor vehicles. The challenge was much more daunting with respect to the ozone problem. It was initially estimated that attainment of the standard would require limiting ozone precursor emissions, oxides of nitrogen (NO_x) and volatile organic compounds (VOCs), to something less than 50 percent of the 1990 level, both within the state and in the upwind area. Using cost-per-ton-removed estimates published by the U.S. Environmental Protection Agency (EPA) and others, the Connecticut Department of Environmental Protection staff estimated the cost of the controls necessary to achieve the target level of emissions at eight hundred million dollars per year.

Early discussions within a governor's cabinet subgroup established to guide policy decisions on clean air issues led to a conclusion that considerable efficiency could be achieved if market-based programs could be successfully implemented. Further, recognizing the regional nature of the problem, it was believed that regional programs of this nature could be even more beneficial. As a result, each new major component of the State Implementation Plan (SIP) was evaluated with the potential in mind for incorporation of a market-based approach, either as an add-on, or as a substitute for a traditional command-and-control mechanism. Initial consideration of other economic incentives such as fees and taxes came to the conclusion that such tools were politically unacceptable.

With this guidance, the Department concluded that cap-and-trade permits and tradable discrete emission reductions (DERs) were the best way to incorporate cost-effective market mechanisms into its programs. The former mechanism, the cap-and-trade concept requiring participation of emitters, is the basis for the regional NO_x control mechanism championed by the state and adopted by 12 of the 13 jurisdictions that comprise the Ozone Transport Commission. An alternative emissions-trading approach has recently been proposed by the EPA as a way to manage NO_x emissions from large sources across the northeast portion of the country. The incorporation of the latter mechanism, the DERs concept allowing for voluntary participation, into several aspects of Connecticut's emissions control program is the subject of this chapter.

The present scope of the program allows, on a voluntary basis, regulated sources of emissions of NO_x to use DERs emissions trading or averaging or a combination of the two as an alternative to the traditional technology or rate-based compliance, or to the use of tradable emission reduction credits, another voluntary program. In addition, the DERs program has provided for innovative responses to air quality threats of a temporary nature. Several of these are described in the case studies at the end of this chapter.

DERs: The Connecticut Design for Emissions Trading

In the next few sections, I will describe the major features of the DERs program and some of the considerations that went into the program's design. I will then turn to the program in action. DERs are emissions reductions generated over a discrete period of time and measured in tons by a valid quantification protocol. They may be distinguished from tradable emission reduction credits (ERCs) which require that the reduction be continuing or permanent. In contrast, tradable DERs are for a discrete amount of emission valid for a discrete amount of time. The motivation for this new program is to create a more flexible trading system and to simplify the complicated rules surrounding ERC trades that have limited their use. However, the Connecticut program does not go as far as the open-market system that places most of the responsibility for assuring the quality of the DERs on the buyer. The Connecticut plan requires demonstrations of this quality on the part of both the seller and buyer, as will be explained later. Both DERs and ERCs are to be distinguished from sulfur dioxide allowances and RECLAIM trading credits. One essential difference is that under the latter two programs, cap-and-trade market designs, emitters are required to participate and are allocated credits that they can trade or turn over to the government for emissions. In contrast, the former two programs provide for credits that are created voluntarily by emitters who can reduce emissions below the requirements or standards of traditional regulation.

DERs must meet most of the traditional EPA policy tests; they must be real, surplus, and verifiable quantitatively. They may be banked for sale or use at a later time within restrictions. Those created before May 1999 will expire between 1998 and 2001, depending on when they were created. Those created after May 1999 may be banked indefinitely providing the program is extended beyond the present horizon date of April 2003. DERs may not be generated by a shutdown or curtailment of activity.

DERs Demand-and-Supply Factors

The major opportunity to explore market options was found in the CAAA'90 requirements for states to implement Reasonably Available Control Technology (RACT) for stationary sources of NO_x and VOCs. Because stationary sources were the traditional sources and users of ERCs, it was only natural that they would be a focus of early efforts to integrate DERs into the state's regulatory programs. The Department's intention was to provide affected sources a cost-effective and flexible alternative mechanism for meeting environmental requirements. The existence of DERs has made the granting of "alternative emission limits," "exceptions," or "extensions" unnecessary. An analysis of the reasons sources could want to purchase DERs as an alternative to installing controls reveals the potential demand for these discrete tradable credits:

1. Emission rates sufficiently close to RACT limits may not justify the expense of additional controls (DERs constitute a "compliance assurance buffer");

2. Inefficient, outdated equipment that will be replaced within the next few years may make DERs a cost-effective option for achieving compliance during the interim;

3. Processes for which controls are not technically feasible or insufficiently developed, for example sludge incinerators, specialized manufacturing processes, etc. may make DERs an attractive alternative;

4. Business circumstances temporarily limiting funds for control equipment may make DERs cost-effective during that period;

5. Delays in installation of control equipment either for scheduling efficiency or equipment supply reasons may create a demand for DERs;

6. Expected business closings or relocation making for a short life of existing control equipment and/or infrequent use of that equipment may make the use of DERs attractive.

On the supply side, an advantage of the DERs mechanism is the incentive it provides to sources to reduce their emissions below the limits that are established under traditional command-and-control regulatory programs. The widely varying marginal control costs among NO_x emitters, and among the industries in which they are located, and the possible innovations in control that could be stimulated, indicate the potential in this regard for substantial cost-savings.

Early in the planning process, the Department chose not to limit the region from which DERs could be obtained. The possibility of trading with other states whose emissions affected Connecticut's air quality had been under discussion for some time. Interstate trading in traditional NO_x ERCs for use in meeting offset requirements and in NO_x allowances under the Ozone Transport Commission (OTC) NO_x budget program were well-developed concepts. However, the Department's initial approach to the use of out of state DERs was conservative. Interstate trades would only be allowed if they met several conditions with respect to seasonality and directionality (for example, sale to downwind locations being prohibited). To date, routine trades have been limited to tradable credits created in New Jersey. A recently approved trade that involved Michigan and Ontario, Canada was accomplished under special circumstances.

DERs Market Rules

The Department approves each tradable credit through the use of a trading order. Trading orders indicating all terms of tradable credit use must be obtained before sources can use this compliance option. For example, those created during ozone-season months (May through September) may be used at any time, but those created during the non-ozone season may not be used during the ozone season. In utilizing DERs, the buyer may only use them at a rate that approximates the rate at which they were created.

The program baseline begins with the Connecticut 1990 base-year ozone emission inventory. This inventory is the aggregate benchmark against which emission reductions are measured by the state. It serves as the starting point for the evaluation of potential control strategies, such as DERs, in meeting the state's clean air attainment goals. The data also become an important element in preparing the computation for a tradable credit. The upper bound is the full-load emission rate (FLER) which is approved for each source and then incorporated into the trading order as an enforceable limit that must not be exceeded. This full-load emission rate is a potential maximum and not the rate set by RACT. Emitters wishing to make use of DERs may acquire and utilize them up to the difference between the FLER and 95 percent of the traditional RACT regulated rate. This 5 percent adjustment is designed to reflect the average level of actual emissions under "not to exceed" regulations.

Another aspect of the program was the combining of DERs with the "averaging" or bubbling regulation already in effect. For the facility with two or more units that generate emissions, an averaging cap is based on the sum, or bubble, of historic (1990) emissions from all units in the averaging set. To allow greater utilization and hence cost-saving advantages in situations where such use would be otherwise constrained by the averaging cap, the facility may use DERs to offset emissions above the cap. Various discounts are applied to assure environmental benefits when these options are chosen.

Enforcement and Monitoring

Fulfillment of the requirements of the trading order are subject to the same enforcement procedures and civil or criminal penalties as other environmental activities subject to regulation. The creator and user are responsible for meeting the terms specified in their trading orders. Compliance is determined based on operating, fuel consumption, and emissions data. Information filed in March of each year regarding DERs use is reviewed by enforcement staff. Calculations are verified and prior ownership is checked. During routine field inspection, fuel records and tradable credit ownership may be checked. Sources were allowed to develop their own record keeping system, making agency review somewhat more difficult.

The open-market approach to the creation of DERs (less up-front Department review of case-by-case transactions) has been advocated by some to reduce administrative time and cost. One such transaction was tried during this period. It did result in a reduction of up-front administrative time and cost for the Department but, because the source relied on an incorrect measure of allowable emissions, the source was later found to be out of compliance. This resulted in significant additional costs to the source and work for the Department. Almost unanimously, sources prefer to have the certainty of pre-approved DERs.

THE DERs PROGRAM IN ACTION

I now turn to a description of the major features of the development of the program. Approximately one-third of regulated major stationary NO_x sources in Connecticut chose a DERs market-based approach to NO_x compliance. DERs, including some created through early implementation of RACT requirements, are also presently being used for the purpose of compliance and for new source review "offsets." Overall, the DERs used represent about 5 percent of the state's point source emissions for the period 1995 through 1997.

The supply of credits generated by creators has totaled 15,778 tons of NO_x approved for use in Connecticut since the inception of the program in 1995 through 1997. The demand for DERs, 3,820, has been much less. Ten percent of DERs have been retired upon creation to assure a net benefit to the environment. Prices have ranged between $750 to $850 per ton.

The demand for DERs has been extended to nontraditional budget and mobile source applications as will be revealed in the case studies at the close of this report. Attempts by mobile and area sources to create credits appear promising, but have yet to bear fruit. Efforts are underway to streamline the program and to integrate it with other programs such as the U.S. EPA NO_x Trading Rule.

Initial Program Development

Late in 1992, the Department began the development of trading regulations based on the EPA's 1986 emissions trading policy. An attempt was made to deal with both traditional ERCs to meet new source offset needs, and DERs for limited application as compliance options. By early 1994, the proposed rule had been through several iterations of revision and review by the Department's Regulation Revision Advisory Committee. The proposal was still considered to be unworkable.

The number of complex issues, seemingly contradictory EPA policy and guidance, and internal promulgation timelines slowed the process considerably. The Department decided that the air toxics issues surrounding VOC trading and the limited immediate interest in VOC trading warranted a focus on NO_x applications, thus simplifying the process. To increase the chances that this NO_x option would become operable, it was decided that each trade would be treated as a single source State Implementation Plan (SIP) revision.

The decision to go the individual SIP route was announced as a "bad news/good news" situation. It assured sources that a market compliance option was available, but compliance through a single source SIP was considered to involve considerably more administrative effort by both the buyer and seller and the Department. In retrospect it turned out to be mostly good news, especially for the sources involved. On the other hand, the case-by-case approach did create a significant workload for the Department's administrative enforcement staff. It created a requirement for the negotiation and preparation of orders and SIP revisions for the more than one-third of the sources that participated in trading and were subject to the RACT rule emission limitation. However, the trading order process did have many benefits that were not originally contemplated. The process of negotiating orders with individual sources provided a degree of flexibility that could never have been achieved under a generic trading rule. It allowed sources to pursue internal emission reductions in whatever manner and to whatever extent deemed practical and to then meet any remaining responsibilities through the use of DERs.

Legal implementation of this approach was accomplished by adding a very simple provision to the Department's rule allowing any source the opportunity to use a trading order with the Department as a substitute means of meeting the emission reduction responsibility otherwise required. Each trading order contains all of the details pertaining to the creation or use of credits—measurement, record keeping, reporting, and so on, that would otherwise be contained in a trading regulation. Under EPA guidelines, the trading orders were a required part of the SIP for each source. The rule did not require a demonstration of the technological or economic infeasibility of traditional controls. In fact, because the trading option was presented as a first order option, some of the usual provisions allowing for exemptions based on economic impracticality were excised from the final rule.

The case-by-case approach left the details with respect to credit creation and use such as eligibility, quantification, reporting and tracking, transfer mechanisms, and auditing to the trading order process and to the traders, subject to government approval. Credit creators, unlike credit users, were generally, larger, sophisticated entities capable of accomplishing most of the analysis and documentation necessary for the trading orders and SIP revisions that were required. Individual creations also tended to occur in larger volumes and at far fewer sources than did individual uses. Thus, much less departmental effort was required on the creation side.

To repeat, the present scope of this program allows regulated sources of emissions of NO_x to use DERs trading or averaging or a combination of the two as an alternative to the technology based compliance traditionally expected under a NO_x RACT regulation. A total of 37 single-source revisions to the SIP, together with the required completion of the Economic Incentive Program (EIA) and the accompanying trading orders, have been implemented. After being subjected to public hearings, they have been submitted to the EPA. Tables 10.1 and 10.2 present information on specific emitters and the DERs supplied or purchased during the period 1995 through 1997.

Monitoring, Record Keeping, and Reporting

For the purposes of DERs use, the majority of buyers are relatively small, calculate emissions based on fuel usage. For

Table 10.1   Supply of DERs Approved for Use (1995–1997)

Company Name (and Control Options Chosen to Create DERs)	Tons Created
United Illuminating Company (low-NO_x, Pre-RACT)	2941.0
Public Service Gas and Electric Utility (PSG&E-New Jersey) (Pre-RACT)	6425.0
United Illuminating Company (low-NO_x system, Pre- and Post-RACT)	754.0
United Illuminating Company (Bridgeport 3, Low-NO_x system, Pre- and Post-RACT)	1216.0
United Illuminating Company (Bridgeport 3, Low-NO_x system, Pre- and Post-RACT)	122.0
United Illuminating Company (Bridgeport 3, Low-NO_x system, Pre- and Post-RACT)	1049.0
United Illuminating Company (Bridgeport 3, Low-NO_x system, Pre- and Post-RACT)	394.0
Algonquin Gas Transmission Company (30 TPY offsets or discrete credits. Order No. 8123)	88.7
Connecticut Resource Recovery Authority (SNCR and combustion modifications)	211.5
Connecticut Resource Recovery Authority (SNCR and combustion modifications)	59.0
PSG&E-New Jersey (Hudson #2 1994)	1412.0
PSG&E-New Jersey (Hudson #1 1994)	136.0
Ogden Martin Systems of Bristol, Inc. (Post-RACT overcompliance (SNCR))	67.0
Ontario Hydro Services Company (Low-NO_x burners 1995–96. Limited approved uses)	538.0
Detroit Edison Company (Low NO_x burners Monroe Power Plan. Limited approved uses)	365.0
Total DERs approved	15,778.2

Table 10.2   Connecticut Sources Using Approved NO$_x$ DERs and/or Averaging

Source Buying: Company Name (and Emission Unit or Technology Using DERs)	1995[a] (tons)	1996[b] (tons)	1997[c] (tons)	Source Supplying
Anchor Glass Container Corp. (glass furnace)			1.0	NA
Allied Signal, Inc. (averaging plus DERs at 3 boilers)		7.0		United Illuminating Company (averaging plus DERs)
American Ref-Fuel Company (fuel resource recovery facility)	51.5	72.0	40.5	PSG&E-New Jersey
Bridgeport Resco (resource recovery facility)	104.4	177.9	199.0	PSG&E-New Jersey
Bridgeport Hospital		5.0	0.0	United Illuminating Company
Bridgeport Hydraulic Company (BHC) (water utility)		0.0	0.6	United Illuminating Company
Connecticut Natural Gas Corporation (using averaging plus DERs)		0.2		PSG&E-New Jersey (averaging plus DERs)
Connecticut Light and Power Co. (20 peaking turbines and diesels)		650.0 (peak)	28.3 783.0 (peak)	PSG&E-New Jersey plus own DERs (260)
Connecticut Light and Power Co. (offsets, summer emergency operations 1996)		432.0		PSG&E-New Jersey and United Illuminating Company
Connecticut Light and Power Co. (auxiliary boiler)	3.5			PSG&E-New Jersey
Connecticut Light and Power Co. (auxiliary boiler)	1.2	3.7	7.7	PSG&E-New Jersey
State of Connecticut (three hospitals)	38.5	10.7	10.5	United Illuminating Company
Cytec Industries, Inc. (averaging, boilers, incinerator, furnace, dryer)		12.4	0.23	PSG&E-New Jersey
International Paper Company (boilers)	56.4	143.1	91.0	United Illuminating Company
FIDCO, Inc. (2-month delay)	2.0			PSG&E-New Jersey
Electric Boat (Division of General Dynamics Corp.) (delayed compliance, eight boilers)	9.0	14.4	0.88	United Illuminating Company
Mohegan Tribe of Indians of CT (offsets of VOC and NO$_x$ from vehicle activity at casino)		120.0	435.2	PSG&E-New Jersey (no VOC DERs available)
So. Norwalk Elec. Works (6 diesel peaking generators)	0.76	1.2	3.9	PSG&E-New Jersey
City of Norwich DPU (peaking turbine)	2.9	0.2		PSG&E-New Jersey
Pfizer, Inc. (6 boilers)	146.9	135.2	23.0	PSG&E-New Jersey

(continued)

Table 10.2   *(Continued)*

Source Buying: Company Name (and Emission Unit or Technology Using DERs)	1995[a] (tons)	1996[b] (tons)	1997[c] (tons)	Source Supplying
Sikorsky Aircraft Corp. (5 boilers)	2.0	4.4	4.8	United Illuminating Company
Simkins (boiler)		7.0		United Illuminating Company plus averaging
Stone Container Corp. (creation and use for boiler)		15.6	0.0	Own DERs
United Illuminating Company (auxiliary boiler)	0.0	0.7	0.15	Own DERs
United Illuminating Company (peaking turbine)	1.2	0.6	0.7	Own DERs
United Technologies Corp. (NSR offsets and RACT Compliance)		69.2	32.4 128.0 (offsets)	United Illuminating Company
United Technologies Corp. (Hamilton Standard) (boilers)	7.4	18.8	20.8	PSG&E-New Jersey
U.S. Naval Submarine Base (peaking diesel)		2.3	3.0	PSG&E-New Jersey
University of Conn. (boilers)		6.5	13.4	NA
Uniroyal Chemical Company (boiler)	4.8	11.7		United Illuminating Company
Wallingford Electric Division (2 peaking boilers)	3.0	1.8	1.4	NA
Yale University (19 boilers, plus DERs)	17.8	19.3	15.6	United Illuminating Company (averaging plus DERs)
Total (tons per year – TPY)	453.26	1942.9	1845.06	

[a] As reported with emission statement March 1996.
[b] As reported with emission statement March 1997.
[c] As reported with emission statement March 1998.

accounting and record-keeping purposes, fuel consumption is determined as accurately as possible, ranging from estimates using hours of operation at maximum firing rate to hourly fuel records. Daily accounting is required of sources using DERs for compliance. The source must always own a stock of unused DERs sufficient to cover the following day's excess emissions. Compliance is audited through normal state reporting and field inspection procedures. This includes emission measurements and inspection of fuel and trading records and reports to ascertain that sufficient quantities of approved DERs were in the user's possession to meet the conditions of the trading order.

Information from these filings on DERs use has been compiled, and each source's information has been reviewed. In general, the quality of this reporting has been good. Initially several sources experienced uncertainty about the methodology for calculating their emission responsibility or were confused about the use of actual data rather than estimates. These problems have generally disappeared in later reporting cycles.

Integration with Other Programs

Following a public hearing, the Department has notified the affected community that it intends to continue the program through May 2003. Sources may cease using DERs at any time if they adopt other strategies that result in compliance with applicable emission limitations. The Department intends to bridge trading with the NO_x budget program for utility and large boilers. The NO_x budget program utilizes a NO_x allowance approach similar to the cap-and-trade sulfur allowance (Acid Rain) program. In this budget program, each allowance authorizes the emission of one ton of NO_x during the ozone season. These allowances are bankable and are tradable throughout the Northeast Ozone Transport Region. However, until difficult questions about substituting DERs for NO_x allowances can be resolved, NO_x allowances will be usable in place of DERs, but not vice versa.

Administrative Procedures and Cost

Implementation of the program took approximately two full years and an estimated five to six person years of Department professional staff effort as well as additional senior management involvement and legal support. Assistance was provided by the New England States for Coordinated Air Use Management/Mid-Atlantic Region Air Management Association (NESCAUM/MARAMA) Emissions Trading Demonstration Project staff and participants. Regulated sources provided considerable technical assistance with the preparation of their SIP revisions and trading orders. As experience with these approaches improved and cases were replicated, the time required has dropped dramatically. It should also be recognized that without the trading program, a considerable portion of the above-noted effort would have been required to negotiate and find acceptable solutions for sources unable to comply on time through traditional means.

The case-by-case approach, as compared to trades that might have been accomplished under a detailed trading regulation such as a cap-and-trade approach, required considerably more staff and management effort on initial cases. On the other hand, the lack of a trading rule provided important types of flexibility. It is unclear, to us, whether overall administrative time and cost would have decreased with a trading rule or another approach to implementation. It is time-consuming to prepare highly specific orders and SIPs for each DERs creation and use, but this served an important function in the early stages of the program by allowing a better understanding of the process and goals by everyone.

Having the experience of the case-by-case approach, the Department is now including self-implementing DERs trading mechanisms in new regulations such as the recently proposed rule requiring NO_x emission reductions from municipal waste combustors. It is also working on rules that will move creation of DERs and ERCs from a case-by-case basis to a generic process.

Banking and Intertemporal Trading Concerns

These concerns about harmful peaking of tradable credit use at the time of highest ozone readings may be allayed by beneficial seasonal shifting of emissions (DERs created in the summer and used in the winter), the minimum 10 percent retirement of DERs upon their creation, and the excess of credits created over those used. There may also be a net environmental benefit from removing pollutants from the air at a time when emissions were at higher levels. Information collected for the initial two years of the program (1995 and 1996) indicates that DERs creation far exceeded their use. One creation source alone (United Illuminating Company, Bridgeport 3 Facility) generated more DERs than all 27 buyers used during the first year. Therefore, the benefits for cleaner air are apparent. Data for 1997 is in the process of final collection and analysis. A review of the preliminary data seems to indicate the same pattern still exists. The retirement of "peak DERs" are an additional benefit to the environment.

CONCLUSIONS AND THE FUTURE

The Department is in the process of final adoption of the NO_x budget or cap-and-trade program developed by the Ozone Transport Commission. This regulation will cover many sources now using and/or creating DERs. As a result, beginning in 1999, some of these sources are likely to find it impractical to create ozone-season DERs and will move to the budget program. The response of other potential creators is uncertain given the thinness of the remaining market. There is an opt-in provision in the program that allows nonbudget sources now using DERs trading to become part of the budget program, but monitoring, reporting, and other burdens are believed to effectively preclude opt-in by the smaller sources currently participating in the DERs market. In addition, because the RACT rule is not replaced by the budget program and because some of the participating sources will likely continue to operate at an emission level above the RACT limits, there will likely be a continuing need for DERs. The Department is proposing to allow the use of NO_x allowances in lieu of DERs as a means of assuring that a continuous source of credits is available. It is anticipated that the introduction of new NO_x emission limits will raise credit prices to some extent (from current levels of $750–$850 per ton) and that the increased value of DERs should elicit voluntary reductions from sources that have not previously participated. The direction other states take with respect to these same policy choices will influence the use of DERs throughout the region.

From the regulatory and administrative effectiveness point of view, the case-by-case approach is time consuming but it allows more flexibility, certainly more than traditional regulation. Other problems arose concerning measurement of emissions where sources were not using continuous monitoring. The discounting of the number of credits generated to compensate for uncertainty in emission measurements in the absence of continuous monitoring is imperfect but the best available method at this time. Although averaging rules are even more complicated than those involving DERs use, requiring considerable agency review and source record keeping, the fact that it rewards cost-effective intrafirm trading has made the effort worth while to a number of emitters. It must be noted in all these situations that time and attention is needed to educate all levels of agency staff unfamiliar with market-based concepts. Their cooperation is essential to cost-effective trading.

Whether the relative success, as we see it, of DERs use in the NO_x stationary source area can be duplicated on a more ambitious basis with VOCs and with mobile and area sources remains to be seen. The Department recognizes the many issues involved but is committed to further development of market-based options in these areas.

The experience and insight with respect to this new program provides a basis for innovative extension of these concepts to several other areas. DERs have been used as offsets for new sources as well as for temporary and emergency generator emissions. They have also been used in several less traditional applications. These include uses such as offsets for mobile source emissions associated with very large new recreational facilities, as an option to compensate for increased utility emissions due to massive outages of nuclear capacity, and even as a performance assurance option in the state's vehicle inspection contract. Each of these case studies is discussed in more detail below and will provide the reader with an understanding of the flexibility inherent in this new incentive approach.

CASE STUDIES OF THE USE OF DERs

Summer Utility Emissions Cap: A Nuclear Problem

In the spring of 1996 it became evident that a large portion of the states electric generating capacity would be out of service for an undetermined period of time as a result of the Nuclear Regulatory Commission concerns over the management of three of the four nuclear units (the last unit was similarly shutdown a short time later). The loss of these units resulted in the prospect that fossil fuel units would be call upon to run at extraordinary levels during the summer. This level of operation would result in large increases in summer NO_x emissions. Further, a significant amount of additional generation capacity would be required to meet the summer demands. The proposal to meet this need was reactivation of retired plants, installation of five new combustion turbines, emergency siting of several large military diesels, and a plan to ask for the operation of customer generation at times when the electric load approached the otherwise available generation.

This plan met the power needs but posed a number of perplexing environmental and regulatory issues. The proposed new units were of a size that required NO_x offsets. One of the retired units had surrendered its operating permit and should have been treated like the new ones.

The challenge facing the Department was to try to come as close to the intentions of the various regulations while at the same time recognizing that these plants would be installed and run (at least for the first summer) without regard for such niceties as offsets. While it is possible that some traditional ERCs might have been found for some of the new units, that possibility did not resolve the larger problem of greater operation of existing units. Recognizing that there would be an inevitable increase in emissions for the summer, the Department proposed a program designed to internalize the social cost of those utility emissions through a market mechanism. It proposed an emissions cap based on 1990 levels of operation and 1996 allowable emission rates, a level well below expected emissions. DERs were allowed to be used to compensate for any emissions above this level. All of the new sources were required to provide offsets in the form of DERs in amounts meeting the New Source Review requirements. The RACT emission limit for emergency generators was waived provided that all emissions above the limits were offset with DERs.

The weather for the summer turned out to be rather moderate. Except for the operation of the new units, which were covered with separate offsets, the emissions cap was exceeded by only a small amount, for which offsets were purchased. The Department considers the effort a success in that clear signals about the cost of increasing emissions had been sent and environmental compensation had been achieved. The Department recognized that most of the DERs came from a bank that had been developed earlier, but was not concerned about it. The Department's view was that market pressures would translate the depletion of the bank into a demand for greater DERs creation in future periods with a corresponding environmental benefit. The experience in Connecticut was the basis for a similar program in Massachusetts in the summer of 1997. Presently, a multi-state approach using DERs is under development for the upcoming summer. Because there will be correspondingly fewer allowances and/or DERs available in the future, the total of future emissions will be lower than would otherwise have been allowed. Thus, the environment will be compensated for the social costs associated with the electric capacity deficiency due to nuclear shutdowns through lower burdens in the years to come.

New Source Offsets: Growth and Environmental Benefit

The provisions of the CAAA'90 regarding emission offsets for new sources are designed to ensure that the process of permitting new activity does not result in emissions growth. Federal law and EPA policy require greater than one-to-one offsets. As a result, each new source is in fact responsible for a net improvement in the emissions picture. In most instances this is a reasonable demand on industry. The 20 percent to 30 percent additional requirement in and of itself may be taxing but seldom is seen as a complete bar to economic operations. If a source is planning on operating for many years, or, if it is reasonably certain that its emissions will be close to the level of emissions that it is purchasing offsets for, the long discount period or the assured salvage value through resale of the offsets makes investment in traditional ERCs acceptable. This is not always the case however, and DERs can provide a reasonable alternative in these situations.

One such case where DERs were successfully used involved the addition of some engine test cells at a large industrial facility. The cells were large enough to be covered by the offset rules, but the nature of the testing activity is such that the annual level of emissions may vary significantly and the lifecycle of the project is uncertain. Rather than require ERCs of a traditional nature, the Department issued a permit that requires the source to purchase sufficient DERs to cover two years of emissions and to submit a timely plan to show how continuing operations will be offset. This approach allowed the source to limit its investment in offsets while still meeting its obligations to provide a net environmental improvement.

Offsets for Mobile Source Emissions: Driving to the Indian Owned Casino

During the period that the DERs trading program was being developed, one of the Native American tribes was seeking approval for construction and operation of a large casino from the appropriate federal agencies. The tribal property was located in an ozone non-attainment area and the issue of sharp increases in motor vehicle emissions emerged during the required Environmental Impacts Statement process. Given the "Serious" non-attainment designation, the lack of an attainment plan for the area, and the need to meet the transportation conformity provisions of the CAAA'90, it was not clear that the issue could be resolved within a reasonable period of time or in a manner that would serve all parties. In a prior legislative session there had been a proposal mandating that sources such as casinos offset traffic emissions. Although this proposal had failed in the legislature, it became the basis of a voluntary program proposed by the Mohegan Tribe of Indians of Connecticut to resolve what otherwise looked like an impasse. The Tribe agreed to offset the emissions of the patron-generated traffic on a continuing basis through the use of DERs. This solution was implemented through a formal agreement between the state and the Tribe. Given the agreement, the federal agencies concluded that the negative environmental impact of patron traffic would be appropriately compensated for and issued the necessary authorizations for the project to go forward. Upon opening the casino, the Tribe commenced purchasing DERs.

An especially interesting aspect of this agreement is that it not only extends the concept of using DERs to mobile source emissions, but it covers VOC emissions as well as NO_x. Presently there are no VOC DERs approved for use in Connecticut and the agreement provides for the substitution of additional NO_x DERs for the required VOC DERs until the latter become available. This market for VOC credits has been of interest to sources, but no credits have been approved to date. The principal effort in this area involved a proposal to supply reformulated gasoline with a lower than required vapor pressure. Credit was being sought for the emission reductions that would have resulted. Considerable effort was expended by EPA, the gasoline refiner, emission trading consultants, and several states that were interested in the effort. The concerns that were never satisfactorily resolved centered on the "baseline" to which the low volatility gasoline could be compared, and the problems encountered in trying to track the various batches of gasoline as they flowed to the several market areas that overlapped state boundaries.

DERs and the Vehicle Inspection Program

Given the difficulties Connecticut (and many other states) have had with implementing the Enhanced Inspection/Maintenance program required by the CAAA'90, it is only natural that attempts to provide flexibility would include consideration of market or credit options. Several of these avenues, including allowing the use of credits as an alternative to the otherwise mandated expenditures on repairs, proved, at least for the time being to be dead ends. Rather than implementing the model program, the state and its contractor chose to implement a more consumer-friendly program designed to provide equivalent emission benefits. As actual implementation approached, the contractor for cost reasons felt compelled to substitute an easier to implement test. This test did not appear to provide the same level of emission reductions as the agreed upon test. The contractor maintained that it would be able to embellish the test to provide equivalent results by the time they became necessary. The amount in question was several hundred tons of VOCs per year. Given the uncertain effects of any attempts to "improve" the program, additional assurances of overall performance were needed. The solution turned out to be a provision added to the contract that requires the contractor to provide for any shortfall through the use of DERs. This contingency approach allowed an otherwise stalled program to move forward to meet critical deadlines.

DERs and Peaking NO_x Emissions

Peaking units are defined as sources with peak daily NO_x emissions greater than three times their average daily emissions during the ozone season. The basic concept of the trading program is that sources with excess NO_x emissions may use NO_x DERs to comply. Although typical sources may use DERs on a mass basis (one ton of DERs to offset one ton of excess emissions) with an acceptable environmental outcome, sources with large variations in emissions from day to day pose an additional problem for ozone attainment planning.

The most common peaking units or "peakers" are electricity generating units that run during times of high electricity consumption. Electricity demand is often the highest during hot, humid days of the summer when the potential for ozone formation is also high. Peakers frequently are major emitters. To the extent that these units produce emissions at exactly the time when emissions need to be reduced to limit ozone formation, allowing peakers to continue to comply with new rate limits through the use of DERs on a ton-for-ton basis will exacerbate this effect. On the other hand, if it can be demonstrated that the DERs being used by peakers were generated on a comparable basis (i.e., during days of high ozone potential), then ton-for-ton use by peakers would be appropriate.

The impact of the emissions from peakers during summer operation is a product of temporal variability as well as mass emissions. Any DERs trade must consider equivalency to the NO_x reductions that control equipment would produce on an ozone day. The protocol defines these relationships and the required computations to maintain air quality.

Protocol

Peaking units are only considered to be a temporal issue for the ozone season months. Ozone season emissions for these purposes shall be calculated based on a mass basis (total anticipated excess NO_x emissions over the ozone season) and a peak-day basis (maximum excess emissions for any day during the ozone season based on the daily *potential* NO_x emissions from a peaking unit).

Sources will be required to provide credits equal to the amount calculated on a mass or peak-day basis, whichever is larger, determined as follows:

1. Mass basis: DERs required will be equal to the total number of tons of excess NO_x emissions over the entire ozone season.

2. Peak (daily rate) basis: DERs (in tons) required will be calculated by dividing one-third of the actual maximum daily excess emissions (in pounds) by 13 pounds/day/ton: the formula divides the peak emissions by three in recognition that a degree of diversity exists with respect to operation of units relative to unhealthful days.

Where maximum daily excess emissions are the difference between emissions at the full-load-emission-rate maximum and 95 percent of the allowable emissions rate as experienced on any of the days projected by the Commissioner to be "moderate to unhealthful," "unhealthful," or "very unhealthful."

The actual "DERs required" will be the greater of the DERs calculated on the basis of (1) or (2). To the extent that the number of DERs used to offset peak-day emissions exceed the total mass of excess NO_x emissions for the ozone season, the remaining mass value of such DERs may be carried forward for use in the winter (non-ozone season).

Costs of NO$_x$ Emissions Control Technologies

VINCENT M. ALBANESE

From Joseph Belanger's contribution we learned that of the 300 major sources that existed in his jurisdiction as a former administrator in Connecticut, 81 were required by regulations to achieve significant NO$_x$ reductions. Of these, only six companies created tradable discrete emission reductions (DERs) greater than 100 tons. The two largest suppliers of DERs were located in New Jersey. Another matter of great interest to me as a supplier of NO$_x$ control technologies is that only two cases are in evidence in the Connecticut program where DERs were created by application of post-combustion control. These two sources of DERs were the Public Service Electric and Gas Utility near Trenton, New Jersey, and the Connecticut Resource Recovery Authority, a municipal waste incinerator in Hartford.

To date, there is not a landslide of interest in development of emissions controls for the purpose of creating surplus emission reductions for sale under this voluntary participation program. In most cases where emission reductions occurred in surplus, the overcontrol was incidental to some existing compliance need or position. My intention in these remarks is to address "end-of-the-pipe" technology for the generation of surplus reductions that holds the potential for expanding the dimensions of voluntary emissions trading in programs similar to that of Connecticut.

NO$_x$ emissions seem to be the "pollutant de jour" given recent developments bearing on their reduction. First there are the acid rain requirements for the two major types of boilers. Then, there is the Ozone Transport Commission's Memorandum of

Understanding leading to that region's cap-and-trade effort to reduce NO_x emissions. Not least is the U.S. EPA's NO_x SIP call and recommended cap-and-trade program for the OTAG 23 fine grid states. In the light of these efforts, I'll focus my remarks on the generation of surplus NO_x reductions for trading, although the generic concept applies to any pollutant whose control is managed within an emissions trading market. In my approach, I will draw on data from my firm's experience in determining the incremental cost of NO_x reduction deploying post-combustion control technologies and compare these estimates to the current market values of tradable credits.

There are, in my view, some current misperceptions surrounding the cost of NO_x control under a trading system. One of them was clearly in evidence when the U.S. EPA modeled the aggregate cost in OTAG states of sources required to meet the 0.15 lb./mm Btu emission standard. In their modeling approach, the U.S. EPA contractors specified a series of representative boiler types and sizes to portray the population of affected boilers. Then an array of control technologies was placed in the boiler types and a cost-effectiveness criterion (a $/ton NO_x metric) was used to select the winning technology for each type and size. The costs of winners for all boiler types and sizes were then summed and recorded.

My belief is that this approach leads to an overstatement of the control costs to the electric utility and other affected sectors. The primary reason for my conclusion is that the U.S. EPA approach utilizes monolithic or one-type-of-technology control on each boiler type and size to meet the proposed limit. However, in most control situations, it is a fact that the incremental performance, and cost, from a baseline increases exponentially depending upon the degree of reduction achieved previously; that is, the incremental cost depends on the degree of challenge. What the U.S. EPA approach does not reveal is the cost effectiveness of combined control technologies, some of which were operating previously below their optimum capability. Thus, there exists a potential for incremental control costs below those estimated by the U.S. EPA.

Today's suite of available NO_x reduction technologies includes low NO_x burners, various means of staged air, combustion tempering, gas reburn, selective catalytic reduction, selective non-catalytic reduction, gas co-firing, neural network controls, and more. We have found in many applications that a combination of two or more of the above technologies, applied in serial fashion, lowers the total cost of compliance for the boiler. Decentralization of these on-the-spot micro-decisions to utilize these control technologies in various optimum combinations is one of the major advantages of emissions trading programs.

To provide an illustration of the range of incremental costs for various combinations of post-combustion NO_x controls, Figure 10.1 presents data that my firm finds valuable in thinking about cost-effective solutions to reduction problems. This figure differs from the textbook marginal control cost curve and requires some explanation.

The horizontal axis measures baseline NO_x emissions in pounds per million British thermal units. The right vertical axis is scaled to represent the costs of a 55 percent reduction. The line connecting circle points is to be read off this axis. Each point on this line has two dimensions, a horizontal dimension measuring baseline NO_x in pounds per million Btu and a

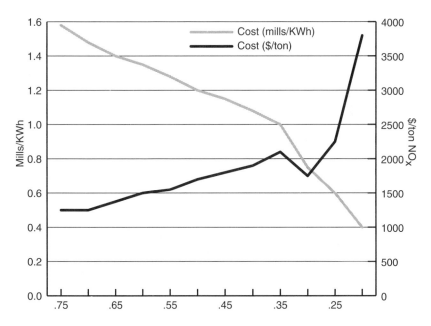

Figure 10.1   Marginal costs of NO_x control.

vertical dimension measuring the cost of a 55 percent reduction in dollars per ton NO_x reduced. The numerators in the variables on both vertical axes are the same conceptually, representing both annualized capital costs and annual O&M costs. The denominators are different: on the right the denominator is pollutant removed; on the left unit production. An example will help: the .75 lb./mm Btu on the horizontal axis is associated with the $1250 per reduced ton on the right vertical axis. As one reduces baseline NO_x emissions along the horizontal axis, the associated points on the right ordinate measure the generally increasing incremental costs of a 55 percent reduction from each baseline point. This 55 percent reduction is achieved by a specific combination of control technologies, not by a single winning technology. It follows that when baseline NO_x emissions are large, the incremental cost of a 55 percent reduction is smaller than when baseline NO_x emissions are small. That is, the cost of a 55 percent reduction from a small baseline, say .25, is large ($2,250) because fewer tons are being removed.

Now, reading along the left vertical axis, the line connecting the triangular points on the figure gives the additional costs in mills per kilowatt hour as 55 percent reductions are achieved at each baseline NO_x emission level. This is the concept most boiler or process owners who purchase control technologies consider first as it is based upon cost per production unit (e.g., mills/kWh for electric utilities). In contrast, regulatory agencies publish environmental policy and write control regulations based upon dollars per ton of pollutant reduced.

The curve connecting triangular points declines as baseline values decline, which may seem counterintuitive. The reason for the decline is that maintenance and operation control activities decline when the volume of emissions is smaller. These control activities typically involve managing the catalysts, in catalytic reduction, or chemical application in non-catalytic reduction. Therefore, the line declines. For example, the costs are 1.60 mills when baseline NO_x emissions are .75 lb./mm Btu and fall to .40 mills when the baseline value is .20. That is, per mill costs decline by 75 percent when baseline emissions decline by about 27 percent in the interval .75 to .20.

We have found it useful to calculate an average cost of a total NO_x control program at each baseline level of emissions by averaging the incremental costs of a 55 percent reduction, as given by the curve in Figure 10.1, with the costs already incurred in getting to the baseline emission level. More control expenditures have been made in reaching .30 lb./mm Btu than .60 lb./mm Btu. For example, if a low NO_x burner were used to reduce NO_x emissions to .45 lb./mm Btu at $250 per ton, that value would be weight-averaged with the incremental $1750 per ton cost required to obtain a further 55 percent reduction. This piecemeal approach gives a sense of the real cost requirements for deep NO_x reductions.

An overall example may illustrate my main point. To reduce the baseline values from .75 to .20 utilizing a low NO_x burner (LNB) plus nonselective catalytic reducer (NSCR) plus selective catalytic reducer (SCR) could require about $795 per ton NO_x reduced.

The post-combustion NO_x control costs depicted in the figure are taken from our (now significant) database of budgetary quotes to utilities. These quotes are based upon combinations of control technologies such as the SNCR/SCR hybrid. In this combination of technologies, the SNCR, operating at its theoretical maximum, provides ammonia for SCR catalyst feed. This combination also allows the SNCR and a specifically tailored SCR to achieve the desired level of NO_x reduction.

Certain basic technical assumptions have been made in these calculations that can be compactly summarized as:

1. $30 /kW capital requirement,

2. 15-year capital recovery,

3. 35 percent boiler capacity factor (reflecting seasonal application), and

4. A reagent normalized stoichiometric ratio of 1.5 (this ratio provides more than the theoretically calculated amount of ammonia or urea required to achieve the NO_x reduction).

The costs presented are total levelized use costs in 1998 constant dollars. That is, capital recovery is annualized and added to annual operating costs to arrive at the dollars per ton and mills/kWh figures.

The conclusions that I reach from these data are as follows:

- The incremental control costs for seasonal NO_x reductions achieved by post-combustion controls in optimal combination with existing technologies is squarely in the range revealed by emissions trading in the ozone transport region (quoted bid and ask prices in late 1998 range from $1200 to 2400/ton NO_x).
- The weighted average cost of NO_x reduction is low based as it is on the prior installation of LNB that average $250/ton NO_x.
- The incremental cost stated in terms of electricity rates seems attractively low to me, ranging from .40 to 1.60 mills/kWh or .5 to 2.0 percent of the average price of electricity.

Emissions Trading in Michigan

LOUIS L. JAGER

Michigan's open-market Emission Trading Program provides for the generation, use, and trading of emission reduction credits (ERCs), as well as statewide emission averaging. The program provides a financial incentive for sources of air emissions (volatile organic compounds [VOCs], oxides of nitrogen [NO_x], and all criteria pollutants except ozone) to voluntarily reduce emissions and register the emission reductions as ERCs. A mandatory 10 percent emission deduction at the time of ERC registration and other safeguards built into the program rules and operational procedures ensure an overall environmental benefit from trading. Other sources may then purchase the ERCs as an alternative means of compliance with various air quality requirements. The Michigan Department of Environmental Quality, Air Quality Division, maintains information regarding the generation, use, and trading of ERCs under the program on a publicly available Internet Registry at the following Internet address: (http://www.deq.state.mi.us/aqd/eval/e_trade/registry.html).

The program became effective at the state level on March 16, 1996, and was submitted to the U.S. EPA as a proposed revision to Michigan's State Implementation Plan (SIP) the following month. The program is currently being revised to address several federal approvability issues raised by the EPA in a September 18, 1997 Federal Register (FR) Notice of Proposed Rulemaking (NPR) publication. Although the EPA proposed approval of our program in the NPR, it was also stated that final action would not be taken until the approvability issues identified therein were addressed. Negotiations with stakeholders and the EPA have since led to mutually acceptable strategies for addressing the approvability issues. The revised program rules and operational procedures have been submitted to the EPA, and timely federal approval is expected.

FEDERAL APPROVABILITY ISSUES

Because the myriad issues associated with the federal approvability of the program are largely outside the scope of this publication, only the more substantive of these will be discussed for purposes of illustration. Experience in Michigan has shown that market activity under a voluntary state trading program is directly related to the federal approvability of the program. The EPA's stance on some of these larger issues is therefore relevant in the context of this chapter.

In general, several factors were considered during development of the program revisions. Although federal approval was desirable from the standpoint of market confidence and participation as stated above, stakeholders and the state were concerned that making some of the changes recommended by the EPA would render the program unusable. "User friendliness" is an important consideration in the context of a voluntary trading program, as the desired environmental and economic benefits will only occur if people choose to participate. It was therefore critical to address the EPA's concerns in a manner that would minimize negative impacts.

While the majority of the EPA's concerns were resolved early-on in the process, others were more difficult to accommodate. Issues rooted in the EPA's belief that emission quantification protocols under trading programs must be more accurate and precise than those under traditional "command-and-control" air programs threatened to impose a double-standard between the trading program and the foundation upon which it was built. Recognizing the unlikelihood of sources voluntarily subjecting themselves to more stringent emission monitoring and quantification requirements as a condition of participation, stakeholders and the EPA were able to agree upon reasonable criteria for judging the acceptability of such protocols in the revised rules. These criteria are largely consistent with those used to judge the acceptability of quantification protocols under the existing air program.

The EPA also raised pollutant-specific geographic concerns which threatened to limit trading to within specific nonattainment or maintenance (sensitive) areas. Such sensitive areas in Michigan currently comprise only a small percentage of the state. The practical effect of such restrictions would therefore have been to create trading zones too small to support robust markets where trading is most needed. This would be particularly true in the case of VOCs, which has been the pollutant most actively traded under the program to date. Given the fact that air quality in sensitive areas is impacted by pollutant emissions in the surrounding areas, discussion with stakeholders and the EPA led to agreement on a system for significantly expanding these trading zones. With respect to VOCs, the new system consolidates contiguous sensitive areas and provides for trading within a defined perimeter which is measured from the outer border of the consolidated area. Other facets of this new system also impose restrictions on the trading of criteria pollutants, but they also provide for the free trading of NO_x on a statewide or regional basis.

Issues related to credit generation through activity level reduction (e.g., source shutdowns and curtailments) were also controversial. The EPA's general stance on such emission reductions is that they are "anyway tons"; reductions which would occur with the same frequency in the absence of a trading program. Stakeholders and the state believe that all reductions benefit the airshed regardless of how they are generated. Further, while load-shifting and other concerns should be factored into the amount of creditable reductions resulting from such activities, they are nonetheless recognized as legitimate strategies for reducing emissions under the federal Clean Air Act. Therefore, our view was that there is no regulatory basis for prohibiting them as a means of generating creditable reductions under a trading program. These issues were eventually resolved through agreement on reasonable use restrictions for these credits (e.g., where the use could jeopardize attainment demonstrations or maintenance plans in sensitive areas) rather than prohibiting their generation altogether.

PROGRAM ACTIVITY

As indicated above, program activity statistics to date closely reflect the EPA's changing position regarding federal approvability. The EPA's initial belief that the program would not be federally approvable was made clear during the initial development of the state rules during the 1994–1995 time frame. Although significant technical support was included with the April 1996 SIP submittal in response to these concerns, the EPA was poised to publish a notice of proposed disapproval by the end of that year. The subsequent debates which ensued between Michigan and the EPA focused on threshold policy issues such as those discussed above, and were highly publicized in environmental publications. Although the EPA ultimately published the aforementioned proposed approval instead of a proposed disapproval, the very clear message which was sent to industry in Michigan during the latter part of 1996 through 1997 was that federal disapproval was imminent.

Consequently, the only significant program activity observed during this time was ERC generation compared with an insignificant activity in ERC use. This ERC use was mainly a transfer of credits from one emissions source to another within a facility. About 38,000 tons of voluntary emission reductions for four different pollutants have been generated or supplied under the program to date, with the vast majority of these occurring during the latter part of 1996 through 1997. Conversely, only 6 companies chose to use or demand ERCs during this time. Only 1 of these 6 ERC uses involved a trade from one company to another, and in this case, the ERCs were used out-of-state (in Canada). Several potential ERC users opted against participation during this time and cited the uncertainty regarding federal approval as the basis for their decision. Clearly, the fear of federal retribution for using a compliance mechanism that was not federally approvable was preventing the development of a robust trading market in Michigan.

All of this began to change in 1998. While the EPA published their proposed approval in September 1997, the proposal carried with it so many requirements for program changes as conditions of approval that most feared federal approval and a workable program would not be mutually attainable goals. It was not until the negotiations with stakeholders and the EPA concluded in January of 1998 that these fears were allayed. The general consensus of stakeholders, the EPA, and the state following this process was that the proposed revisions would make the program federally approvable, and would also retain the key features necessary to keep the venture practical and usable. This view is reflected in program activity statistics for the first quarter of 1998.

For example, while only 13 notices to trade ERCs between separate companies have been received by the state since program inception on March 16, 1996, 12 of these were received during the first quarter of 1998 (program submittals include notices to trade, generate, or use ERCs). As previously stated, the one transfer which occurred prior to 1998 was part of an out-of-state ERC use. These statistics show that traditional market activity in Michigan has increased dramatically since the program became "federally approvable."

PROJECTIONS

Another conclusion which may be drawn based upon the above statistics is that, while current market activity trends in Michigan are increasing, relatively few trades have occurred overall. Michigan's air trading market is clearly in the early developmental stages when compared to established markets in states such as Connecticut and California. It is therefore difficult at this early stage to predict how the market will behave in the years following formal state and federal approval revisions. However, it is possible to identify and discuss the various factors which will likely influence market performance.

One important consideration is the timeliness of federal approval. In short, the sooner formal federal approval of the program is granted, the sooner potential participants will have complete confidence that federal enforcement action will not result from their participation. Another factor is the ease of participation under the revised program. While stakeholders involved in the rules development have indicated that the program will remain practical and usable under the proposed revisions, it remains to be seen if this will actually be the case. As stated above, "user friendliness" is a key consideration in the context of voluntary trading.

Regulatory drivers are a necessary component of any trading program. Outside of the retirement market, there is little incentive to purchase ERCs without a need to use them for regulatory compliance. Michigan is unlike Connecticut and California in that the vast majority of the state is currently attaining air quality standards. Consequently, more stringent applicable requirements may not come to bear in Michigan until measures to address the new ozone and particulate matter standards are implemented in the state. Since the program provides for the trading of the ozone precursors, VOCs, and NO_x, as well as the criteria pollutant PM_{10}, it is very likely that the inevitable requirements to strengthen regulations for sources of these pollutants will result in an increased need for trading. Of course, the law of supply and demand dictates that increases in the use and trading of ERCs should also result in increased ERC generation activity in the state. The general outlook in Michigan is that having a federally approved trading program in place will be an important part of the state's strategy to attain and maintain compliance with the new standards in the most efficient and cost-effective manner possible.

VOC Emissions Trading from an Industrial Perspective: Past, Present, and Future

THOMAS W. ZOSEL

The concept of emissions trading evolved from an interpretive ruling that required new emissions in nonattainment areas to be offset by decreased emissions from existing sources. The Clean Air Act of 1970 arguably prohibited increases in emissions in nonattainment areas. If that truly was the Act's requirements, it would have prohibited any industrial growth in those nonattainment areas. This outcome would have created political problems that far outweighed the air quality benefits.

In response to this potential problem, EPA interpreted the Act to require no "net" increase in emissions. Consequently, in order to construct a new source that created new emissions, a facility would need to find an existing source within the nonattainment area that was willing to decrease its emissions by an equivalent amount. The new emissions were offset by the decreased old emissions. The concept of emissions trading was born.

While the development of this offset concept evolved in the 1970s and was codified in the Clean Air Act Amendments of 1977 and 1990, a robust market in the sale of emission reduction credits (ERCs) of volatile organic compounds (VOCs) has never developed. There are some emission trades that take place in different areas of the country but these trades are few and far between. Even in Southern California, where some trading has developed, the amount of trading in relationship to the total number of sources is actually quite small.

A rational for the failure of a robust market for VOC ERCs to develop can be seen through an analysis of the "value" of the ERCs to a potential seller. If a company has reduced its emissions below the level required by the regulations, that company has developed a quantity of emission reduction credits. U.S. EPA's test for credits requires that they be real, surplus, permanent, and enforceable. Real means that they were emissions that actually occurred in the past and have since been reduced. Paper offsets or reductions in permitted emissions that never really occurred in the past are not acceptable. Surplus means that the emission reductions were not required by regulations. They are voluntary reductions that go beyond the requirements of the regulations. Permanent means that the reductions are created in a manner that is not temporary or intermittent. Installing control equipment or shutting down a line are permanent reductions. Enforceable means that the reductions or the means of achieving those reductions has been incorporated into a federally enforceable permit.

Once a company has created the ERCs, they could be sold to another company in order to allow that company to expand. The generating company could also keep the ERCs in order to be able to offset its own future expansion needs. In the majority of cases, companies have chosen to hold their ERCs for future internal use, even if they had no immediate plans for expansion. In addition, since there was not a robust market in VOC ERCs, there was no way to guarantee that if a company sold their credits there would be others available for sale if they needed them in the future. Thus, the lack of a market inhibited others from selling. Essentially, the "value" of the ERCs is greater for allowing the company future expansion than the monetary "value" that is gained through a sale.

Many of the past intercompany trades are from companies that have either shut down or have permanently closed a portion of their operations. In these cases, there was no value of the credits for future expansion and the company could cash in on the monetary value of the credits as another asset to be disposed of. Consequently, when we look at the past history and present situation regarding the intercompany trading of VOC emissions, we see that some trading has occurred but a robust market in which frequent trades are taking place has not developed in any part of the country.

An overlay to the issues of the value of the VOC ERCs for expansion versus monetary gain through a sale is the issue of a negative image of emissions trading that has developed in the environmentalist community. Selling pollution is not viewed as the environmentally proactive thing to do. This issue of image has been a major driver in 3M's approach to the use of VOC ERCs. Since 3M's goal is beyond compliance performance, many of 3M's facilities have generated VOC ERCs. 3M has adopted a corporate policy not to profit from the sales of ERCs. In a majority of the cases, 3M has returned these credits to the appropriate agency for air quality improvements. In some of these situations, we have been able to claim a tax deduction as a donation for the value of those credits.

There are two notable exceptions in which 3M worked with its stakeholder communities in order to develop community value through the innovative use of these credits. The first case was in Camarillo, California, in Ventura County, which is located just north of Los Angeles. In this situation, 3M sold ERCs to Procter and Gamble for an expansion of their Ventura County facility. The selling price of those credits was $1.5 million. 3M then donated the $1.5 million to the Ventura County Air Pollution Control District. The APCD Board was the gatekeeper for the use of the funds after recommendation from their citizen's advisory board. This allowed the District and the County to develop and implement innovative air pollution control projects that could not be funded through conventional means.

It is anticipated that by the time the $1.5 million is completely spent the projects that were funded will achieve emission reductions that are far greater than those that 3M sold to P&G. In other words, this sale, the creation of the fund, and the projects implemented through the fund created a net air quality benefit. While this project has produced definite air quality improvements, it remains the only fund of its type ever established.

In a second case, 3M donated 300 tons of VOC credits to the City of Chicago for urban redevelopment. One issue with Brownfield's reutilization was that companies would need to offset emissions from the site remediation and from any facilities that were then located on that site. This need for offsets was stated as one impediment to Brownfield's reutilization. 3M's donation to the City of Chicago was an attempt to eliminate that issue for Brownfields in the Chicago area.

The City of Chicago's Department of the Environment used these credits to create an innovative emission bank. Chicago is presently the only city in the nation that has an emission bank that has real deposits of VOC ERCs that can be used at the discretion of the city. Other so-called banks exist but they are in actuality merely a listing of companies or entities that hold title to ERCs. A user or purchaser of ERCs must then negotiate with one of those titleholders. Chicago has eliminated that problem. A person seeking to expand or locate in Chicago has essentially one-stop shopping. Everything they need is available to them from the city. Chicago has already completed one deal in which a company will expand its operations into a remediated brownfield site. From 3M's perspective, this proves that the concept behind our donation to Chicago is valid and has produced the intended result.

These are just two examples of how ERCs could be used in innovative mechanisms to either improve air quality or support secondary environmental benefits. While both cases involved extensive stakeholder involvement and negotiations, the end result in both cases was environmental improvement.

Now let's look into the future. Illinois is about to embark on an innovative Emissions Reduction Market System (ERMS) for the Chicago ozone nonattainment area. This ERMS system will require each major VOC emission facility within the designated area to have emission allotments that are equal to their ozone season emissions. The ozone season is defined as the five summer months of May through September. The allotments are based on the facility's historic emissions with a reduction for future air quality improvements. This is essentially the future attainment strategy for the Chicago area. Chicago will be the first area in the nation to have an attainment strategy that is developed based upon a market-based system.

However, rather than replacing the existing technology based strategy (the requirement for RACT, BACT, LAER) with a performance based strategy (ERMS), the U.S. EPA has required compliance with both systems simultaneously. These dual compliance requirements greatly reduce the potential effectiveness and benefit of the emission market system.

It is readily apparent that the existing centralized technology-based system has produced significant environmental benefits in the past 30 years. However, it is also clear that this command-and-control system is not adequate to drive the future environmental improvement that will be needed into the twenty-first century. It is time that we move into the future. Innovative environmental agencies like the Illinois EPA and the City of Chicago should be allowed the leeway and freedom to experiment with new and progressive ideas that will create the foundations for future environmental management systems. To treat these innovative ideas as overlays on the existing system rather than as total replacements greatly reduces not only their effectiveness, but also our ability to learn the benefits and shortcomings of these new ideas.

The ERMS market approach is one of the few efforts in an ozone nonattainment area that establishes a performance-based system. We would anticipate that there would be a market for the tradable credits and that some trading will develop. However, we also believe that this new system will not achieve its maximum potential for air quality improvement because of the fact that it is an overlay on the existing technology-based command-and-control system.

This basic concept of emission trading has been with us for close to 30 years. In the SO_2 area it took congressional action (the Clean Air Act Amendments of 1990) to establish a system that works. The price of SO_2 credits is far lower then anyone originally predicted. Consequently, the nation is getting greater environmental protection at a lower cost under this market-based approach.

While a market-based approach has proved workable with SO_2 emissions, no area of the country has yet proved that it will work for VOC emissions. The Chicago area ERMS program will be the first. We hope that everyone that is truly interested in air quality improvements will be committed to making this new system work. It will take innovation and support at both the state and federal level. It's a system that could pave the way for environmental management in the twenty-first century.

PART SEVEN

A Perspective on Emissions Trading

11

The Significance of Incentive-Based Regulation

Michael Moskow

Regulators are moving away from command-and-control strategies toward market- or incentive-based regulation. The environmental sector is one of the most important areas where these changes are playing out.

Our goal is to apply the experience we have gathered to improve environmental regulations currently being written and designed. As a regulator of financial institutions, I am also looking to learn from market-based environmental regulation as it provides important lessons for the financial services industry. Recently, regulators of financial markets have been discussing ways to improve the International Monetary Fund's ability to enhance financial stability by introducing additional elements of incentive-based regulation. Closer to home, the Federal Reserve Bank of Chicago has proposed ways to use an incentive-based approach in regulating banks. The goal is to determine a level of regulatory capital that applies to a specific bank based on that bank's market risk.

This shift to incentive-based regulation came about largely because of the many problems with traditional command-and-control regulation. One of the most fundamental problems with command-and-control is an asymmetry in information and expertise. Command-and-control regulations tend to require information from the regulated firm that cannot be obtained reliably and at reasonable cost. Thus, firms often have a significant advantage over regulators in this area. Regulated firms also tend to have far more expertise in how best to achieve the desired goals. As a result, command-and-control regulations are difficult to implement. More importantly, the regulations tend to be far more simplistic than the activity they regulate. Too often regulations are "one-size-fits-all" rules that involve a host of cost inefficiencies.

I have observed the regulatory process, both from inside the government and outside the government, for more than 25 years. Unfortunately, in my experience so-called regulatory "innovation" has usually meant looking for better ways of applying the existing rules. In most cases, regulators are well-intentioned and creative people, but they are limited by the rigidity of the laws they are required to carry out.

Currently, we are looking at a completely different approach—a truly innovative approach. Incentive-based regulation draws on the expertise and self-interest of firms to meet public policy goals. This approach helps address the asymmetry problems I mentioned earlier. It also helps create a cycle of continuous improvement as firms have an incentive to constantly develop new and more efficient methods of achieving regulatory goals.

An additional point I would like to make is the need for regional solutions to regulatory issues. This is one of the principal findings of the Federal Reserve Bank of Chicago's comprehensive study of the trends facing the Midwest economy. We held a series of workshops featuring leading experts who presented research on a wide range of issues. The study looked at various aspects of the regional economy—global linkages; the labor force and education policy; the rural economy; tax and regulatory policies; the performance of metropolitan areas; and changes in the manufacturing sector. One of the strategies that emerged from this project called for greater attention to developing public policies on a regional level. Going forward, it is important that we search for ways to sustain this region's very strong economic performance.

Environmental regulations designed to meet and exceed the required goals in the most cost-efficient manner are certainly going to contribute to this effort. And I am quite sincere when I say "exceed the required goals." The Midwest will need to do all it can to improve its quality of life for its inhabitants if it is to continue to attract America's increasingly particular workforce. This includes having clean air and water.

Fortunately, emissions trading programs are taking this regional approach. One of the studies of this volume features Connecticut's experience in emissions reduction trading. Another describes a program for the Los Angeles basin, where permits have been traded for over four years. Here in the Midwest, regional efforts have been underway as well. The states in the Federal Reserve Bank of Chicago's district, Iowa, Illinois, Indiana, Michigan, and Wisconsin, are part of the Ozone Transportation Assessment Group (OTAG). Under the leadership of the Illinois EPA, this group of 37 states in June 1997 proposed regional solutions to the ground-level ozone problem.

Incidentally, the Illinois experience with emissions trading provides some interesting lessons regarding designing regulation. More than five years ago, the Illinois EPA began to develop a regional emissions trading program for the Chicago area. The IEPA originally considered a program designed to control nitrogen oxide emissions. Later, air quality modeling found that the first priority for controlling ground-level ozone in Northeast Illinois was not reducing nitrogen oxide, but rather reducing volatile organic compound emissions. The modeling revealed that, unlike Los Angeles, the Chicago area would actually experience an increase in ground-level ozone concentrations if local sources reduced emissions of nitrogen oxide. In response, the IEPA switched from nitrogen oxide concerns and developed what is the nation's first emissions trading program in volatile organic matter. This program is called the Emissions Reduction Market System (ERMS). It has been signed into law and its first reduction requirements will become effective in the summer of the year 2000.

This example illustrates the need for regional solutions in air quality regulation. Air is a transportable element whose quality can be affected by upwind sources. Air quality does not respect state or municipal boundaries. When we want to control it, we must consider a regional, or national or—in the case of green-house gases—an international approach.

Our approach to cleaning up the environment, much like our approach to economic growth and development, should involve working together across much wider geographic boundaries than we are used to. And we will also need to cross intellectual and cultural frontiers.

The conferences on which this book is based have attracted a large and diverse audience, including regulators and the regu-lated community, public interest groups and academics. The lively discussion and exchange of ideas that resulted have been captured in this volume by inclusion of the panel commentaries.

Acronyms

ALA—American Lung Association

AQMP—Air Quality Management Plan

ARCO—Atlantic Richfield Company

ATS—Allowance Tracking System

ATU—Allotment Trading Unit

BMP—Best Management Practice

BP—British Petroleum (British Petroleum Amoco—ARCO)

CAA—Clean Air Act of 1970

CAAA—Clean Air Act Amendments of 1990

CAFE—Corporate Average Fuel Economy

CARB—California Air Resources Board

CBE—Citizens for a Better Environment

CBOT—Chicago Board of Trade

CCA—Coalition for Clean Air

CDM—Clean Development Mechanism

CCEEB—Californian Council for Economic and Environmental Balance

CEMS—Continuous Emissions Monitoring System

CFC—Chlorofluorocarbon

CO₂—Carbon Dioxide

COHPAC—Compact Hybrid Particulate Collector

COP4—Fourth Conference of the Parties (Framework Convention on Climate Change)

CTO—Certified Tradable Offset

DERs—Discrete Emission Reductions

EAC—Emissions Averaging Credits

ECOS—Environmental Council of the States

EDF—Environmental Defense Fund

EDI—Electronic Data Interchange

EIA—Energy Information Agency

EIP—Economic Incentive Program

EPA—U.S. Environmental Protection Agency

EPRI—Electric Power Research Institute

ERC—Emission Reduction Credits

ERMS—Emissions Reduction Market System

ESP—Electrostatic Precipitator

ETPS—Emission Trading Policy Statement

FGD—Flue Gas Desulfurization

FLER—Full Load Emission Rate

GHG—Greenhouse Gases

IAMs—Integrated Assessment Models

ICF—ICF Resources International

IEPA—Illinois Environmental Protection Agency

LAER—Lowest Achievable Emission Rate

LNB—Low NO_x Burners

MIT/CEEPR—Massachusetts Institute of Technology/Center for Energy and Environmental Policy Research

MSW—Municipal Solid Waste

NAAQS—National Ambient Air Quality Standards

NAPAP—National Acid Precipitation Assessment Program

NATS—NO_x Allowance Tracking System

NESCAUM/MARAMA—New England States for Coordinated Air Use Management/Mid-Atlantic Region Air Management Association

NGR—Natural Gas Reburning

NO_x—Nitrogen Oxides

NPR—Notice of Proposed Rulemaking

NRC—Nuclear Regulatory Commission

NRDC—Natural Resources Defense Council

NSPS—New Source Performance Standards

O_3—Ozone

OFA—Overfire Air

OTAG—Ozone Transport Assessment Group

OTC—Ozone Transport Commission

PJBH—Pulse Jet Baghouse

RABH—Reverse Air Baghouse

RACT—Reasonably Available Control Technology

RECLAIM—The Regional Clean Air Incentives Market

RFP—Reasonable Further Progress

ROG—Reactive Organic Gases

SCAQMD—South Coast Air Quality Management District

SCR—Selective Catalytic Reduction

SIP—State Implementation Plan

S&L—Sargent & Lundy LLC

SNCR—Selective Non-Catalytic Reduction

SOAPP—State-of-the-Art Power Plant (Technology Modules)

SO_2—Sulfur Dioxide

SO_x—Sulfur Oxides

STAPPA/ALAPCO—State and Territorial Air Pollution Program Association/Association of Local Air Pollution Control Organizations

TIW—Trading/Incentives Workgroup
TVA—Tennessee Valley Authority
UAM-V—Urban Airshed Model Five
UNOCAL—Union Oil of California
VOC—Volatile Organic Compound
VOM—Volatile Organic Materials
WSPA—Western States Petroleum Association

Contributors

Vincent M. Albanese is vice president of sales and marketing at Fuel Tech, Inc. He was formerly vice president of external affairs for Fuel Tech's predecessor, Nalco Fuel Tech, and prior to that spent 15 years with Nalco Chemical Co. His assignments concerned fuel properties and air pollution control. He has served as a member of the U.S. EPA's Acid Rain Advisory Committee and, more recently, the Ozone Transport Assessment Group. He has authored articles and technical papers relating to pollution control, and he currently holds seven patents in that area. The writer received his B.S. in chemistry from Manhattan College and his M.S. in physical chemistry from Villanova University.

Joseph A. Belanger, until his retirement in April of 1998, served the Connecticut Department of Environmental Protection as the director of planning and standards for the Bureau of Air Management. He was among those responsible for the design and implementation of Connecticut's regulatory programs required to comply with the Clean Air Act Amendments of 1990. He was a member of The Ozone Transport Commission (OTC), served as chairman of the OTC Stationary and Area Source Committee, and represented Connecticut on the Ozone Transport Assessment Group where he focused on economic incentive and trading issues. He served on the Federal Clean Air Act Advisory Sub-committee on Ozone, Particulate Matter, and Regional Haze. The contributor received a B.A. in economics from the University of Connecticut and holds M.A.s in public administration and management from the University of Hartford and the Hartford Graduate Center/Renesselar Polytechnic Institute.

Holly M. Biggs is an undergraduate biological sciences major at the University of Illinois at Chicago and a research assistant for the Workshop on Market-Based Approaches to Environmental Policy. She is a member of the Honors College and the Guaranteed Professional Programs Admission (GPPA) program which will lead to study at the University of Illinois College of Medicine. During the fall semester of 1999, she studied at Universidad San Francisco de Quito in Ecuador.

Dallas Burtraw is a fellow in the Quality of Environment Division, Resources for the Future, and has been on the staff of that institution since 1989. He specializes in the analysis of incentive-based environmental regulation, the theory and measurement of social costs, and public finance. Two primary areas of research have been the analysis of incentive-based environmental regulation and the theory and measurement of social costs associated with electricity generation. He is an adjunct lecturer at Johns Hopkins School of Advanced International Studies and Georgetown University and has served as a consultant to state and federal agencies, electric utilities, environmental organizations, and international lending and economic assistance institutions. The author received his Ph.D. in economics and Master of Public Policy degree from the University of Michigan.

Rayenne Chen is a policy analyst with the U.S. EPA's Acid Rain Program. Her work focuses on the analysis of the SO_2 emissions trading program, evaluating the compliance strategies of electric utilities, assessing the environmental impact of the program, and analyzing the SO_2 trading market. She has worked on emissions trading with the EPA since 1996. Prior to that, she worked in environmental strategy consulting at Arthur D. Little. She received her B.A. from Harvard University.

William DePriest is the manager of Environmental Services in the Fossil Power Technology Business Group of Sargent & Lundy LLC. He has over 25 years of experience in the power industry with a professional focus on environmental aspects of fossil combustion technologies. His experience with environmental control technologies includes research and development technology application and O&M. He received a B.S. in chemical engineering from Michigan Technological University.

A. Denny Ellerman is executive director, Center for Energy and Environmental Policy Research (CEEPR) and senior lecturer, Sloan School of Management, MIT. Formerly he served as vice president, Charles River Associates; executive vice president, National Coal Association; and deputy assistant secretary for policy analysis, U.S. Department of Energy. He also served on the staffs of the National Security Council, the Energy Research and Development Administration, and the Office of Management and Budget. He was elected president of the International Association for Energy Economics for 1990. The contributor's CEEPR-supported research focuses on productivity change in the coal industry and the effect on coal prices, as well as the interrelation between coal and emission allowance prices.

Mary A. Gade is a partner in the Environmental Practice Group at Sonnenschein Nath & Rosenthal. Prior to joining the firm, she served as director of the Illinois EPA from 1991 through 1998. She previously was deputy assistant administrator for Solid Waste and Emergency Response at the U.S. EPA. She has received a number of awards for her leadership of the Ozone Transport Assessment Group, a 37-state collaboration to deal with the problem of ground-level ozone. As Illinois EPA director, she directed the development of the Emissions Market Reduction System. She led an international outreach program that provided an exchange of views and professional expertise and technology with China and three Baltic nations. The author received her law degree from Washington University School of Law.

Gary R. Hart is manager of Clean Air/SO$_2$ Allowances at the Southern Company. He is a Certified Management Accountant and a past president of the Birmingham Chapter of the National Association of Accountants. He has over 20 years experience with the company, where he has held positions such as assistant to the vice president and comptroller of Alabama Power Company. He is also an officer and board member of the new professional association dealing with emissions trading known as the Emissions Marketing Association. He is a graduate of the University of Alabama with a B.A. in finance and accounting.

Louis L. Jager is a senior environmental engineer with the Michigan Department of Environmental Quality, Air Quality Division, and does program development work in the Strategy Development Unit. He is currently the coordinator of Michigan's air emissions trading program. Previously he did project engineering and manufacturing work in the private sector. He has a B.S. in chemical engineering from the University of Michigan.

Roger A. Kanerva is environmental policy advisor to the director of the Illinois Environmental Protection Agency, where he leads that agency in developing proposals for market-based approaches to state environmental policy. He was a co-chair of the design team for the trading plan for stationary source hydrocarbon emissions in the Chicago nonattainment (ozone) area and principal author of the final design proposal for ERMS. He also chaired the Trading Incentives Workshop of the Ozone Transport Assessment Group. Prior to joining the IEPA, he was deputy director for the Maryland Water Resources Administration. The author received a B.S. and an M.S. in watershed management from the University of Arizona.

Thomas H. Klier is a senior economist in the research department of the Federal Reserve Bank of Chicago. His research concentrates on issues pertinent to the economy of the Midwest, especially structural changes in the manufacturing sector, and environmental policy and regulation. He contributed to the Bank's yearlong study, "Assessing the Midwest Economy" and coauthored its report of findings. Current research projects include analysis of the spatial clustering of supplier networks around assembly plants, primarily in the auto industry, as well as examining evidence on the workings of the RECLAIM market for NO_x. He received his B.A. and MBA from Friedrich-Alexander-Universitat, Erlangen-Nurnberg, and his Ph.D. from Michigan State University.

Richard F. Kosobud is a professor of economics at the University of Illinois at Chicago, where he specializes in environmental economics. He is director of the Workshop on Market-Based Approaches to Environmental Policy, which has been supported principally by the John D. and Catherine T. MacArthur Foundation and the Acid Rain Division of the U.S. EPA. His research, currently in the area of market incentives and the economics of climate change, has been widely published and has been supported by, among other sources, the National Science Foundation and the National Institute for Child Health and Human Development. He received a Ph.D. in economics from the University of Pennsylvania.

Joe Kruger is chief of the Energy, Evaluation, and International Branch at the U.S. EPA's Acid Rain Division. He directs studies and assessments of the environmental and economic impacts of the Clean Air Act's Acid Rain Program. His branch is also involved in implementation of the U.S./Canada Air Quality Agreement and development of administration positions on greenhouse gas emissions trading and electric utility restructuring. Before his present position, he was an energy and environmental analyst at the Investor Responsibility Research Center in Washington, DC, and, prior to that, he was a research assistant at the Argonne National Laboratory, U.S. Department of Energy. He has an M.A. in public policy from the University of California at Berkeley and a B.A. in economics and government from Cornell University.

James M. Lents is director of corporate affiliate programs and environmental policy in the College of Engineering, Center for Environmental Research and Technology (CE-CERT), at the University of California, Riverside. He is a consultant to regulatory agencies and private industry on adoption of new technologies to control air pollution. From 1986 to 1997, he served as executive officer of the South Coast Air Quality Management District (SCAQMD). In a previous position, he was director of the Colorado Pollution Control Division in the Colorado State Health Department. He holds a B.S. in engineering physics and an M.S. in physics and infrared spectroscopy from the University of Tennessee, Knoxville. In addition, he earned a Ph.D. in physics and ultraviolet spectroscopy at the University of Tennessee Space Institute in Tullahoma.

Brian J. McLean is director of the Acid Rain Division within the Office of Air and Radiation at the U.S. EPA. He directs the government implementation of the national Acid Rain Program under Title IV of the Clean Air Act Amendments of 1990. He is also working with states to develop and implement an emissions trading program for NO_x for the eastern United States, and advising on the development of international emissions trading efforts to control greenhouse gases. He has been with the EPA since 1972, working as an air program specialist in the Philadelphia office from 1972 to 1979; as an air program analyst and manager addressing transportation, emissions trading and acid rain issues in Washington, DC from 1980 to 1990; and as director of the Acid Rain Division since 1990. The author holds a B.S. in electrical engineering from Lafayette College, a master's of city and regional planning from Rutgers University, and a Ph.D. in city planning from the University of Pennsylvania.

Michael H. Moskow is president of the Federal Reserve Bank of Chicago, in which capacity he rotates as a voting member of the Federal Open Market Committee, the Federal Reserve System's key monetary policymaking body. He has held a number of senior positions with the U.S. government, including undersecretary of labor at the U.S. Department of Labor, director of the Council on Wage and Price Stability, assistant secretary for policy development and research at the U.S. Department of Housing and Urban Development, and senior staff economist with the Council of Economic Advisors. In 1991, President Bush appointed him Deputy United States Trade Representative, with the rank of Ambassador. He was a professor of strategy and international management at the

J.L. Kellogg School of Management at Northwestern University at the time of his appointment as president of the Chicago Reserve Bank. Prior to these undertakings, he was president and chief executive officer of Velsicol Chemical Corporation; vice president of corporate development for Dart and Kraft, Inc.; and vice president of strategy and business development for Premark International, Inc. He is the author of seven books and more than 20 articles. He received a B.A. in economics from Lafayette College, an M.A. in economics, and a Ph.D. in business and applied economics from the University of Pennsylvania.

William D. Nordhaus is Whitney Griswold Professor of Economics at Yale University, New Haven, Connecticut. From 1977 to 1979, he was a member of President Carter's Council of Economic Advisers. He was provost of Yale University from 1986 to 1988 and served as Yale's vice president for finance and administration from 1991 to 1992. He is a member and senior advisor of the Brookings Panel on Economic Activity, Washington, DC, and is a fellow of the American Academy of Arts and Sciences. He serves on the National Academy of Sciences Committee on National Statistics and is chairman of the Academy's Panel on Integrated Environmental and Economic Accounting. He has been active as an editor of several scientific journals and has served on the executive committee of the American Economic Association. His current research focuses on economic growth and natural resources, on the question of the extent to which resources constrain economic growth, and on the economics of global warming. He is the author of many books and articles. After completing his undergraduate work at Yale University, he received his Ph.D. from the Massachusetts Institute of Technology.

Kenneth J. Rose is a senior institute economist in the Electric and Gas Research Division of the National Regulatory Research Institute of Ohio State University. He has worked primarily on studies concerning electric utility regulation, and has contributed to many reports, papers, articles and books. He is engaged as a project leader and principal investigator in studies of the implications for electric utilities of the Clean Air Act Amendments, environmental externalities, and industry restructuring.

Before coming to the NRRI, he worked on energy-related issues at Argonne National Laboratory. He received his B.S., M.A., and Ph.D. in economics from the University of Illinois at Chicago.

Richard L. Sandor is chairman and chief executive officer, Environmental Financial Products LLC, a risk management firm specializing in derivative market applications. He was second vice chairman of the Chicago Board of Trade. He has served on numerous committees and boards including those of the Chicago Mercantile Exchange, the Banking Research Center of Northwestern University, and the Columbia University Futures Center. He was named "Father of Financial Futures" by the CBOT and the City of Chicago. He is an expert and advisor to the U.N. Commission on Trade and Development on tradable entitlements for carbon dioxide emission control. He received a Ph.D. in economics from the University of Minnesota.

Douglas L. Schreder is an advanced candidate for a Ph.D. in economics at the University of Illinois at Chicago. His primary research interest is market-based approaches to solving environmental problems, with particular focus on emissions trading. He assisted with the organization of the two workshops in 1998 which are the basis for this publication. He has extensive work experience in the areas of engineering, sales, and marketing, as well as in teaching economics, quality assurance, and management communications. He lived in Spain and France for seven years, gaining an international perspective on business and work experience in management consulting and teaching. He has an MBA from IESE, Barcelona, Spain, and a B.S. in industrial engineering from the University of Toledo (Ohio).

Kevin F. Snape is executive director of the Clean Air Conservancy, a not-for-profit organization dedicated to reducing air pollution by retiring marketable pollution rights. He has been an environmental policy analyst and educator for the past decade and has recently worked to develop community consensus building through a U.S. EPA-funded comparative risk program. He served as board president of the Environmental Fund of Ohio, representing 26 environmental organizations in Ohio. He holds a Ph.D. in political science and public policy from the

University of Kentucky, an M.A. in urban politics and urban planning, and a B.A. in political science, both from the University of Rhode Island.

Robert N. Stavins is professor of public policy and faculty chair of the Environment and Natural Resources Program at the John F. Kennedy School of Government, Harvard University. He is a university fellow at Resources for the Future, the chairman of the Environmental Economics Advisory Committee of the U.S. EPA's Science Advisory Board, a member of the EPA's Clean Air Act Advisory Committee, and a participant on the Intergovernmental Panel on Climate Change (IPCC). He has been a consultant to the National Academy of Sciences, the World Bank, the United Nations, the U.S. Agency for International Development, among other agencies. His current research includes analyses of technology innovation, environmental benefit valuation, political economy of policy instrument choice, and econometric estimation of carbon sequestration costs. His research has appeared in numerous refereed journals, other scholarly and popular periodicals, and several books. The author holds a B.A. in philosophy from Northwestern University, an M.S. in agricultural economics from Cornell, and a Ph.D. in economics from Harvard.

Sarah M. Wade is a member of the Environmental Defense Fund's Global and Regional Air Program and is working on the design, demonstration, and implementation of markets for environmental commodities. Her most recent experience was with the consulting firm, Hagler Bailly, where she worked with electric utilities to implement continuous emissions monitoring (CEM) programs and assisted natural gas utilities with strategic planning to address industry deregulation. In addition, she has worked on solid waste disposal with the Departments of Environmental Protection in the states of Connecticut and Massachusetts. She holds M.A.s in public and private management and in environmental studies, both from Yale University.

Michael J. Walsh is a senior vice president of Environmental Financial Products LLC. He previously served as a senior economist with the Chicago Board of Trade where he directed the

Chicago Board of Trade's efforts to develop exchange-based environmental markets. In this capacity he directed annual auctions of SO_2 emission allowances conducted on behalf of the U.S. EPA, and directed the establishment of the CBOT Recyclable Materials Exchange. Prior to his position with the Chicago Board of Trade, he was a financial economist in the Office of Tax Policy in the U.S. Department of the Treasury. He has been on the faculties of the University of Notre Dame and the Stuart School of Business at Illinois Institute of Technology. He has written extensively on energy markets and the economics and implementation of energy efficient programs. He holds a Ph.D. in economics from Michigan State University and has attended the University of Chicago Graduate School of Business.

Thomas W. Zosel was, before his death, manager of environmental initiatives in 3M's Corporate Environmental Technology and Safety Services organization. He was responsible for following major environmental legislative and regulatory activity, developing a proactive response to assure beyond-compliance performance, and coordinating 3M's environmental stakeholder communications. He served on the U.S. EPA's Clean Air Act Advisory Committee and was past chair of the American Institute of Chemical Engineers Center of Waste Reduction Technologies. He also chaired the National Pollution Prevention Center Advisory Board and served on several National Academy of Science Committees. He held a degree in chemical engineering from the University of Wisconsin.

Index